SIPPING G
SUNLIGHT

SIPPING
SUNLIGHT

A MEMOIR

BERNARD ROSS

atmosphere press

Published by Atmosphere Press

ISBN 979-8-89132-200-4

Cover design by Ronaldo Alves

Atmospherepress.com

I dedicate this book to my spiritual Master, Sant Kirpal Singh Ji Maharaj, whom I met when I was 23 and had the great good fortune to be with him in his ashram for five glorious months. He turned my life around and continues to guide and bless me. I'm also grateful to Sant Kirpal's successors, Sant Darshan Singh Ji Maharaj and Sant Rajinder Singh Ji Maharaj, for their unfailing love and guidance.

I also dedicate this book to my amazing family, whom I love with all my heart, and especially to Rosie, my dear wife and life partner.

INTRODUCTION

This manuscript began as a small creative project to pass the time as my corporate career wound down. I thought it would be fun to write about my crazy youth as a hippie in the early '60s when I was a pioneer adventuring in the land of LSD.

It was fun recapturing those crazy times, early in the youth movement, when drugs opened our minds to worlds and universes beyond our limited consciousness, free love was all the rage, peace and love became more important than war and conquest, and our social consciousness expanded, colliding with the rigid morality of previous generations.

What began as a trip down memory lane morphed into the realization that my story was a search for my life's meaning. As I wrote and reflected, I realized my life was a spiritual quest leading to a higher purpose and that my life's events were all interconnected as I trudged on this curved, convoluted path leading to the possibility of self-realization.

What began as a creative writing exercise for my amusement became a memoir I want to share. I hope my story will entertain and inspire others to see that life can be a spiritual journey if only we expand our vision.

BOOK 1

THE HIPPIE

"Run from what's comfortable. Forget safety. Live where you fear to live. Destroy your reputation. Be notorious. I have tried prudent planning long enough. From now on, I'll be mad."

-Rumi

❧1❧

Little did I realize that day would be a game-changer. On that day, in the autumn of 1963, I was destined to meet someone who would change the course of my life. I began the day once again bemoaning my job because I felt like a con artist going to the poorest neighborhoods, guilt-tripping people into buying a crappy set of encyclopedias. And if the family didn't have school-age kids, I tried to saddle them with a big, fancy family Bible.

I felt terrible after each sale because I knew what it was like to be part of a poor family. I'm a child of Holocaust survivors. My family came to New York with nothing when I was five. We settled in the South Bronx, and it took years of hard work and sacrifice to dig ourselves out of that neighborhood.

The company sent me out every morning with our manager and two other young guys also working through college. Our manager, Abe, was an old geezer who taught us the sales pitch and coached us on how to close a sale.

The only good thing about this crappy job was meeting Florin. On that day, we were working in the Bedford-Stuyvesant area of Brooklyn, a depressed, predominately Black neighborhood. I was in a five-story apartment building without an elevator. The halls were clean despite cracked floor tiles arranged in a black-and-white hexagonal pattern. I could smell the disinfectant as I entered the hallway and saw the beige paint peeling off the walls. There were six apartments per floor, and all the doors were metal, painted dark green, with multiple locks and a peephole.

Though I didn't want to be there, I went from door to door,

ringing each doorbell. Most people weren't home. Those who were home would shout through the closed door, "What do you want?" And when I told them, they'd yell, "Not interested." But when I rang Florin's doorbell, I saw the peephole darken and knew someone was checking me out. Then I heard two locks opening. A Black woman stood in the doorway and said in a calm and confident voice, "Can I help you?" She was of medium height with light brown skin and black wavy hair starting to turn gray. She had a high forehead, pointy chin, clear penetrating eyes, and full lips fixed in a slight smile, almost an amused look. She stood erect, like a dancer. She wore a floral housecoat and fuzzy slippers.

I knew she was too old to have school-aged kids, so I started to pitch the family Bible. I usually kept eye contact during my presentation, but with her, I couldn't. I rattled off my pitch and expected her to turn me away. But instead, she said, "Okay, young man, show me what you got."

I followed her into her tidy apartment. We went through a long hallway, past her kitchen with avocado-green appliances, and into a dining room. The walls of her apartment were all painted beige, and the floors were worn wood parquet. Her dining room had an old walnut cabinet and a large table with six matching green upholstered chairs. On one wall was a nicely framed picture of Martin Luther King. She introduced herself as Florin, and I told her my name.

It was November 22, 1963. I laid my sample bag on a chair, opened it, and took out the big, white King James Bible with the gold-leaf lettering. As I was ready to expound on this once-in-a-lifetime opportunity to own an heirloom Bible, we heard distressed voices from the television in the other room announcing there was an attempt on the life of President John F. Kennedy.

A shockwave ran through me. Could this be true? Florin and I hurried into her living room and quickly sat on her couch as if we were old friends. All the usual social conventions, such as asking for permission to sit, didn't seem necessary under such dire circumstances. We became transfixed as the horrendous details spewed out of Florin's black-and-white TV.

The first news flash came from a visibly shaken Walter Cronkite, who delivered the devastating details. He stated that three shots were fired at the president's motorcade as it traveled through the streets of Dallas. The shots hit Kennedy and Texas Governor John Connally, and both were taken to the hospital. It was so surreal hearing this shocking news while sitting in that darkened room with this older Black woman. We witnessed this tragedy together, and it brought us closer. I felt a weird kinship with her as we sat in silence, hearing newsflash after newsflash about this horrific act.

I thought about the few things I knew about our president. I admired his courage during the Cuban Missile Crisis and for getting the Soviet Union to sign a Nuclear Test Ban Treaty. But mostly, I admired his humanity and how he cared for all people, which manifested in his commitment to strengthening civil rights laws. He was the first political figure I admired. As a young man, I hadn't paid much attention to politics until Kennedy inspired me. Now, his life was hanging by a thread.

The TV commentator stated that a priest delivered the last rites to Kennedy. The news was grim. Hope was fading fast.

"Who would do such a thing? Who would shoot such a wonderful president?" I asked.

"There is lots of hate out there. I don't know why he was shot. Perhaps it was because of his stance on civil rights. Kennedy introduced major legislation to Congress this year that would end segregation and protect voting rights," Florin answered.

Stating the obvious, I said, "Yes, discrimination is terrible in the South."

"In the South, Black people generally know where they stand. It's clear to them that they can't live in that neighborhood or get that job. Those are for Whites only. In the North, it's worse. Here, they shake your hand, take your job application, and smile, but you still don't get that job or the lease for that nice apartment. Here, discrimination is underhanded, equality is an illusion, and Blacks live in ghettos. Everybody knows that Harlem and Bed-Stuy are Black ghettos. Black people are constantly harassed by the police, not only in the South, but in every state. That's why we need new laws."

I looked at Florin and nodded my head in agreement. Her words resonated with me, and her eyes said much more. For the first time in my life, I started to understand the plight of Blacks. I felt compassion for their struggle. As a Jew, I knew a bit about discrimination. As a child of Holocaust survivors, I knew what focused hate can bring. I understood how hate can slowly erode the minds of ordinary people and embolden bigots, and how unspeakable atrocities can become the norm over time. Black people in the United States didn't need a yellow star on their sleeve to identify them. Their yellow star was their skin.

About a half-hour after the shooting, Cronkite announced that Kennedy was dead. He died at 2:00 p.m. EST. Hope for a miracle was now shattered. I sat there in shock and started to contemplate the meaning of death for the first time in my life. It was undeniable that I would die one day, which terrified me. At this point in my life, death had never really affected me. I had never seen a dead person or even went to a funeral. I heard about death a lot from my parents. I heard the horrific tales of Nazi execution squads killing my relatives and the suffering my parents endured, but I never contemplated my death. Now, I felt the sharp claws of death shredding my frail consciousness; my own mortality stared at me with lifeless, indifferent eyes. What's the point of living if I'm just going to die? I wondered. The anxiety started to build. I was quickly spiraling into a hole of despair when Florin spoke to me.

I don't know if she knew the state of my mind at that point, but she looked at me and said, "Death is not the end for us. Only the body dies; our soul is eternal."

I looked at her and saw compassion in her eyes. She continued, "When we die, the soul leaves the body and lives on in a different world."

I said, "I don't know if I believe that. I don't think there's a God. I don't believe in the soul."

"That's understandable," she said. "You can't truly believe anything unless you see it for yourself. I don't believe in blind faith. But many people have had experiences of their soul. I have, and I'm certain that God and the soul are real."

"Well, I haven't," I said a bit defiantly.

"The question you should be asking is how can I experience my soul," she said.

"Okay, how can I experience my soul?"

"Some people are born with that gift. Some people experience it after years of penance and study. And some people get it by taking a psychedelic drug like peyote or mescaline, which is usually given by a medicine man or shaman," she said.

I was now finding our conversation more interesting. I was glad that Florin wasn't lecturing me about the Bible, Heaven and Hell, or the need to convert to Christianity. I was relieved to leave my hole of despair behind and focus on something else. I could see a slight smile on her face and some fire in her eyes as she continued.

"Have you heard about LSD and the work that Timothy Leary is doing?" she asked.

"Sure," I answered. "Wasn't he fired from Harvard just a few months back because of his work with LSD and psilocybin?"

I had read that in *The Realist*, an underground newspaper I subscribed to. I also read about Leary's trip to Mexico, where he took psilocybin a few years earlier.

I continued, "I remember reading that Leary said he learned more about his brain and its possibilities in five hours on psilocybin than in fifteen years of study and research at Harvard."

Then Florin said, "Yes, these drugs can have a profound effect on our consciousness. I see a change coming. I think your generation will change people's outlook and values. Many of your generation will embrace LSD, and people will expand their awareness; people will see that there is more to reality than what they thought."

11

"I agree with you," I said. "My generation sees the world differently. We disagree with the values of our parents. Most of us are against the war in Vietnam and support civil rights. All I know is our wonderful president, who was going to bring about change, is dead. This country is so screwed up."

Florin nodded and said, "Yes, this country is screwed up. Our country is divided. There's a lot of hate out there. But many of your generation believe in love and peace. Many of your generation will try LSD, and you will as well. And when you take LSD, you will experience a profound change."

What? Did I hear right? I wondered. Did she just say I would take LSD?

"I'm not sure I'm ready to take LSD. I heard it can mess people up," I stated emphatically.

"Yes, it can. But it can also open you up to amazing realizations. I think you will soon begin a journey to find out why you are here on earth and who you really are. And that will start with your first LSD experience."

This was now blowing my mind. Florin went from generalities about my generation to speculations about my future. I was starting to feel uncomfortable. *How the hell could she know what my journey would be? She only met me a couple of hours ago.* No way was I going to take LSD based on her recommendation. Maybe this old lady was some kind of kook.

This was getting too weird. I needed to get out of there and get back to Abe. I needed to return to normalcy as I knew it.

I said, "I don't know about that, ma'am. But I have to get back to my boss. I've decided to quit this shitty job."

"It was nice meeting you, Bernie." She smiled, looked me in the eyes, and said, "Perhaps there was a reason that you took this shitty job. Hold on one minute. I want to give you something."

She went into the kitchen, opened a drawer, took out a pen and paper, and wrote something on it.

"Here's my phone number. Put it in your wallet and call me when you take LSD. I think we will meet again," she said.

I found myself complying with her wishes. I took out my wallet, carefully folded the paper, and put it away. Now, I started to feel even more vulnerable and a little shaky. This meeting was way past my comfort level. I could feel Florin's power as she looked at me, though it wasn't menacing or anything like that. It felt like she could see through me. I wanted to get out of there as quickly as possible and return to my normal, boring life. This whole afternoon was an emotional roller coaster. I felt drained.

I gathered up my big, white St. James Bible, put it back into my sample case, and walked out of there as quickly as possible. I was sure I would never see her again, but I was wrong. The next time I saw Florin was absolutely phenomenal.

I managed to meet up with Abe and the others at about 4:00 p.m. I told Abe this job wasn't for me. I didn't have the stomach for it.

Abe said, "I'm not surprised. You don't have the temperament to be a successful salesman."

Everybody was badly shaken by Kennedy's assassination as we drove back to Queens in silence. Once I got home, I learned the assassin was apprehended a mere seventy minutes after he shot Kennedy. The Dallas police did a great job catching the killer; however, they did a terrible job protecting our president. A couple of days later, the assassin, Lee Harvey Oswald, was shot by Jack Ruby, a Jewish gangster. This whole catastrophe was getting stranger by the minute. Some of my friends felt there was more to this tragedy than was reported. Conspiracy theories were cropping up like mushrooms.

Once I was back in my Middle Village, Queens, neighborhood, I started thinking about some of the things Florin said. I realized there were no Blacks where I lived. Middle Village was a lily-white neighborhood even though it had affordable housing. People would say, "Blacks won't move here because we're surrounded by cemeteries." What a crock of shit. Discrimination and racism were alive in my own back yard.

❧2❧

It took about a year and a half for Florin's prediction to come true. It was Perry Robinson who encouraged me to try LSD.

I first met Perry in 1965 while he was visiting Steve's apartment in Middle Village. Steve Tintweiss, a longtime friend, was now being acknowledged as an up-and-coming jazz bass player. He played with Perry quite often, and they developed a close friendship. Perry was known as the Maestro, a musician's musician who motivated and inspired many young and established artists.

When I met him, Perry was already a well-known jazz musician. *DownBeat* called him one of the top jazz musicians for his instrument seven times, and his album, *Funk Dumpling*, was well received. But Perry was more than a musician. He was a philosopher, a talented magician, and a fun guy to have around.

Perry resembled the textbook image of the scrawny jazz beatnik, with his soul patch goatee, long hair, beret, and little glasses. He always wore colorful clothes and had an infectious smile. He was a free spirit who generated positive energy everywhere he went and was loved by everyone who knew him. He took a genuine interest in everyone he met and was open, funny, and authentic.

He often liked to amuse us with magic tricks. Whenever something serendipitous or coincidental happened, Perry would make a tiny globe of the earth materialize out of thin air and say, "Small world."

I saw Perry numerous times at Steve's place and in concert. There was always weed available at Steve's, and we would get stoned and have great conversations. Perry was well-read and knowledgeable about many topics. He was a kind soul, and I came to trust him completely.

I admired Perry's ability to capture the essence of any book he read and clearly and succinctly convey the fine points so you truly understood them. Sometimes, I would talk about a book that Perry explained as if I had gotten that clarity and insight from reading it myself. One of the first books Perry turned us on to was *Stranger in a Strange Land* by Robert A. Heinlein, a science fiction novel that became extremely popular throughout the hippie community. Heinlein created a new word, "grok," in that book, and the hippies embraced it. To grok something was to understand it deeply and thoroughly, at an intuitive level. It amazed me how quickly that word was adopted into our everyday speech. People were saying, "I totally grok that."

One day, our conversation turned to LSD and other psychedelics. Perry had taken LSD about a year earlier and told me about his incredible experience. He said it made profound changes in his life. He spoke about the love and connection he felt with everyone and everything during his trip.

"After you take LSD, you will know what 'We Are All One' really means," he stated.

I was apprehensive about taking LSD because I'd read conflicting reports about its effects. Some articles touted its benefits, while others warned of severe brain damage. Perry said he knew many people who took LSD, and the key to a good experience was to be in a safe place with a good guide. He offered to be my guide and promised to stay with me the entire time. Perry assured me everything would be fine.

Having a mystical experience was something I longed for after reading Aldous Huxley's *The Doors of Perception*, in which he describes his psychedelic experience under the influence of mescaline. He wrote that these experiences could offer great psychological benefits and lead to mystical insights. That book and Perry's experience helped me feel ready to try LSD. I also remembered my conversation with Florin and how sure she was that taking acid would change my life. I hadn't thought of her since the day JFK was assassinated. Finally, her prediction was about to come true.

In the summer of 1965, Perry and I piled into my Corvair and drove up to Woodstock, NY. This was well before the name Woodstock became world famous for its rock concert. We found a lovely glen in a wooded area.

Perry said, "This is what I learned from my trips. All your fears, emotions, intuition, and senses will be heightened to the max. It's like complete enlightenment; it's like the first day of your life. It will open you up like a book. The key is to not let anything that comes up get to you. The worst thing is to fight any of those feelings; just accept them no matter what they are. That's the spiritual teaching of life anyway; it's a great lesson in terms of discipline, to just go with whatever is happening."

Perry then gave me a sugar cube laced with LSD, and thus began a truly miraculous experience.

It was a beautiful day with a mild temperature, blue skies, and puffy white clouds, and I was very relaxed. Perry made me feel like we were on an exciting adventure in a new world. The first thing I noticed as the LSD kicked in was how beautiful everything was. Every one of my senses was heightened. The colors of everything around me became much more vibrant. I was aware of all the sounds around me ... the flutter of bird wings, the buzzing of insects, the whisper of the wind through the trees. I could smell the sweet grass and the rich earth below and feel the gentle breeze caress my body. Perry watched me, and I just smiled and nodded; there was nothing else to say. He knew I was in a good place.

I saw an energy field around everything. It was very subtle, and I felt a deep connection to whatever I saw. When I saw a bird, I felt like I was one with the bird. When I looked at a tree, I felt its leaves quiver in the wind. A tiny ladybug was a miracle to behold. A new world of wonder was opening to me. Or was this how the world truly was? Every place I looked was magical.

These were the eyes I wanted to have, not the dull eyes lost in the shadows of my limited brain. Every thought I had was profound, every experience a revelation.

Then I looked at Perry and saw him as a universe of light made up of billions of shimmering specks spinning, vibrating, and changing color. He was beautiful beyond description, and I felt love flowing between us—a warmth resonating from my heart. He was separate from me and yet part of me. He smiled, and the light around him changed to a beautiful pink-purple glow. Perry then started playing his clarinet. The notes were a new language, which took me on an incredible journey of sound and light—all bursting with meaning. His music told a story—a call to the cosmos full of joy and sorrow, pleasure and pain, longing, love, rapture, and a thousand other emotions not yet named. I felt a deep connection to Perry as he poured his soul into his music, which was the most beautiful sound I had ever heard.

I started to peak, and the hallucinations were utterly delightful; explosions of color and shape permeated my vision. This symphony of light constantly changed, forming intricate patterns. I could feel the colors and caress the shapes as I accelerated through this glowing maze, which then erupted with an explosion of light thousands of times greater than any fireworks. It was exhilarating; it was enchanting. I was in a world of wonder and magic.

There was no fear; nothing was weird or even strange. Everything was like it always had been and would be, just more vibrant, more beautiful, more real. I always knew this truth, but had forgotten it. I was me, I was my soul, I was everything, and everything was me. There was no separation, no duality; I was one with everything. The tapestry of life was exquisite.

After a while, I stood up. I now experienced my body in a new way, like I was standing for the first time. It was amazing, feeling my legs and arms, my muscles, my bones, the air in my lungs, the beating of my heart, the blood flowing through my body, all so new and incredible.

Perry said, "Okay, just relax now; you're there, you're cool."

I was in bliss. I had never experienced anything so beautiful, magical, and profound in my entire life. There were no questions or answers needed. I started wandering through the forest and met another person on an LSD trip. We never exchanged names; there was no need. He knew me, and I knew him. Speech was unnecessary. I felt a deep connection to him and knew he felt the same. We wandered together for a while and then went our separate ways. Perry was there the whole time, keeping an eye on me and ensuring I was okay. I was better than okay; I was ecstatic.

It was about seven or eight hours since I took the acid, and I was starting to come down. I felt great. I was now aware of another reality, a reality that felt primal, like it was TRUE REALITY. I realized that what we perceive as reality during our day-to-day existence is but a shadow, a reflection of a reflection. I was convinced that LSD was the gateway to spirituality. How could this drug be anything but a great boon to humankind? I wanted everyone to experience what I had. If they did, I was convinced that there would be no hatred, war, hunger, or poverty and that people would love one another. I was ready to become a true believer, a bona fide acidhead. Up until this point, Perry hadn't asked for details of my trip. His presence was a comfort and a joy. On our ride back from Woodstock, Perry asked, "How was your trip?"

I said, "Man, it was fantastic. I became everything. I was part of everything, and everything was part of me. It was incredible, it was so beautiful, everything had meaning. I was blown away."

Perry exclaimed, "Shoooo, you had a high trip. You connected with the universal consciousness, man. You became one with the cosmos. Totally uni." He became animated when he spoke and exuded so much happiness for me.

Perry had lots of idiosyncratic expressions; "uni" was one of his favorites, which I think encompassed oneness, universality, and uniqueness.

"Aren't most trips like that?" I asked.

"No, man, that was a high trip. You experienced oneness. On

most trips, you experience incredible things, but you are separate from the experience, duality, man. Most trips have some highs and lows. Suddenly, you can sink into some dark shit. That's why it's a good idea to have a guide. Man, you should be a guide after you've had a few more trips," Perry suggested.

"Maybe I will. I think acid is going to change the world. What an amazing gift we've been given. Thank you for being with me."

"Yeah, man," Perry replied. "Acid is already changing the world. Even the jazz greats like Trane are turning on. Check out his album, *A Love Supreme*, totally uni, man."

"I love that album. It's like a beautiful prayer," I said.

When we got close to his pad on the Lower East Side, I asked him how much he paid for rent and was amazed at how inexpensive rent was in this area. I decided it was time to leave the 'burbs and have my own place.

On my drive back to Middle Village, I once again thought about Florin. It had been about eighteen months since our meeting. I remembered her vividly and recalled she wanted me to call her after I took LSD. But what would I tell her? She predicted I would take LSD and that it would change my life. It looked like she was right. So ... what else could she say? Maybe I didn't want to find out. I decided not to call. But as fate would have it, Florin and I would reconnect several years later in the most extraordinary way.

❧ 3 ❦

Fifty bucks a month. That's what my first apartment cost, with no broker fees and only a one-month security deposit. I sold my beloved Chevy Corvair and had enough money for many months. The apartment was on the corner of 11th Street and Avenue B in the East Village. I moved there in September 1965 while still attending the Bernard Baruch campus of City College of New York on 21st Street and Lexington Avenue, a twenty-minute walk from my apartment.

The East Village in lower Manhattan was known for its run-down tenements and cheap rents. In 1965, it was still a working-class neighborhood, the home of Ukrainians, Poles, African Americans, and Latin Americans. Many longtime residents were moving into the city-sponsored high-rise buildings with modern appliances, reasonable rents, and the promise of a better life, known as "the Projects," leaving a glut of empty apartments and even entire empty buildings. As the original tenants moved out, beatniks, hippies, musicians, and writers moved in. But in 1965, it was still a neighborhood where generations co-mingled. Teenagers played basketball in the park, children were on the swings at the playground, older people walked their dogs, and stoned hippies wandered the streets, smiling at everyone. Everybody got along; everybody minded their own business.

But things were changing quickly. The counterculture was moving in, and many hippies rented these cheap apartments while others squatted in abandoned buildings. They came in droves, and soon, the East Village became the epicenter of the

NYC hippie scene. Young people flocked to the East Village, leaving Mom and Dad in their suburban homes, and took Timothy Leary's advice to "turn on, tune in, drop out." This was the new mecca for the hippie movement in New York, where the faithful could easily get LSD and safely trip in one of many crash pads. This was where free jazz flowed freely out of Tompkins Square Park, and beat poetry flourished in the local bars and clubs. This was where new music, like underground rock and folk, could be heard in the bars and coffeehouses every night of the week. This was where The Fugs got their start. Writers and artists lived here, and Allen Ginsberg held court at St. Mark's Church. This was my new home and community, and I couldn't have been happier.

My apartment was nothing to look at; in fact, it was a bit of a dump. It was up one flight of stairs, and when the door opened, you'd walk right into the kitchen. Right in front of the door was a clawfoot cast-iron bathtub with a plywood plank on top that served as a makeshift kitchen table. To the right was a toilet with a sink but no shower; thankfully, the room had a door.

The living room was to the right of the kitchen, and my bedroom was past the living room. It was an L-shaped apartment with one window that looked out into an air shaft; all you could see was a brick wall down the alley. The flat even had some furniture from the old tenant: a bed, which I prayed didn't have bedbugs, and a ratty old armoire that was perfect for the few clothes I owned. The living room had an old couch against one wall and a beat-up iron cot against the other, providing a good seating arrangement when friends came over. This was my new home, my first apartment, and the center of my newfound freedom.

I was in the second semester of my second year at Baruch, and up to that point, I attended classes regularly and maintained an A average. I majored in accounting, which was practical but uninspiring. However, my liberal arts classes taught me to appreciate poetry and inspired me to try my hand at writing poems.

Now that I had my own pad, I was getting stoned every day.

At first, I attended classes, but soon, I was cutting them, and before I knew it, it was time for midterms. I had no desire to study, so I dropped out of all my classes right before the midterms. Dropping my classes meant I would get an incomplete rather than an F, thereby maintaining my A average. Even in my stoned haze, I had the good sense to preserve my college accomplishments.

Dropping out of school was also a red flag for the draft board. In time, I knew they would send me the dreaded draft notice. The war in Vietnam was raging, but I didn't care. I was living for today, and if I got drafted, there was no way I was going. But why worry now? I would deal with the draft in the future.

<h1 style="text-align: center;">❧ 4 ❧</h1>

Exploring my new neighborhood was a joy. The dirt, the stink, and the rundown tenements didn't bother me one bit. The neighborhood was alive with my people—hippies and beatniks, musicians, poets, and artists—and most of them were as stoned as I was. People acknowledged one another with a nod or a smile in passing. Everyone was cool; even the locals seemed relaxed.

Making friends in the East Village was easy. I met Andy, who lived down the street and made a living dealing LSD, which was sold on sugar cubes. Andy was a skinny Jewish kid who grew up in Brooklyn and had a wild mop of curly black hair, a thick mustache, and dark, penetrating eyes. He looked a lot like Cheech Marin. He lived in the basement of his tenement building, and you needed to open an iron gate and walk down a few stairs to get to his apartment. Andy was kind and generous, with a wry sense of humor and a goofy smile. His main passion was getting stoned, staying stoned, and getting others stoned. We became great friends.

Mike lived up the street from me, in the same building as Perry. Mike was our local philosopher. He was very serious and rarely laughed or smiled. Mike was over six feet tall, with a strong athletic build, long and straight brown hair, and a bit of peach fuzz on his face. He came to New York from Baltimore, and I was surprised to learn he was raised as an Orthodox Jew.

Mike dealt weed and hashish, and there were always interesting people at his apartment engaged in stimulating conversation and sampling the merchandise he happily supplied. Mike was very interested in Eastern mysticism and other spiritual matters. He read a lot and introduced me to many topics, including karma, reincarnation, meditation, yoga, and past-life regressions. The Age of Aquarius was alive and well at Mike's.

Mike adopted an older East Indian guy named Ravi, who was well-versed in Hindu philosophy and yoga. He claimed to be a disciple of the Indian mystic, Yogananda. Ravi was short and very thin, much like Mahatma Gandhi after his famous Salt March. He had an air of sadness and always looked slightly disheveled, wearing clothes a few sizes too big.

Ravi was a fixture at Mike's. He would perform his yoga routine while we were getting stoned. He had conversations with us while standing on his head. He smoked with us and then entertained us with stories and quotes from the *Bhagavad Gita*, the best-known Hindu scripture.

Ravi said the main message of the *Bhagavad Gita* was that a person whose mind is free from desires and attachment could attain supreme perfection. As if being desireless was even a remote possibility for a bunch of stoned hippies basking in a world of newfound freedom and free love with great drugs. The *Bhagavad Gita* sounded good and noble, but none of us were ready to lead a spiritual life, with the possible exception of Mike.

Ravi also liked to expound on how to meditate properly or the fine points of yoga, showing off poses that turned him into a pretzel. He would share his vast wealth of knowledge with anyone who listened. If he got your attention, you were in for a long conversation.

During one acid trip, Mike convinced himself that Ravi was his guru. Mike gave him his bedroom and slept on the couch. He would show him great reverence and even wash his feet as a sign of devotion. But when Mike discovered that Ravi was addicted to cough medicine, he was so disappointed he threw him out. Ravi wasn't very profound when he was under the influence of codeine; he wasn't even coherent. It was unfortunate because he had a great mind and meant well. I really felt sorry for him. He wasn't a con artist or anything; he was just a guy trying to find his place in a changing world. I never saw Ravi again. Maybe he found new disciples. Hopefully, he kicked his Robitussin addiction.

* * *

Another friend I met at Mike's was Gene Bloom, the poet who published a monthly poetry magazine, *Entrails*. The magazine's full name was *Entrails: The Magazine of Happy Obscenity and Captured Dragons*. His publishing house was Whisper Shit Press.

Gene gained notoriety because the first edition of *Entrails* had a baggie with parsley stapled to the back cover, which looked just like a nickel bag of weed. The magazine contained some surprisingly good avant-garde poetry from New York and around the country. *The New York Times* book review listed his magazine as one of the decade's five best underground poetry magazines. Gene was getting famous, and many beat and concrete poets[1] submitted poems for his consideration.

Since I fancied myself a poet, I sought him out and found him approachable, caring, and encouraging. He gave me many pointers about my poetry in his thick Brooklyn accent and even invited me to his apartment on the Lower East Side, which was often full of interesting people. He was kind enough to include one of my poems in the second edition of *Entrails*. The poem didn't have a title, so Gene gave it one, "Hypocrisy." I don't remember how the poem went, but I remember thinking the title fit.

* * *

Over on Second Avenue was a rundown movie theater, with seating for over two thousand people, that occasionally held

---

1 According to *Encyclopedia Britannica*, the poet's intent in concrete poetry is conveyed by graphic patterns of letters, words, or symbols rather than by the meaning of words in a conventional manner; see https://www.britannica.com/art/concrete-poetry

lectures, poetry readings, and stand-up comedy by such celeb-rities as Allen Ginsberg and Lenny Bruce. One day, I went there to see Timothy Leary's lecture on LSD.

Leary was introduced and entered the stage to great applause from a packed house. He was a thin man in his 40s, medium height, clean-shaven, expressive eyes, a beaming smile, and a calm and soothing voice.

He said, "My sermon will begin with a hymn from a mod-ern-day holy man—Bob Dylan—, from his psalm "I Ain't Gonna Work on Maggie's Farm No More." That statement drew a laugh from the audience.

Leary continued, saying, "Like Maggie's mom, I will talk tonight about God, man, and love."

The main points of the talk were:

The realm of God is the human body, and the gates of Eden are our senses.

Christ said that the kingdom of God is within. Each of us is God. I am God, and you are God as well. This concept is not a new one. In India, people greet each other with Namaste, which means "I salute the God in you." Each one of us creates our own universe. Each one of us can change our consciousness by using sacraments. Sacraments bring us closer to our divinity. LSD is my sacrament of choice because it changes us molecularly and allows us to explore endless realms within.

He encouraged the people in the audience to turn on, tune in, and drop out. He explained that turning on is taking the holy sacrament. Tuning in is focusing on your body and gain-ing the incredible wisdom within. Dropping out means no lon-ger accepting conformity and being open to change—for peace, civil rights, women's rights, freedom, and love.

Besides promoting the virtues of LSD, he also plugged his new church, the League for Spiritual Discovery. He announced to the young men in the audience that any draft-age guy could join the church and claim conscientious objector status with the draft board and not go to Vietnam.

Leary ended his talk to thunderous applause.

Since I was already an LSD devotee, this information was fortuitous. I hung around after the show to speak to Tim about his church. He thought I would make an excellent disciple. There was only one catch — I had to move to Millbrook, New York, the estate where Timothy Leary lived. At this point, I wasn't ready to leave the East Village. He said to let him know if I changed my mind. I took him up on his offer many months later.

* * *

The East Village was a magnet for mystical movements, philosophies, and esoteric teachings. Storefronts were dedicated to assorted spiritual, political, and health movements. One of my favorites was The Paradox, New York's first macrobiotic restaurant, where you could get a delicious meal and learn the principles and benefits of a macrobiotic diet. Macrobiotics stresses eating a properly balanced diet to make physical, emotional, and spiritual progress. In other words, you could eat your way to enlightenment. I loved going there. The food was simple but delicious, and the atmosphere was zen-like and peaceful, with Japanese music playing softly in the background. My favorite dish was miso soup and brown rice with perfectly prepared root vegetables. *Zen Macrobiotics* had just been published and was sold at the restaurant,[2] and the macrobiotic-devoted employees were happy to share their wisdom.

In the 1960s, the East Village became the counterculture's center for all things political, spiritual, philosophical, psychological, and mystical. Coffeehouses were populated with seekers discussing Zen, Taoism, Yoga, Theosophy, and a host of spiritual fare. The Samuel Weiser Bookstore in the East Village encompassed two floors and offered a huge selection of books on the occult, mysticism, esotericism, and Eastern philosophy, including

---

2 Michio Kushi and Aveline Kushi, *Zen Macrobiotics* (Tokyo: Japan Publications Trading Co., revised edition, 1993).

many rare volumes. It was an amazing place to explore the dark arts as well as the many paths to enlightenment.

I bought a few books but wasn't ready to embrace any of the teachings. To succeed in anything, especially spirituality, you need to work at it; you need discipline, perseverance, focused concentration, and a good attention span. Of these, I was lacking. At this point in my life, I couldn't even finish the books I bought. I did absorb a bit of understanding from them, though, enough to have a few good talking points and to sound cool while stoned. But somehow, the seeds were planted, seeds containing the possibility of higher consciousness, seeds that could someday sprout.

❧ 5 ❧

Magic was in the air on that exquisitely sunny day in the spring of 1966. I felt like something remarkable was about to happen, and then I saw Gretchen walking toward me. She was about 5'6" with long brown hair, bright hazel eyes, skin the color of cream, and full, beautiful lips that seemed to form a perpetual smile. Her happiness was infectious. Once she was in my line of vision, I didn't want to look at anything else. There was a sweet aura, a positive energy coming from her. She had a very relaxed way of walking, almost gliding down the street in her bright Indian-print dress. I thought she was the most beautiful woman I'd ever seen. Once our eyes locked, I could see her smile become bigger.

I walked up to her and said, "Hi, I'm Bernie. I live up the street."

She answered, "Hi, I'm Gretchen. I live down the street." And we both laughed.

We experienced a strong connection without having to say much. We both smiled and started to walk together like old friends. I was a bit stoned on grass, and I suspected she was too. I knew I had just met a kindred spirit, and all I needed to know about her was in her eyes and smile. We walked together into Tompkins Square Park as if we'd done it a thousand times before.

Sun Ra and his band were playing at the bandstand on the other side of the park. We walked toward the music and started holding hands. We listened to free jazz played by one of the masters of the genre. Gretchen, new to jazz, was having trouble getting into it. I'd been a jazz enthusiast for a while and

29

had learned to appreciate free jazz by listening to Perry and his friends perform.

I told her, "I know free jazz can be difficult to appreciate. It frees the artist to improvise and create new sounds on their instruments. It allows the artist to get primitive, go wilder, be primal, be free of structure. It breaks the old rules. You have to let go of your preconceived idea of what music is and just go with it to fully appreciate it."

Gretchen said, "I get what you're saying, but I find it hard to listen to. It's so wild and angry. I guess I just like music that's easier to listen to."

"I had trouble at first, too, I said, but I learned to like free jazz, but I know it isn't for everyone."

Still holding hands, she asked me if I'd ever done LSD. I told her about my amazing acid trip in Woodstock and my four other trips since then. I must have sounded like I was an expert at tripping.

She looked at me for a long minute and said, "I haven't dropped acid yet, but I think I want to try it. Would you do acid with me?"

I smiled and said, "Sure, we can trip today if you want to."

She nodded yes and smiled a little apprehensively.

Hand in hand, we went over to Andy's house. He knew why we were there without us saying a word. He welcomed us into his house with a big smile and had us sit on his old, ratty couch.

"Gretchen, is this your first trip?" Andy asked. She nodded, and he continued trying to make her comfortable. "The acid I'm giving you is really pure, and I think you're going to enjoy it."

He took two sugar cubes out of his fridge, asked us to stick out our tongues, and distributed the holy sacrament. I almost expected him to say a benediction or prayer to the lord of dope. Andy was our high priest, and I mean that literally and figuratively.

With the sweetness of the holy sacrament melting in our mouths, we headed back to her apartment at 6th and C.

On the way, I said, "Gretchen, I want you to know that I am here for you. I want you to feel safe, and I want you to tell me if you feel weird or scared in any way. It's best not to have pre-conceived ideas about LSD and just go with the flow."

By the time we reached her apartment, the acid was just starting to kick in. We began kissing, and the kisses were the most sensual, wonderful ones I had ever experienced.

Playing the role of an experienced guide, I said, "Let's take it real slow. No need to rush. Let's get comfortable."

Gretchen turned on her record player and introduced me to a piece of music that was completely new to me: Erik Satie's *Gymnopédies*. This was very different from the frenetic, wild sound of Sun Ra. Satie was also avant-garde but from a classical perspective. It was slow and unhurried; it was magical. The term *Gymnopédies* comes from ancient Greece and refers to an important rite of passage dedicated to Apollo. In Sparta, the youths danced naked and displayed their artistic and martial skills in an elaborate dance. With that perfect piece of music, we did a dance of our own.

Our elaborate dance began as the acid trip intensified. We started to experience everything in super slow motion as we explored a new universe of wonder and delight. Every sensation was an explosion of endless joy and bliss. It was like we were newborns experiencing another person for the first time. Every touch was an orgasm. The music of Erik Satie was a perfect complement to our lovemaking.

We wound up naked on her bed and started making love slowly, unhurriedly, as the LSD flowed through our bodies and into our consciousness. I could feel the warmth radiating from her body, and I could see the glow of subtle colors surrounding her like a misty shroud. Around her head was a pale pink aura that pulsated and became reddish at times. The colors changed like a kaleidoscope as they emanated from the various contours of her body, sometimes yellow, sometimes shades of green or blue. It was another delightful dance in perfect symmetry to Satie's music.

I spent what seemed like an eternity exploring the universe called Gretchen. I held her close and was delighted by the smell of her hair, which was more fragrant than any rose.

I could smell patchouli and lilac and lavender and other aromas beyond description. I closed my eyes and deeply drank in these perfumes. As I moved to other parts of her body, the scent changed; sometimes, it was sweet, and sometimes, a rich, musky fragrance, but always a delight.

I kissed her neck and marveled at the shape of her ear. It was a work of art, a masterpiece, and a joy to behold. The lobe was so much softer than the helix and perfect for nibbling on. I could see the colorful musical notes captured by these marvelous devices. A world of wondrous and subtle sounds filled the air. I was amazed at how these sounds could create emotion and meaning. They were filling me with such joy, and I was sure they were just as alluring to Gretchen.

My awareness was riveted on her, marveling at each part of her, kissing and licking her magnificent full breasts. Suddenly, my attention shifted to her touching me. Our lovemaking was a beautiful dance. Sometimes, my focus was completely on her, and I'd get lost in her beauty for what seemed an eternity. Then, suddenly, my focus shifted to the pleasure she was giving me, and I got lost in that ardor.

The intensity of our dance peaked when we locked our eyes. The experience was so much more than seeing her beautiful hazel eyes subtly change color from green to brown. It was so much more than the joy I could see coming from her. It was more than the love radiating from those wide-open, trusting orbs. I felt like I could see her essence, and she could see mine. I felt like we both had nothing to hide. It was exhilarating. It was enchanting. I felt like we could see each other's souls, which were pure, open, and innocent.

Then I entered her. It felt like a sacred act as I slid into that magical place, that temple of creation. Her eyes opened wider, rapturous with love and longing. Her face took on a new glow, with auras of pinks, reds, and purples flowing all around her. I felt the beating of her heart intensify and the quickening of her breath. Then, finally, the climax, an explosion of a billion stars illuminated my darkness. As I came, I heard her low moans and felt her spasming, and her orgasm convulsed throughout her body. She drew me closer, holding me more tightly. I felt complete, the yin and yang united at last. We were one as we lay in each other's arms, content and spent. We fell asleep entwined in each other's embrace.

We awoke to smiles and laughter. The acid had worn off, but we were high on the afterglow. I could see that she was as moved by this incredible experience as I was. Had I met my soulmate? We showered together, still enamored by each other's bodies. We couldn't keep our hands off each other. We made love again and again.

We saw each other almost every day after that night of bliss. But we could never again capture the joy and wonder of being so completely connected to one another, the sheer bliss of a touch, the intoxication of a smile, and pure and unadulterated love.

After about a month, we started to drift apart. We were free-spirited hippies, and neither of us was ready for a committed relationship. In the East Village, hippie relationships didn't last very long. There were too many distractions and temptations to ignore. There was always another trip to take, new highs and lows to explore, new people to fuck. No sense in getting attached. Nothing was permanent in the acid world, certainly not love.

But during that incredible LSD trip, I experienced something pure, something unsullied, something magical. By luck or happenstance, I fell into it. Somehow, I transcended my little, egotistical self and landed in an unadulterated realm, a realm beyond the ego. This latest trip and my first trip showed me the possibility of a state of being in which one is capable of pure love, where one experiences a realm beyond the physical, where there are no limitations and no separation. The question was, how could one attain that state permanently? The mystics teach that one can achieve the state they call enlightenment in a flash of profound realization. Once that hallowed state is reached, it becomes one's permanent state of being, and all love and wisdom are ours.

It seems that LSD may give you a glimpse of it if you're lucky, but we always come down. We always descend back to our limited, egotistical, selfish selves. I hoped and prayed that perhaps my next acid trip would provide that breakthrough—enlightenment.

⮞6⮜

Crash pads were popping up all over the East Village. These were places where you could get stoned, meet new people, and have a safe place to sleep if you didn't mind crashing on a dirty mattress with several other people in the room.

Eric, the chemist, had a crash pad on 10th Street between Avenues B and C. I don't know if he had a degree in chemistry, but he sure knew how to make fine psychedelic drugs. Eric looked more like a science nerd than a hippie, with short brown hair and thick glasses. He resembled a human bean pole, thin, pale, and more than six feet tall. But nobody cared how Eric looked; he was our medicine man, and his finest creation was DMT, which he distributed for free.

Short for "dimethyltryptamine," DMT is a powerful psychedelic drug that, when smoked, induces incredibly intense and colorful hallucinations. All one needs is a small amount in a hash pipe. Someone always held the pipe because you're gone the minute that shit hits your lungs. When smoked, you find yourself traveling at warp speed through a tunnel of intense light with incredible shapes and colors. You're in a state of euphoria and completely unaware of the outside world. Each trip is unique and usually lasts for less than a half hour, but you are unaware of time while under its influence. I loved tripping on DMT and usually went over to Eric's a couple of times a month to ride that psychedelic roller coaster.

DMT is also known as the spirit molecule. According to some researchers, it induces mystical and transcendent experiences.

Shamans in the Amazon used ayahuasca, which contains DMT, in their healing rituals. It also occurs naturally in our bodies, produced by the pineal gland, a tiny pinecone-shaped organ at the brain's center. The pineal gland has been called the seat of the soul and is believed to cause mystical and out-of-body experiences.

Eric's two-bedroom apartment was the holy temple of DMT in the East Village. There were usually a dozen people in various states of consciousness, sprawled out on chairs, lounging on couches, or lying on one of the many mattresses covering the bedroom floors. It was clear that Eric didn't live there. Where he lived and manufactured his drugs was a complete mystery. How Eric supported himself was also a mystery. The drugs at St. Eric's were always free. We speculated that perhaps he was independently wealthy or a professor at a university.

I met Renee at Eric's. I returned from one of my magical trips, and the first thing I saw was the beautiful Renee looking at me. I was still high, and her incredible eyes drew me in. They were beacons of blue light, warm and inviting, silhouetted by a shroud of long, curly, flaming red hair. She met my gaze with a smile and a bit of nervous laughter.

"It looks like you enjoyed that," she said.

"Seeing you made it even more enjoyable," I answered.

She smiled shyly, not knowing how to respond to that compliment. I introduced myself, and we started a wonderful conversation. Renee was an artist who had just arrived from Woodstock and planned to visit for only a few days. She was here to buy paints, get stoned, and maybe find some inspiration. She was a beautiful and voluptuous woman with a shroud of red hair, bright blue eyes, and a freckled face. She had a very expressive oval face with full ruby-red lips. She was slightly plump, with magnificent breasts. She wore a colorful Indian skirt, a loose-fitting top, and sandals.

We hit it off immediately, and I invited her over to my apartment. Renee was a free spirit. All she had was a small overnight bag and a case with her paints and brushes. We walked the few short blocks to my place and started to make out the minute we entered my apartment. Making love to Renee was a joy. She was so responsive to my touch. For a couple of days, we didn't bother with clothes. We would make love, talk, smoke dope, listen to music, and have sex again. We even took a bath in the old cast-iron bathtub in my kitchen. She also loved to paint in the nude.

My living room had a large bare wall about nine or ten feet long. Renee asked if she could paint a mural on that wall. I said I would love her to. Renee began painting a pair of open thighs about eight feet long from toe to toe, with the most provocative and seductive vagina you could imagine. Georgia O'Keefe would have been proud of that rendition. Renee was pleased with the mural, and I was delighted to have her art to remember our incredible weekend.

Later that day, Renee told me it was time to return to her home in Woodstock. She gave me her address and said I should look her up next time I'm there.

"How are you getting back?" I asked.

"By bus from Penn Station," she said.

"Are you hungry? I know this great Polish restaurant that's a few blocks away."

"I'm famished," she admitted.

We walked to the restaurant, a tiny place that served great food. It had five or six tables with yellow oilcloth tablecloths, a small counter, and a heavenly smell wafting out of the kitchen. Their pierogies were out of this world, and the liver and onions were fantastic. We feasted.

Then I went with her to Penn Station, and we said our goodbyes.

When I returned to the apartment, I looked at the mural for a long time and saw that she indeed left me with a most fitting remembrance of our time together.

Many friends came over, enjoyed smoking weed, listening to jazz, and experiencing that incredible mural, which would move around or change color depending on how stoned you were. One night, my friend Howie came over with a strobe light. Shining it on the mural provided a new perspective. Now, the mural seemed to detach from the wall and float in mid-air.

"What should we name this masterpiece?" asked Steve.

Howie suggested "The Big Snatch."

"Pussy Monster," called out Andy.

Perry proposed "Vagedelic."

"I got it," yelled Gene. "Hole in the Wall."

"That's it, Gene! So, we are the Hole-in-the-Wall gang." We all agreed and laughed.

The Hole in the Wall was delightful to behold, not only to young horny males, but some women appreciated it too. For a few days, I felt like I had an art gallery.

A few weeks later, the phone rang at about 9:00 or 10:00 a.m., well before I usually awoke. It was my mom announcing that she, my dad, and my thirteen-year-old twin sisters were coming over in about an hour. It was only a few months since I left home, and they wanted to see where their son was living. This was Sunday morning. Half asleep, I dragged my ass out of bed and walked into the living room, passing the colossal vagina mural on my way to the bathroom. Suddenly, the enormity of my situation exploded in my mind.

I ran back into my bedroom and immediately called my mother to reschedule the visit. But it was too late. They must have left right after she called.

How the hell do I cover this up in the next hour? Shit, what do I do? I can't let my parents see this! It's bad enough I'm living in a fifty-dollar-a-month shithole with one window that overlooks a brick wall.

I had bedsheets that would cover the mural, but no way to fasten them. I didn't have a hammer, nails, thumbtacks, masking tape, or anything. And it was Sunday morning, and my parents would be in my apartment in less than an hour. My brain was scrambling for a solution, and I finally could think of only one. I grabbed the mattress off my bed and laid it vertically against the wall. The only problem was the two enormous legs sticking out of the sides of the mattress.

Then I heard the doorbell ring. My heart was racing. I had to open the door. My mom and dad were dressed in their Sunday finery. My two little twin sisters, Nancy and Marion, wore matching coats, all ready for a Sunday visit with their cool big brother.

The four of them came through the front door leading into the kitchen with the bathtub.

I said, "My apartment is a mess. How about going to Katz's for lunch? There's really nothing to see here."

But my father was curious and wandered in with my mom and sisters in tow. It was clear they wanted to see the rest of the apartment. Reluctantly, I led the way into the living room with my father right behind me. He took one look at the mattress lying against the wall with the two enormous legs sticking out of the sides. *Oh, shit* was all I could think.

Without hesitation, he turned around and said, "I've seen enough. Let's go to Katz's."

My father led everyone out of the apartment before my mom and sisters could see the masterpiece. We had a nice lunch together, and my dad never mentioned the mural again.

❦ 7 ❧

There was always something new and exciting happening in my neighborhood: new adventures to have, new people to meet, new drugs to try. One night, there was a party at Gene's pad on the Lower East Side, which was bound to be fun. Gene had the best parties, attended by interesting people from all walks of life, not only poets and hippies. One was ensured to meet musicians, political radicals, producers, intellectuals, and beatniks, all attracted to the stimulating company and free dope. Gene liked to think of himself as a hippie poet provocateur.

Steve and Perry were already enjoying the festivities when I arrived. There were about eight people there. The distinct smell of weed permeated the air, and I lit a joint, which added to the blue aromatic cloud of smoke engulfing the small room.

Shortly after I arrived, some weird, uptight dude came in looking for Gene. I don't think Gene knew him, but he sold him some weed anyway. A few minutes later, the door burst open, and a few beefy, plainclothes cops barged in with guns drawn, shouting that we were all under arrest and ordering us not to move. They corralled us into a corner of the room so they could take control of the apartment. One of them watched us while the others searched for evidence. They opened drawers, threw the contents on the floor, knocked down bookcases, and generally made a mess of Gene's apartment.

The shift in the energy level was dramatic. In a few seconds, we went from a nice buzz to total fear. It was surreal. I knew that weed and LSD were illegal, but somehow, the possibility of jail

40

seemed remote, especially living in an area where everyone we knew smoked and almost everyone dealt a bit of weed. Now, reality had arrived, and I had no idea what trouble it would bring.

Everyone seemed frozen in the corner of the room, with the uptight cop guarding us as if we were dangerous criminals. No one spoke, and no one moved. After what seemed an eternity, they herded us into a few cop cars. While we were being led away, the weird guy that Gene sold weed to earlier was standing in the hall. No doubt he was an undercover cop or informer.

They took us to the Tombs, the notorious jail in lower Manhattan. Once there, the men and women were separated, and they put us into a large holding pen with about fifty or sixty other people—the unlucky ones scooped up on that cold, miserable night by the long, uncaring arm of the law. Some looked dangerous, some looked like winos, and some were bummed-out, peace-loving hippies.

Soon, Perry, Steve, and I huddled together in the overcrowded holding pen. Steve looked really scared as he reached into the pocket of his winter coat and took out a glove. He showed us the glove, and we could see the tip of a joint sticking out. We were huddled in such a way that hardly anyone else saw it. Perry grabbed the joint in a flash and made it disappear in one fluid motion. Another one of Perry's many magic tricks, this one was designed to keep us safe. Steve seemed relieved. Perry must have swallowed the joint before anyone could see it.

The cops took us into this large, ugly green room where we were processed. They asked for our identification and photographed and fingerprinted us. I didn't want to use my NYC address, so I gave them my Middle Village address and told them I was a student.

After processing us, we were separated and searched. Fortunately, I didn't have any dope on me. We were then led to jail cells, which held only a few people. Perry and I were in the same cell, and Steve was placed in one next to us.

I spent a sleepless night in that cold cell. Perry managed to lie on the cot and grab a few hours of sleep. Maybe Steve's joint was working its magic in Perry's dreams.

In the morning, we met with a public defender, a chubby little guy in a cheap suit and stained tie who told us we were free to go. Only Gene would be charged because the party was at his apartment, and the police had found drugs.

This was my first time being arrested. It wasn't that bad, but it made me realize we hippies were being watched. There were people among us who seemed cool but would sell us out at the drop of a hat. Also, some of us were under active surveillance. Gene was probably in that category, not only because of *Entrails* but also because of his strong political views that he expounded at every opportunity. Gene—ever the provocateur!

The utopia of love and freedom is always under attack by the dark forces of suppression and control, not only during the hippie revolution but throughout history. That realization was enough to make any peace and freedom-loving person paranoid. But I was determined not to let it drag me down.

Two days later, my mother called.

"Bernie, were you arrested?"

I was in shock. How the hell could she have known?

I asked, "Mom, where did you hear that?"

She said, "Someone at the cleaners said they read in the newspaper that you were arrested at a party."

I said, "Yes. It was no big deal. I was never charged."

Somehow, miraculously, Gene wasn't convicted. Maybe the bust was illegal. Maybe he beat it through a technicality. Soon, Gene was back, ready to publish another edition of *Entrails*. As the editor, publisher, contributor, and financier of the magazine, Gene was always struggling to keep the enterprise afloat. The magazine's cover price wasn't nearly enough to cover the expenses. He originally started dealing a little weed to help stay solvent, but now, after the bust, he had to be careful.

Months passed, and his financial woes worsened. One day, he came up with the idea that one big drug sale could solve his financial problems for a long time and free him to focus on his art. Then, miraculously, an opportunity presented itself to sell thirty pounds of marijuana. Gene was excited. He had a good customer and a trusted supplier. This one deal would make him lots of money. It was all coming together beautifully. Maybe too beautifully, for as it turned out, the customer was an undercover cop, and Gene was once again busted. This time, it was serious.

He was already on their radar because of the publicity his magazine generated. It probably was easy to entrap Gene because he was so trusting and naïve. The feds and the state were fighting over who would take credit for getting this dangerous criminal off the streets. Luckily, he wound up sentenced to only one-and-a-half to three years in jail because he had a "good Jewish lawyer" (Gene's words). While incarcerated, Gene published a book of his jailhouse poetry. He got out in two years and moved to California, where he lives today. He still writes poetry, performs at various venues, and remains a provocateur.

❧ 8 ❧

Saturday night was the party night in the East Village. There were always parties in the neighborhood. Word spread quickly, and lots of people from various backgrounds would come together to get high. None of my friends were around, so I decided to go to the party alone.

The party was in a pad above McSorley's Old Ale House on East 7th Street. Standing in front of McSorley's brought back fond memories of my friends and me consuming pitchers of Guinness and eating sandwiches with the hottest mustard I had ever tasted. McSorley's has been around since 1854 and was (and still is) the oldest Irish saloon in New York. The walls were covered with incredible memorabilia, old newspapers, political buttons going back to the turn of the century, handcuffs that Houdini supposedly used, and scores of other interesting things filling every nook and cranny. The bar at that time didn't allow women. It was a place where men could drink, laugh, and fart without worrying about offending women. (It wasn't until 1970 that women were allowed in). Tonight, the party was in an apartment above the bar, and I hoped this evening would be as enjoyable as my many trips to McSorley's.

I walked up three flights to join the party. The small apartment was jammed with people. One of the guys at the party was handing out caps of LSD, and I happily popped one. This was my thirteenth trip. I'm not superstitious, but still, I crossed my fingers and hoped it would be a good one.

It wasn't long before the acid kicked in. At first, it felt nice and familiar, like the dozen trips I had already taken. Then things started to get weird. Everything seemed to have a red hue, as if I were looking through a dark red lens. My mind began jumping all over the place like I was on speed. I couldn't get centered, and everything looked surreal, freakish, and foreboding. I was having trouble identifying everyday objects like a stove or fridge. I was lost in a fog of forgetfulness and started to feel terrified. When I looked at people, they became menacing and ugly. I couldn't understand what people were saying. I also couldn't find my voice. I felt insignificant, vulnerable, and scared. I was looking for someone I knew or could relate to, but everyone looked ruthless, some even vicious. Faces became caricatures, more hideous by the minute. I was terrified and knew I had to get out of there. I had to escape and find someplace safe. But first, I needed to find my body and get my legs moving. I finally stood and somehow navigated through this horde of monsters and demons without being captured, tortured, or killed. It seemed like an eternity until I finally made it to the street.

It was dark and cold outside, but at least no one was looming over me. I walked past the façade of a building, and bricks turned into snakes and started jumping out of the wall to bite me. I tried desperately to keep it together. Just a few more blocks until I'd be home. I walked down 7th Street instead of St. Marks to avoid people, but there were still plenty of people around, and they all looked like hideous monsters. I wanted to sit down and curl up into a ball, but I knew that would make things worse. The last thing I wanted was for these monsters to notice me and do me harm. I had never felt such fear in my life. It seemed to take forever, but somehow, I made it to my door.

I laid down on the couch, closed my eyes, and tried to calm myself. *This is bad acid.* I told myself, "It will wear off soon." Now, with my eyes closed, I started seeing horrible visions of people running in fear as soldiers shot at them indiscriminately, bullets splattering skulls, mothers with children being gunned down, faceless Nazis shooting randomly, and pits full of dead naked

Jews. I saw concentration camp scenes and barbed wire dripping with blood. I saw people as thin as skeletons with bulging eyes dressed in rags. Death and dying were everywhere. It came in like a flood, and I was drowning in grief.

Then, I started experiencing myself as a baby. I was with my mom and dad in a dirty cattle car. I was in a lot of pain. My skin was burning, and I was very hungry. I actually felt all this in my body.

I could see my mother's face, her young face. Why wasn't she feeding me? Every time I began to cry, I felt my mother put her hand over my mouth to stop me. Why was she silencing me?

I felt her holding me close and shushing me. The warmth of her body comforted me, and I heard the rolling train again. The motion calmed me, and I thankfully fell asleep.

I awoke again, and the hunger was more intense, and the pain of my skin burned more severely. I tried to cry, but once again, her hand was covering my mouth. Why was she torturing me? Why wasn't she loving me?

I felt rage; I felt hatred toward her.

She doesn't love me. She doesn't love me! She never loved me.

The rage was boiling up, red hot. I saw a knife, a thin, sharp stiletto. I took it, and in a moment of madness, I raised it high and stabbed my mother in the heart.

This was a very real and deliberate action vividly ingrained in my mind. I was shocked. What had I done? How could I do this? I'm a monster. And suddenly, something broke within me, as if the dagger also punctured a dark, painful boil deep in my psyche. The dark bile of anger and hate oozed out of me, and I felt released from that ancient wound. Exhausted both physically and emotionally, I was finally able to fall into a blessed sleep.

I often heard the story of our escape from Poland on a freight train heading for the American sector in Germany. My mother had to keep me quiet, or we could have been discovered and arrested. I was very sick when we finally arrived at a displaced persons camp, where the doctors revived me.

The next morning, after the bad trip, my mother called me. She was very concerned about me. She hadn't heard from me for a few weeks, not since my family's visit to my cheap rundown apartment. Strange that she'd call today. *Did she feel something, too? Did my horrible experience affect her somehow?* That morning, I truly heard my mother. I felt her love and concern. I felt a closeness that I was blind to until now. I told her, in a caring and gentle way, that I was fine and not to worry.

I believe I relived a childhood experience, and as harrowing as my rage was, it was liberating.

❧ 9 ❧

Acapulco gold is primo weed, the best I've ever tried. I had scored four ounces and planned to sell much of it in nickel bags. I had a few regular customers, mostly from college, who would come to my pad to buy some dope. I wasn't the type of dealer that stood out in the street, hawking wares. I was strictly small-time and only interested in having a supply for me and my friends and making a little extra to cover some of my meager expenses.

One afternoon, Perry came over to sample the new weed. I loved it when Perry came over; we always had great discussions. That day, he was particularly philosophical.

Perry said, "Be kind, for every person you meet is fighting a hard battle. You realize as human beings that we have an amazing challenge; we're part of the universe, yet we have this individual sense of being cut off from everything, and it's an incredible dichotomy. That's what we feel as spirits living in a condensed body. We feel only certain emotions, like physical love, as opposed to universal love. We have to get over our separation and loneliness because life is preparing us for an incredible journey."

We had just finished smoking another joint and enjoying the wonderful high when we suddenly heard a loud knocking at my door. With some effort, I got up to check the door. I didn't have the foresight to ask who it was or even check the peephole because I was in a very peaceful and trusting place. I just opened the door, and two big, burly men pushed me aside and forced their way into my apartment. I realized right away these were the notorious narcs, and once again, I was getting busted.

These guys brandished guns and waved badges while yelling loudly, "Nobody move; nobody fucking move, or we'll shoot."

I don't know if they had a search warrant. These guys were prepared for resistance, but Perry and I, being mellow hippies, just stood there stunned, not moving. That didn't stop them from treating us like we were dangerous criminals. They pushed us against the wall and handcuffed us in no time flat.

I said to Perry, "Is this the incredible journey life is preparing me for?"

One of the narcs said, "Shut the fuck up."

They ransacked my place and easily found my meager stash, which consisted of about twenty caps of LSD and the weed. They also found my money and pocketed it. It was about three hundred dollars, which would have covered six months' rent.

I treated my drug dealing as if it were no big deal, especially since lots of my friends did a little dealing on the side. Clearly, I was too sloppy, too cavalier, and didn't take the necessary precautions. I must have aroused suspicion, and now I got caught. It was my own damn fault.

Perry and I were led out in handcuffs like common criminals and taken once again to the Tombs, a jail in lower Manhattan. This is where they took murderers, rapists, and first-time drug offenders. The Tombs was known as the Manhattan House of Detention and ranked as the worst of the city's jails in overall conditions and overcrowding. It held an average of 2,000 inmates in spaces designed for 925.

We were booked, searched, and fingerprinted. They took our belts and shoelaces so we wouldn't hang ourselves. The jail was enormous, with many floors. We were led through many iron gates with fierce guards glaring at us. Bleak fluorescent lights illuminated the drab walls with their peeling green paint and water stains. We passed hundreds of cells, all filled with miserable faces, the unluckiest of the city.

There's no buzzkill like getting busted. It all seemed unreal, like we were playing a role in some bizarre grade-B movie. We were led to our cell, a six-by-eight room with metal benches and a metal toilet. Once the steel door slammed shut, misery kicked in. *What the fuck do I do now?* I wondered. I was certain I was headed to jail. Four ounces of weed was a felony, and I would face years in prison. It felt like my life was over.

I said, "Man, now I'm truly fucked. I'm going to jail for a long time."

Perry said, "You don't know that, Bernie. Did they have a search warrant? Man, stay cool. We never know what the universe has in store for us."

Perry was the best cellmate one could hope for. His positive attitude and calm demeanor helped me calm down. He took a very philosophical view of our situation and talked me off the ledge.

We only spent one night in prison. Perry's charges were dropped since he had no drugs on him. I was charged and assigned a public defender. Since I was a student and this was my first offense, I didn't need to post bail. I was free to go and was told the city would notify me of my court date. They had my address and my parents' address. I begged them not to tell my parents.

Since we had no money on us, we walked the few miles back to the East Village. It was such a relief being out of that shitty jail. They let us out around noon. The day was gray and cold, and we were hungry but glad to be free. I got back to my apartment in about an hour.

As I walked up the stairs, I realized I didn't have my keys. I also realized I had never locked the apartment door. (It would have been hard to do while in handcuffs, and it wasn't like the cops were thoughtful or obliging.) As I approached my apartment, I was shocked to see my door was wide open. I could see right away that my apartment was ransacked and burglarized. I didn't have a lot of stuff, but they took almost everything. My precious record collection, gone. Not one record left. Some of the records were irreplaceable, like my Sheila Jordan album, *Portrait of Sheila*, which she had autographed so beautifully, "To

Bernie, my biggest fan. Love Sheila" ... gone.

I remembered seeing her perform at one of the clubs on MacDougal Street in Greenwich Village back in 1963. She was a jazz vocalist, and all she had backing her up was a bassist named Steve Swallow.

I went to hear her with Steve Tintweiss, who was studying bass with Swallow. I can still hear her sing, "Falling in love with love is falling for make-believe. Falling in love with love is playing the fool." I loved her voice and remembered we sat through both sets. She came over after the second set to talk to us. We were the last customers in the club.

A couple of weeks later, I returned to hear her again, bringing her 1962 Blue Note album. After the set, she signed it, and I was smitten. Now it's gone, and all I had left were the memories.

They took my record player, my silver flute, and even some clothes and kitchen utensils. I was hoping to learn the flute and play jazz like Eric Dolphy. Thankfully, my beautiful pussy portrait, the colorful "Hole in the Wall" lovingly painted by Renee, was still there to remind me of happier days.

I was cleaned out. Fortunately, Daniel, my next-door neighbor, the drummer and conga player for Richie Havens, and a real stand-up guy, had salvaged a few items.

When my friend Andy heard of the robbery, he gave me his radio. It wasn't just any old radio; it was a top-of-the-line Grundig Majestic radio with AM, FM, and shortwave. The sound was spectacular, much better than my old record player. And now we had music again. Symphony Sid would play great jazz late at night, as did WKCR out of Columbia University. The British Invasion was in full swing, and great music was heard again at Bernie's.

My court date was set for about a month after the bust. Several days before I was to appear in court, a brand-new psychedelic drug, STP, arrived at Eric's. This drug was the latest created by Owsley Stanley, the famous underground chemist. Timothy Leary labeled this drug "Serenity, Tranquility, Peace." It was too tempting, and Andy and I decided to try it. I felt sure I'd be fine for my trial. An acid trip never lasted more than eight or nine hours. How long could this drug last?

Quite a while, it turned out. STP was a different kind of drug. It didn't have the intensity of LSD, but it lasted many days. It came on slowly. At first, I felt a tingling throughout my body. Soon, I felt super conscious with clarity and understanding I never had before. It was like being enlightened and all-knowing. I was able to smoke DMT with little effect. I could communicate telepathically with Andy. We would answer each other's thoughts. We had deep conversations without saying a word, or so it seemed to me.

I was aware of and understood everything. Fear and uncertainty didn't exist. Was this the next stage of human evolution? *Homo sapiens* were like Neanderthals compared to us, at least for a few days.

I saw my friends in a new light and saw the greed, anxiety, and insecurity in them. I didn't feel superior, nor did I feel concerned for them. Compassion and caring weren't ingredients of this drug. If they took STP, I thought they would rise above these trifling feelings and be free.

It had been four days since I first took STP, and I was still very high. Today was my court date. I had no fear. What could these mere mortals do to me? Andy accompanied me to the courthouse. We sat there quite detached while watching the proceedings. I felt nothing when my case was called. I was detached even when I stood before the judge.

The judge threw out the case due to a lack of evidence. It was clear those narcs took the weed for themselves and turned in the LSD caps, thinking it was heroin, which would be enough to put me away for a long time. The narcs pocketed the real evidence and my money, and now they had no case; lucky me. As I understood it, the lab tested the caps for heroin and found nothing. Presumably, the test for heroin involved heat that destroyed the LSD inside the capsules. I was extremely lucky and was free to go. Since I was on STP, I considered the whole affair no big deal.

One problem with STP is that it's hard to sleep. I was high

for about five days with very little sleep. When I could finally sleep, I slept for a long time. When I awoke, the drug had worn off, and I was my old self, my old insecure, fucked-up self. So much for enlightenment. That drug took a toll on my body and mind. I was exhausted for days.

❧10❧

It was just another Saturday night on the Lower East Side of Manhattan, late autumn of 1966. It was acid night at Eric's apartment. Good old acid, no more STP. It took weeks for that shit to leave my system. I was ready for a safe, garden-variety LSD trip (if there was such a thing).

Some of the gang was already there; Andy, Mike, and Carol were starting to trip. I took my hit and joined the party. Taking acid was a bit of a crapshoot because each trip could differ wildly. Sometimes, it's love and peace; sometimes—as I'd recently learned—it's paranoia and demons. Often, it's a mix of both. I'd taken lots of acid—no big deal. *Let's see what tonight brings.*

My high was already starting when I felt something very different and abnormal. Something was coming, something ominous. *Bernie, relax. You've taken lots of acid. You love tripping; don't start by bumming yourself out.*

About an hour into my trip, I realized what the night would bring. *I'm going to die tonight. Death, the final trip.* The thought was terrifying, but at least I would have the answer to the eternal questions: Is death the end of life? Is there a God? Is the soul immortal? Will I go to heaven or hell, or will I reincarnate into a new body?

Tonight, I'll find out. Tonight, I'll have all the answers, but I won't be able to share them with anyone.

But I don't want to die. Why do I have to die? I want to die when I'm old and gray. But the voice in my head said, "You don't control your destiny. Your soul won't die. Your body is like an old rag that the soul discards."

I had read some books on mysticism. *The Tibetan Book of the Dead* was popular in my circle. It talks about death and rebirth and the importance of being fully conscious at the time of death to experience the clear light. All the Eastern philosophies speak of the soul and reincarnation.

Don't be scared, I told myself. But I was frightened. I was starting to freak myself out. I tried to be pragmatic and told myself, "Bernie, calm down. This is just a trip. I'll get through it. I've had bad trips before."

"This is the end. This night really will be your last. You will not come back from this trip," I heard a voice in my head that I didn't recognize, a voice that spoke with conviction and finality.

"This will be my last trip," I told myself. With tears in my eyes, I saw my friends happily tripping, oblivious to my predicament. I wanted to say goodbye to them; I needed to say goodbye. But I didn't want to be a downer. I gave Andy all my money and said goodbye. "Okay, dude, I'll see you later," Andy replied.

"Okay, it's time," I told myself. I laid down on the floor, spread-eagle, and said, "Okay, God, take me." I expected it to be easy; I'd just close my eyes, and off I'd go. I was ready to let go; I had no choice. I wondered whether it would be light or darkness.

"Not here. You can't die here. Your body is going to freak people out. Go up to the roof," I heard the voice command.

"Okay, that's cool. I'll go up to the roof," I replied to the voice in my head.

Eric's apartment was on the second floor of a six-story tenement. This building has no elevators, so I walked up the four flights to the roof, past the smell of weed and piss, a broken sink in the hall, and a dirty mattress in a dark corner.

People often go up to the roof, but thankfully, that night, I was alone. I laid down on the cold asphalt, spread my arms out, and said, "Okay, God, I'm ready. Take me."

The answer was clear, "Not here; the ledge."

The ledge? Sit on the fucking ledge? That's crazy. I could accidentally fall. I was very stoned. But for some crazy reason,

I complied. I carefully sat on the ledge with my legs dangling downward. I didn't dare look down. I looked out at the tenement buildings across the street and saw silhouettes in the windows, people living their lives. The sky was getting a bit lighter. I saw the smoke rising from tenement smokestacks, dark gray ribbons commingling with the pale gray sky. I heard a distant ambulance and a dog barking. I saw the traffic lights changing from red to green and back to red. I sat for what seemed an eternity, not daring to look down. I felt a chill in my bones. It was early Sunday morning, and the city was eerily quiet, too quiet.

I finally looked down, way down to the street far below. "This is crazy. I'm too fucked up to be here," I thought. And suddenly, I saw myself falling, falling toward the cold concrete. I felt myself accelerating with the wind on my face and hair; the street was getting closer and closer, way too fast. But I didn't hit the concrete. What I felt instead was a body of water. Cool, pure water, ocean water. I tasted the salty brine. I dove deep into the water. Then, the scene changed. I was no longer in the water; I was at a graveside. My mom, dad, and my two sisters were at my grave. My mom was crying, my dad was grief-stricken, and my sisters were sad beyond belief. I saw them so clearly that I could almost touch them, but there was no time to say goodbye. I didn't have much joy in my childhood, anyway. Time to move on. Now, I was back in the ocean, continuing my descent deeper into the cold water, deeper into the darkness. Suddenly, I righted myself. I started swimming upward, upward toward the light. The light was not far off; the light was getting brighter. My lungs felt like they were about to explode. And then I broke through. I was free from the ocean. *I'm no longer drowning. No longer in darkness. I'm surrounded by light, bright golden sunlight. I breathed in. I'm alive. I'm alive! I made it.*

All around me were the most beautiful people I'd ever seen, beautiful golden people. Men and women were cheering my bravery, welcoming me with open arms. I looked around. I wasn't on the Lower East Side of NYC, but in a tropical paradise.

The sun was warm, and the air smelled sweet. I was on a beach with white sand and palm trees swaying in the breeze. I was welcomed, accepted, and loved. I was in my new home, starting a new life. Free of all worries or cares. And I finally understood.

This is a possibility.

This could be mine.

This could be real if only I lean a bit forward. Just a tiny bit forward. That's all it takes. A small leap of faith.

Holy shit, holy fucking shit. I need to hold on to something. Don't lean forward, schmuck! Hold on.

"But you know you are not the body," the voice told me. "You are the soul. You have reincarnated thousands of times. What's the problem? Let go. Just a slight lean forward, and it's all yours. Paradise and eternal happiness will be yours."

I considered letting go, leaning forward, claiming my paradise.

But a small voice of reason was crying to be heard. "This is not real. Some demon is fucking with your mind. You don't want to die. You don't fucking want to die."

I prayed in fear and desperation, "Oh, God, please tell me if this is real. Do you want me to jump? Please give me a sign, not in my head, but in the real world."

And out of the quiet, from what seemed a long distance, I heard, "Juuuuummmmp, juuuuummmmp."

Holy shit—no fucking way. Was I hearing this in the real world, or was it still just in my head?

I then said to God, "If you want me to die, come here in person and push me. I don't believe this is real. I believe a demon entered my head, and I want him out. I want to live."

I got off the ledge ever so carefully. I stayed on the roof until the sun rose. It was a cold morning in late autumn, but it was the most beautiful day of my life. It was a new day after a nightmare that had traumatized me to my core. I felt like a man after a long, debilitating illness. My legs were not quite steady, but I felt alive. My fingers were frozen, and I was shivering, but

I was alive! More alive than I had felt in a long time. I fought the demon and won. I was lucky. It was a close match. It could have gone either way, but I won and was elated to be alive in the Lower East Side of NYC.

The hard question was whether the demon was real or if it was my mind trying to destroy me. It was easy to see it as a demon, but what if it was my creation? What would that say about me? Was there a self-destructive element to my nature that could resurface? I had no way of knowing. I always thought of myself as a happy, easygoing person. At this point, I'd taken more than fifty trips and saw acid as a crapshoot—sometimes it was ecstasy and other times misery, but I had never imagined it a possible death sentence.

❧11❧

My luck or fate had changed for the worse. My happy hippie days had gone dark. My world was falling apart, and I didn't know what to do. It had been about eighteen months since I first took LSD and became a true believer, a bona fide acidhead. Now, after my arrest, after finding my apartment burglarized, and after my brush with death, I had sunk into depression. When would things improve? When would this losing streak end? Not right away, it seemed. My draft board physical was scheduled for the next day.

In late December 1966, I dragged my ass down to the draft board. The Selective Service finally caught up with me six months after I dropped out of college. The draft board physicals were held downtown on Whitehall Street, and I was there along with a thousand other terrified boys.

Andy advised me not to wear underwear. He said, "They don't allow people to walk around bare ass. So, you'll keep your pants on while everyone else is walking around in their shit-stained white undies."

My friend Howie and I had our physicals on the same day, so we went together. As hard as I tried, I couldn't fail the physical. During the written test, I deliberately tried to answer every question incorrectly. I passed with flying colors. Not even a genius could deliberately fail that test since the passing grade was close to zero.

I asked to see the Army psychiatrist and told him I was addicted to drugs and was stoned on LSD right now. He replied with a sneer, "Don't worry, son, the Army will straighten you out." It was the height of the Vietnam War, and they had a quota to fill.

I left the physical, depressed as all hell, sure that I would get drafted. As I walked down the dirty streets, I suddenly had an idea—it was time to call Timothy Leary. After all, about a year ago, he offered to accept me in his LSD church, the League for Spiritual Discovery. Once I became a member, I could apply for conscientious objector status. A sliver of hope cut through my gloom. My pace quickened as I rushed home to call the "pope of dope."

Tim and his followers lived in a 64-room mansion in upstate New York in a town called Millbrook. The Hitchcock family owned the estate, including its 2,400 acres. Billy and Peggy Hitchcock were siblings and heirs to the Mellon fortune; they were young jet setters, patrons of the arts, and confidantes of the well-known and eccentric. They mingled with race car drivers, actors, writers, and celebrities of all kinds. The Hitchcocks were also acidheads and friends of Tim Leary and rented this incredible mansion to him for only one dollar a year.

I got Tim on the phone after explaining my situation to several people. I reminded him of our conversation at the Second Street Theater and how impressed I was by his illuminating talk about the virtues of LSD. I reaffirmed my willingness to join his League for Spiritual Discovery and apply to the draft board as a conscientious objector. I told him I was ready to burn my draft card and become enlightened under his guidance. He finally permitted me to come to Millbrook to discuss the possibility of acceptance to this noble institution. I wasn't out of the woods yet, but I had landed an interview.

In early January 1967, I took a train from Grand Central Station to Millbrook, which took about three hours. It had snowed earlier in the week, and a blanket of white glistening snow covered the grounds. Finally, the castle came into view in the late afternoon fog. It was painted white, and the tall pine trees behind it were mostly white from the freshly fallen snow. The structure was grand, with two large turrets, an enormous wrap-around porch, and a green slate roof. Greeting me was a massive clown-like face painted on the front of the building. It felt surreal and unearthly, like an apparition.

A blonde woman in a red cape asked who I was. I told her my name; she checked her list, and sure enough, I was welcomed. She introduced herself as Carol and led me through a large double door into a spacious vestibule. Carol took my coat, and we went up a magnificent, wide, curving staircase of burnished oak to the second floor, where there was a large sitting room and dining area. I couldn't help but notice an enormous oval mirror framed in gold and a massive crystal chandelier that hung from the ceiling. I marveled at the splendor of this castle. Carol then led me through French doors, up another flight of stairs to a large sliding door of Tiffany glass.

She slid the beautiful floral panel door open, and we entered Tim Leary's spacious private quarters. Here, I met the lord of the manor. Tim was dressed casually, his long white hair framing his narrow face. His piercing blue eyes assessed me, and he said, "Welcome to Millbrook. You will be part of

The Hitchcock estate in Millbrook, NY, circa the mid-1960s

the Bill Haines group. I hope you are happy here." End of interview. I thanked him for allowing me to come.

Carol then took me to meet Bill. I had no idea what it meant to be assigned to the other group. Was I not accomplished enough to be part of the League? Was I being sent down to the minors?

On our long walk to meet Bill Haines, I was told that Tim had limited membership to the league to 360 core members, and all the slots were taken. This helped soften the abrupt, almost unwelcoming meeting with Tim.

Bill's group was already established as Sri Ram Ashram. They lost their lease sometime earlier, and Tim allowed them to share the mansion. His group consisted of about 25 members, most of whom were young, hippie-ish folks who embraced psychedelics as the holy sacrament, along with practicing yoga and studying Hindu philosophy.

We entered the ashram area, a large room filled with many Indian prints on the walls and a few oriental rugs covering the oak floors. Fragrant incense permeated the atmosphere. Bill and his group were already seated, mostly on floor cushions.

Bill was a well-built man of about forty, of average height, with a round, clean-shaven face, short black hair, and dark, penetrating eyes. He was sitting in a half-lotus position, wrapped in a large gray wool meditation shawl, with his followers around him in a circle.

After being introduced to Bill, I sat in the circle, and Bill continued his sermon for the day. It had been a long day for me. I was exhausted and promptly fell asleep during the sermon. I woke up just as he was finishing. I was embarrassed. This wasn't a good way to start my first day at Millbrook. To his credit, Bill just looked amused.

Bill introduced me to some of his disciples. One was Bali Ram, who wore translucent gold Indian attire. He was short, thin, and muscular, with a very handsome face and big dark eyes. Bali Ram was a Nepalese temple dancer. Bali's family had given him to the temple when he was six years old. Bill had met him in Nepal and somehow got him out of the country. When Bill introduced me, Bali took my hand in both of his and looked me over like I was a delicious piece of meat, which made me uncomfortable. This amused Bill. Later, I learned that Bill and Bali had once been a couple.

I was assigned Richard Alpert's old room on the top floor. Alpert was an associate of Tim Leary's at Harvard and worked with him to promote LSD. Shortly after Alpert left Millbrook, he went to India, where he met his guru, took the name Ram Dass, and published a well-known book, *Be Here Now*. This work is considered instrumental in bringing spirituality, yoga, and meditation to the West. Ram Dass spent the rest of his life spreading yogic teachings.

Mostly, I hung out with Bill's group. I found them more to my liking, and Bill was quite the character, not what I imagined a guru to be. He was loud, brash, vulgar, and hilariously funny. He was well-versed in Hindu scripture and Buddhism, having studied in India for nine years, but didn't take any of it too seriously.

Bill didn't spare anyone. He would lash out at someone for the slightest infraction. He would yell and curse them out in front of the group, which would usually get a laugh. For some disciples, it was a lesson of tough love, but most didn't take his jibes seriously. They would talk back and make a joke out of it. The group loved to joke. The group was more like the Merry Pranksters than devotees in an ashram.

Bill's most devoted disciple was Saraswati, a skinny, young white woman in Indian attire and a crew cut, who proved to be a thorn in his side. Her devotion was epic and almost all-consuming. At one point, she slept on the floor in front of his bedroom door. She always tried to get close to him, and he would yell and push her away with his cane. "Saraswati, you crazy bitch, leave, I can't stand the sight of you." He would yell, much to the amusement of the group. She would respond, "Oh, guruji, stop kidding around. I know you don't mean it."

And so, she would defuse each one of his affronts, much to his dismay. It appeared that he was stuck with her.

One day, I happened to wander into Saraswati's bedroom by mistake when she wasn't there. On her nightstand, next to her bed, was a bronze statue of the Buddha. Surrounding the statue were about a dozen hypodermic needles, carefully arranged around the Buddha, with the needles pointed inward. I heard that she was once addicted to heroin. Now, she was addicted to Bill Haines.

I spent about three months at Millbrook, and what amazes me is how little I remember of the place and people. In the East Village, I connected with people and made close friendships. I certainly connected with lots of ladies. I can't remember making one close friend at Millbrook or sleeping with any of the fine ladies. Perhaps I was depressed. For whatever reason, I mostly hung out by myself.

Most of the fine ladies were in committed relationships, and many were married with children. There were about a dozen kids at Millbrook, ranging in age from toddlers to teenagers. The folks here were older and more established and accomplished. There were various business operations, including a printing press that published booklets, newsletters, and pamphlets. There were also a couple of sandal makers, jewelry designers, and various artists. Being here made me appreciate that family life and committed loving relationships were possible in the hippie world. I hoped one day to find my true love and have a family.

Millbrook turned out to be a blessing. It provided a nice place to rejuvenate my body, recharge my brain, and nourish my soul. I had a pleasant, private room at the top of one of the turrets, three fine meals each day, fresh air, and nobody bothered me. I was asked to do some chores, which I happily did. Sometimes, I ate communally, but often, I would grab some food out of the enormous walk-in refrigerator in the kitchen. Sometimes, I joined Bill's group for meditation or a lecture, but I don't recall participating much in discussions. I smoked grass and dropped acid occasionally. I must have been perceived as a loner, possibly someone without much to offer. As a result, people pretty much left me alone, which was fine.

I remember one particularly sleepless night near the end of my stay. While lying in bed, I started thinking about how I didn't score with any of Millbrook's fine ladies. I was living an ascetic life and missed having a lover. To make myself feel better, I started thinking about all the incredible women I had screwed while living in the East Village. I couldn't remember all their names, but I was often able to recall how they looked or some other aspect of our connection. These recollections brought an overdue smile to my face.

As my count approached fifty different women, I was getting very drowsy. Finally, I could embrace the sweet arms of sleep.

But what was sad was that other than Gretchen and Renee, none of these ladies meant much to me. I didn't remember the names of more than half of them. Most were one-night stands. At the time, I considered these a great achievement, but in reality, it wasn't much more than making someone's acquaintance at a party. I'm sure most of them didn't remember my name either. Free love was all the rage in hippiedom. It was free of commitment, free of genuine caring, and also free of love. Someday, I hoped to experience genuine love.

In the early afternoon, one day, I decided to return to the East Village. I needed to leave for a week or two to get out of my slump and get back in the saddle. When I got to the kitchen, someone said Tim wanted to see me. I hoped I wasn't about to get kicked out of Millbrook.

ᔒ12ᔕ

I was escorted into Leary's comfortable suite. He greeted me kindly and explained there was a nightly ritual at Millbrook that required one member of the community to drop acid and trip in the meditation house. This person was the designated gatekeeper, assigned to keep out evil spirits and elevate the vibration of the entire community.

He said, "Bernie, I would like you to be the gatekeeper tonight. Are you ready to keep good vibrations flowing and bad vibes out of Millbrook?"

I said, "Yes, but I don't know how to do that."

Tim said, "It's easy. Be in a good frame of mind and let the acid guide you."

I said, "Okay, I'll try."

He opened the cupboard and took out a vodka bottle filled to the brim with pure Sandoz acid. Sandoz Pharmaceuticals originally synthesized LSD, and what Tim had was pure acid straight from the manufacturer. There must have been thousands of trips in that bottle, and who knows how many more bottles of acid he had in that cupboard.

Tim extracted a couple of drops and placed them on my tongue. He said a few more things to prepare me, but I don't recall the specifics. Tonight's ritual took place in the meditation house, about a hundred yards from the main house. I looked forward to spending a night in that beautiful stone structure.

It was an early mid-March evening, and snow was still on the ground. I trudged to the meditation house with my flashlight, winter coat, and boots. The meditation house was a well-insu-lated stone structure with a large fireplace, fine wooden floors, and a few windows from which I could see a field of pure white snow. A warm fire was burning brightly in the hearth, and there were plenty of logs to keep the fire raging all night. There was a couch and a couple of easy chairs in front of the fireplace. It was a comfortable room with extra blankets, a kaleidoscope, and some books, all perfect for a beautiful trip. I took my coat and boots off and settled cozily on the couch, feeling the heat of the fire and enjoying the serenade provided by the crackling wood. There was no radio or record player. I guessed the pur-pose of this room was to meditate and focus on the inner self, which was fine by me. I was ready to try the meditation tech-nique Bill Haines taught.

I could tell this was pure LSD; the high was euphoric. I was happy to be enjoying a good acid experience again. But about four hours into the trip, while I was still very high, Florin appeared to me in her astral form. The same Florin I met the day Kennedy was assassinated. That That dear African-American grandmother who told me about spirituality and encouraged me to take LSD, saying it would change my life. I remember her saying, "I think we will meet again." But I never imagined it would be like this.

She appeared much as I remembered her. I could see her entire body, which was translucent, sparkling with an unearthly light. She wore a white flowing robe, stood straight and tall, and had radiant eyes that were beautiful and bright. She spoke to my mind. I couldn't hear her with my ears, but I under-stood everything she said.

"Tell Timothy Leary I want to meet him," was all she said.

Then she was gone, and my trip abruptly ended. Very weird. It was still night and eerily quiet in the meditation house. By my calculation, I still had a few hours left of my trip. I was a bit freaked out by the experience; nothing like this had ever hap-pened to me or anyone else I knew. What the hell was that? It must have been a hallucination. But why would I imagine her? I hadn't seen or thought about her in years. It didn't make sense. Could she somehow have triggered the experience in me? Is it possible for someone to simply will themselves into someone else's consciousness? The thought scared me.

I sat in the meditation room until morning, pondering this experience. I vividly recalled the incredible meeting with Florin. She said that we are not the body; we are the soul, and we can experience our soul. I could imagine experiencing my own soul, but experiencing someone else's soul seemed farfetched. In the final analysis, I concluded this must have been a crazy hallucination. After all, I had taken a large dose of pure Sandoz LSD. Hallucinations can be very convincing. I still shudder to think about the night on the roof that almost cost me my life. I still recall seeing my family at my graveside and me popping out of the water to a new life in a beautiful new land.

Florin had given me her phone number, which I had kept in my wallet all these years. That morning, I found the folded piece of paper and thought about calling her. It seemed weird to call after all these years. Would she even remember me? I almost decided not to. But what if she was really contacting me? I needed to know, and the only way to find out was to call. It was too early to call, so I decided to call her later that day.

I went into the grand house and had a nice big breakfast. All was quiet. I wondered if I had been a successful gatekeeper. Did I keep good vibrations flowing and bad vibes out of Millbrook? I didn't think Florin's visit or hallucination was a bad vibe.

I called Florin early that afternoon and said, "Hi, I'm sorry to trouble you, ma'am. Are you Florin?" When she replied yes, I said, "My name is Bernie Ross. Do you, by chance, remember me?"

I expected there to be some hesitation, but she replied right away. "Yes, Bernie, I remember you well. You tried to sell me a Bible the day Kennedy was assassinated. Now you're in Millbrook, right?

I was floored by her answer and replied, "Yes, how do you know that?"

She then said, "Did you ask Timothy Leary if I could come visit?"

Holy shit, it wasn't a hallucination. I almost fell over. This was real; no doubt she knew I had seen her the night before.

I told her, "I haven't had a chance to ask him yet. I will call you back when I do."

Florin said, "Oh, you first wanted to check if you hallucinated seeing me last night? I can't blame you. What you experienced is called astral projection, and the first time you experience it can be frightening."

I replied, "It wasn't frightening; it was totally mind-blowing. I've never experienced anything like that before. I saw you just like I remembered you the day Kennedy was assassinated. I will try to speak with Leary today and get back to you as soon as I know."

She said she appreciated my call and looked forward to speaking later.

After the call, I thought about astral projection. I wondered if I would experience it again. LSD introduced me to endless possibilities within our consciousness. Florin showed me there are planes beyond the physical that offer extraordinary powers for those who master them. I felt Florin was way beyond LSD and wondered why she wanted to meet Tim.

I went to Tim and told him about my trip in detail. And I asked him if Florin could come to visit, and he said yes. He didn't ask questions about the astral projection, which surprised me. Maybe he knew all about it, and it's not a big deal. I also thought it would be a good idea for Perry to accompany her. I told Tim about Perry, noting he was a famous jazz musician. Tim agreed to allow both to come, but only for the weekend.

I called Perry, and he was happy to accompany Florin to Millbrook, even though he didn't know her. Next, I called Florin, and she was delighted that Leary gave her permission to come and pleased that Perry would accompany her next weekend. She said this was very thoughtful of me.

When I told Bill Haines about my experience, he had a different perspective. He explained that Florin appeared to me because I entered the astral plane during my acid trip.

He asked, "Were you doing Sri Ram meditation like I showed you?"

I said, "I'm not sure. I was having a great trip until she appeared."

He continued, "Florin could enter your trip because you crossed into the astral plane. She must be a shaman or master to contact you through astral projection. That's a very rare gift. I can't wait to meet her."

"The astral plane is the first plane beyond the physical. This plane is so vast that it's many times larger than the physical universe. When we die, our spirit leaves the body and goes to the astral plane. There are many regions in the astral plane, some beautiful and heavenly and some terrible hells. The spirit goes to a region based on one's karma. You know about karma?"

"Not much," I answered.

"You know the saying, 'as you sow, so shall you reap'? Your spirit gets rewarded for good deeds and punished for bad ones. So, depending on how you lead your life, you go to either an astral heaven or an astral hell or somewhere in between. Our spirit stays in the astral until it's ready for rebirth in the physical plane. The type of life we get when we are reborn also depends on karma. We are reborn with karmic debt; some call it our fate or destiny. We may be reborn into a wonderful, caring family or into some horrible situation. Karma is a bitch; it spares no one. A person you abused in your past life can be a family member in the current life and treat you like shit."

"Are you saying that all the horrible things that happen to people are because of karma—because it's the person's own fault?" I asked.

"It's not that simple. We have free will, which could change our karma or someone else's. Someone can do bad stuff to you, and your suffering isn't because of your karma. People can start wars, causing countless suffering to innocent people because of free will. But our individual karma must be paid off, and that's almost impossible since we are creating new karma every day. We're stuck on the Wheel of Transmigration, continually reincarnating, until we gain enlightenment."

"Wow, that's incredible! What you're saying is we are trapped on this wheel. If we do good things, we reap the rewards of our good karma. If we do bad shit, we return to pain and suffering. You say the only way to get off the wheel is to get enlightenment. How do we get enlightenment?" I asked.

"I lived in India for nine years and studied with several gurus. Each one said that to gain enlightenment, you must master their meditation or yoga method, which required renouncing the world and meditating in some remote ashram or a cave in the Himalayas for decades. By renouncing the world, you no longer create karma, and by perfecting the meditation practice, you rise to higher spiritual planes. When you reach the highest plane, you gain full enlightenment. Well, I wasn't ready to spend my life in some ashram, so when I returned to America, I discovered peyote. In one trip, I went further than any meditation. I realized enlightenment could be ours by taking psychedelics, and then I started the Sri Ram Ashram."

"Did you attain enlightenment?" I asked.

"There are degrees of enlightenment. It's a process. Taking the sacrament, meditating, and leading a disciplined life of love and understanding leads to enlightenment."

It was clear to me that Bill, with all his knowledge, was not enlightened, but his description of karma blew my mind. It was a neat theory that explained everything. To embrace it, one needed to believe in reincarnation and accept that our soul has been migrating to various bodies for eons, evaluated for all our actions, rewarded for our good deeds, and punished for the bad ones—never to gain freedom until we attain this elusive thing called enlightenment. Something seemed missing from this theory. It seemed severe and unforgiving—a never-ending prison sentence. It scared the shit out of me. Who created this karma thing? What about God? I wondered. Was there a God? I didn't want to keep on coming back to some shitty earth existence dealing with disappointment, pain, and death. I didn't want to be on an endless wheel, hoping that my next trip would free me. But what about what I experienced, like Florin's astral form and being one with all things? There must be more to learn. There must be a purpose to my life, or so I hoped.

* * *

Florin and Perry were scheduled to arrive on Saturday. I hung out near the front door to greet them upon their arrival. It was early afternoon when they came, and Florin looked much as I remembered her, a beautiful, strong, powerful Black woman. She wore a long, flowing dark blue robe and a white turban on her head. Perry wore a colorful shirt and a fez. I couldn't help but smile when I saw Perry. He conveyed pure positive energy, and I could see he and Florin were now fast friends.

Florin came over and gave me a big hug like we were old friends. I had a new reverence for Florin and felt very close to her since seeing her radiant astral form. Clearly, she was a shaman or master in her own right. I asked her about entering my trip, and she said it was easy once you knew how. She said she sometimes thought of me and could see my state of being. She knew I was on acid and was open to seeing her without freaking out. She said it was a gift that works only with certain people, and I was open to her.

This freaked me out a bit. I asked. "Can you read my thoughts and see what I'm doing?"

She said, "No. I check in only on rare occasions, and I don't read minds."

We were then escorted into Leary's inner sanctum. After introductions, Tim spoke to Florin for a few minutes and excused himself. It seemed like he deliberately tried to avoid her for the rest of the weekend. Perhaps he was a bit intimidated.

Bill Haines and Florin hit it off and had some good discussions. Then I showed her and Perry around the big house, and I introduced them to people; some were Tim's followers, and some were Bill's. Florin was regal, always comfortable and confident. People were impressed with her. She was interested in each person, and people enjoyed speaking with her. I learned more about these folks in the few minutes Florin talked to them than in the months I lived at Millbrook. People intrinsically trusted Florin and shared their lives and hopes with her.

Mostly, we hung out with Bill's group. That night, some of the group lit up joints and passed them around. This was some fine shit, and soon we all enjoyed a nice buzz. Perry started to play his clarinet, and soon, folks joined him on bongos, tablas, and flutes. Perry was a master at bringing out the musician in everyone, and soon, everyone was feeling the music. Then Bali began to dance. Soon, others joined the dance. Some people howled as Perry's playing grew more intense and Bali's movements became more exotic. It was a wonderful evening, with laughter and joy. When the frivolity ended, more weed was smoked—the perfect end to a perfect day! Florin and Perry were then shown their rooms. After dropping off Perry, I asked him what he thought about Florin.

"Man, she is amazing. What a beautiful soul. She is a powerful, enlightened woman—a shaman or goddess. We had incredible conversations. I learned a lot about spirituality from her. She's totally out there, man, completely uni. I told her she should start her own ashram." Perry answered.

That night, I thought about my time at Millbrook. Over the weekend, I felt like I had finally woken up after a long sleep. Before this, I hadn't connected with anyone, not even the ladies, my specialty, or so I thought. I needed to get away for a bit. I missed my friends in the East Village. I needed to get laid. Maybe I could return more connected to the scene if I took a vacation from Millbrook. Perhaps I could start over and be a contributing member of this crazy community.

The next morning, I asked Carol if I could leave for a week or so.

She said, "This is your home. You can come and go as you please." This statement truly touched me.

Florin, Perry, and I headed back to the city that afternoon. During our ride back, I told them about what I learned about karma from Bill.

I said, "If karma is for real, it is some severe shit."

Florin replied. "Yes, the law of karma is for real, and it spares no one. It's a just law; we are held accountable for our actions. But there's another law—the law of grace. God's grace can lessen the effects of karma and get us through hard times. Faith, humility, and prayer attract God's grace."

I asked, "What is God? Is he some guy in Heaven like in the Bible?"

"No, God is a power, a conscious power that controls all of creation. It's difficult to explain; it needs to be experienced. There are so many levels to it, so many planes of creation. I'm just at the threshold," Florin answered in all humility.

After dropping off Florin at Port Authority, Perry and I took the subway to 14th Street and headed back to our apartments. I learned so much during the last few days. I'd broken through my depression, and I had a new perspective on life. I was looking forward to keeping positive energy flowing.

❧13❧

Before I left for Millbrook, I had sublet my apartment to Carla, a classically trained cellist. Carla was getting into jazz and occasionally jammed with Perry and others.

Without knowing how long I would be at Millbrook, I gave her the keys and explained how to pay the rent. There was no formal sublet agreement, and the landlord didn't care as long as he got paid. Now, I was back for a few days in New York City, and Carla was kind enough to let me sleep on the cot in my living room.

It wasn't a surprise that my friends and the Village scene were very much the way I left them, with everyone still hanging out, getting stoned, getting laid, and making music. Eric's crash pad was still supplying DMT, and Mike's place was still great for spiritual discussions and good weed. Everyone wanted to hear about my experiences in Millbrook. They were blown away when I told them about astral projection.

One of the first things I did was get laid. I reconnected with some of my old flames and also found new ones. In the East Village, getting laid was easy; smoke a little dope, shoot the shit, screw, and move on, just like I thought I liked it. But I'll confess, it was starting to feel a bit empty.

Of all the new faces in my group, the one that stuck out was Patrick. He stood out like a sore thumb from the usual band of scrawny hippies because he looked like a linebacker—tall, strong, and powerful. Patrick was movie-star handsome, 6'3", with dark brown shaggy hair, bright blue eyes, and a strong square jaw. He wore love beads around his muscular neck and army boots on his big feet. He was a fun guy who enjoyed getting stoned and joking around. He liked being the center of attention and was currently sleeping with Carol, one of my former lovers. He was completely ensconced in the hippie scene.

One blustery cold evening, we all dropped acid, and at about 2:00 a.m., Patrick thought it would be fun to enjoy the great outdoors. About six of us wandered out into the brisk, crystal-clear February night.

As we walked through Tompkins Square Park, a bunch of Puerto Rican kids attacked us, yelling, "This is our park, you fuckin' hippies. We're gonna kick the shit out of you."

Within a split second, Patrick jumped into action. He punched one kid in the face, kicked another in the chest, lifted a big steel trash can, and hurled it at the remainder of the group, who ran for their lives. We stood there, stunned. Thankfully, none of us were hurt, and our admiration and gratitude for Patrick grew considerably.

Once we were back in the apartment, we asked Patrick where he learned to fight like that, and he told us his incredible story. Patrick had grown up in a small South Carolina town. He had been a God-fearing redneck and the captain of his football team. When none of the colleges offered him a scholarship, he had joined the Army. After basic training, he was recruited to the Green Berets, the army's elite fighting force. These are the guys who get sent to the world's hot spots to engage in unconventional warfare, counter-insurgency tactics, and other warmongering activities. After his Green Beret training, he was asked by Army intelligence if he wanted a special assignment.

The undercover assignment was to infiltrate Millbrook and bust Timothy Leary. He was told that Leary was the most dangerous man in America, corrupting the youth of our great country. Patrick said it would be an honor to bring this criminal to justice. Patrick was Irish, and maybe the military brass thought that sending an Irish kid to confront the Irish Leary would be a good game plan. This assignment required special training, and to fit in, he had to learn to be a hippie and get used to taking drugs. Some shrink gave him LSD and weed and taught him hippie lingo. For the first time in his life, he listened to folk music, learned about the civil rights movement, and understood why the hippies were against the Vietnam War. After several months, with longer hair, love beads, and a few trips under his belt, they felt he was ready to start his mission.

He was sent to San Francisco to test the waters. He hung out in Haight-Ashbury, met lots of people, took lots of acid, and began to feel comfortable in his new role as a hippie. After a couple of months, he headed to New York and found his way to Millbrook with groovy stories about the scene in Haight-Ashbury to cement his hippie cred. He got into Millbrook and was invited to stay. Tim took a liking to him. Most of the men in the League were scrawny intellectual types, and maybe Tim envisioned this brawny Irishman as a potential personal bodyguard.

Patrick was transformed at Millbrook. He found love, acceptance, and freedom there, but mostly, he latched on to Tim, whom he saw as a father figure (since his father was mostly absent). He took a few acid trips at Millbrook, and during one memorable trip, he came clean. With tears in his eyes, he explained why he was at Millbrook, but noted that Tim had shown him the light. He told Tim that he loved him and all the people at Millbrook and would never do anything to hurt them. He wanted out of the Army; he was ready to desert.

What he got instead was the boot. He was asked to leave the next day and never to return. Patrick was devastated. He told us that he wanted more than anything to return to Millbrook and again be in Tim's good graces. And that's where I came in. Patrick begged me to take him with me when I returned to Millbrook. He was sure he could convince Tim to let him come back.

"What can I do? I'm just a grunt there. I have no influence," I told Patrick.

"Just get me in the gate is all I ask. I'm sure they'll see I'm not a threat."

Well, sometimes I'm not too bright and am usually way too trusting, so I took him with me the next day. We got through the gate and to the main door, where Carol, one of Tim's lieutenants, acknowledged us. But when she got closer and recognized Patrick, she flipped her lid.

Looking at me with dagger eyes, she screamed, "Who the fuck gave you permission to bring Patrick to Millbrook? Do you know who he is? He was sent by the Army to bust Tim. Did you know that? We threw him out months ago. And now you dare bring him to our door." She was hopping mad.

Patrick tried to say something, to explain himself, but it fell on deaf ears. I was told I was no longer welcome in Millbrook either and to retrieve my shit, get the hell out, and never, ever come back.

I was in shock, never expecting this kind of reaction. I tried to explain, but it was of no use. I took one last walk up the long staircase to my old room, gathered my few belongings, and headed back down. Thankfully, I didn't see anyone, or I would have cried. My Millbrook experience was over. Talk about burning bridges!

Carol was waiting for me inside the front door. She didn't want to stay outside with Patrick and listen to his desperate pleas to see Tim. I tried to say something, but she stopped me in mid-sentence and said, "I called a cab. You can wait outside with your narc friend."

They say no good deed goes unpunished. Well, what I did wasn't exactly a good deed; it was a stupid deed. *How could I be so fucking naïve to think they would accept a spy back in their fold?*

It was a long, sad train ride back to the city. Patrick tried to talk, but I asked him to be quiet. I wasn't in the mood for conversation. As the train rumbled along, I wondered what the fuck I was supposed to do now? Soon, I would be drafted, and there was no way I would go into the Army. I knew I couldn't stay in New York. I figured my only options were Canada or California. Things hadn't turned out as I had hoped. Everything was turning to shit, and I was seriously depressed.

*   *   *

Sometimes, what we perceive as great misfortune turns out to be fortuitous. I was lucky to be kicked out of Millbrook because several months later, the Dutchess County sheriff began an aggressive campaign to bust Leary and his followers. There were months of raids, arrests, and grand jury testimony, culminating in the eviction of the Millbrook residents. Leary moved to California, and the Bill Haines group relocated to Arizona. The Millbrook experiment was history.

❧14❧

I'm not sure what was happening to me, but I felt different; much of my naïve enthusiasm was gone. Maybe the experiences of this year had taken their toll. Maybe I was disillusioned with the scene, and maybe the whole draft thing was getting me down. I had returned to the East Village, and Carla reluctantly agreed to let me stay at my apartment. I knew I could have kicked her out, but I felt my time here was almost over.

Then, the dreaded letter arrived from the Selective Service, ordering me to report to Fort Dix, New Jersey—a fitting end to my East Village experience. I decided to pack it up and go home to Mom and Dad.

But first, I needed to say goodbye to Perry and Andy. They were true friends, and I felt sure I would never see them again. But Perry told me not to be so pessimistic. He said, "You never know what the future will bring." Even at this sad juncture, he was brimming with hope and positive energy, relieving the burden in my heart. With Andy, it was just a big hug and a sad goodbye.

My father came with his car to help me move back home. Besides my clothes and a few books, I only wanted the Grundig Majestic Radio. I was anxious to play it for my dad since he loved music. We installed it in his workroom in the basement of our house. I found a classical station to listen to, and my father was so happy. He loved that radio.

To my surprise, my parents were very understanding and supportive. They did not want me to go to Vietnam. They had experienced too much war in their lifetime and wanted their only son safe.

My father had a cousin, Harry, who lived in Toronto. Dad called him, and I was welcome to stay in their home until I could establish myself.

There were still a couple of weeks before I was scheduled to report to Fort Dix. I booked a flight from JFK Airport to Toronto, and at the airport, I met a young guy named Bill, who was also escaping the draft. He told me about an organization in Toronto called SUPA (Students Union for Peaceful Action) that helped draft dodgers and gave me its address near the University of Toronto.

After a short flight, I arrived at Pearson Airport, navigated the Toronto subway system, and miraculously found Cousin Harry's house. Harry was a Holocaust survivor, about the same age as my parents. He was married to Ruthie, had one daughter named Rachel, and lived in a small brick house on a tree-lined street in Richmond Hill, a suburb of Toronto. Harry gave me Rachel's old room (since she was married and had a home of her own) and made me feel welcome and comfortable.

The next morning, I took the subway and found the SUPA office. SUPA was a leftist organization founded in Canada, with branches near almost every Canadian college campus. Its mission was to help abolish war, racism, and poverty. SUPA staged sit-ins, protests, and demonstrations and organized community events to voice their opinions and objections to society's injustices.

The SUPA folks welcomed me with open arms. They helped many US draft dodgers and deserters safely settle in Canada. SUPA advised me to return to the United States and fly back to Montreal. Once in Montreal, they told me to apply for landed immigrant status, and when asked why I wanted to immigrate, I was to tell the immigration officer I was against the war in Vietnam. Quebec had a long history of being against conscription, and I was assured this would work.

I decided to take SUPA's advice and flew back to New York. The date for reporting for active duty was less than a week away, and I decided to spend these last few precious days with my family in Middle Village. Since moving back home, I had been able to see another side of my parents. They were so caring and loving and would do anything for their children. I'm sure they were always like that, but I had been so blind and self-centered that I didn't realize it before. I appreciated every minute with them, knowing I might never see them again. After all the horror and suffering they had been through, they were now saying goodbye to their firstborn. My heart was breaking.

During those precious final days, I asked them about their lives. I wanted to know about my grandparents and about what life was like in Poland. As a child, I heard many stories and pieced together fragments of their lives. Now, I wanted to listen to the whole story. So, we all sat at the kitchen table, talking late into the night.

❦15❧

My ancestors had come to Poland a thousand years ago. For centuries, it was a bastion of peace and tolerance where the Jewish religion and culture thrived. At one point, Poland was home to the world's largest Jewish community. By the seventeenth century, persecution had increased, and atrocities by Cossacks and others fueled by religious intolerance resulted in the murder of hundreds of thousands of Jews. These atrocities continued, culminating with the Holocaust, in which the vast majority of the European Jewish population was slaughtered.

My immediate family settled in the eastern section of the country, close to the Ukrainian border. My maternal grandfather, Beryl, lived in a small *shtetl* (town) called *Potok*. He barely eked out a living as a milkman. He had five children; the oldest was my mother, Hancha. Despite being poor, their lives were rich with love, tradition, and a strong faith in God. All of that changed because of the Holocaust.

One day in 1942, the *Einsatzgruppen* (Nazi death squads) came to *Potok*, taking the Jewish population by surprise. In this part of Poland, there were no train tracks to herd Jews and stuff them into cattle cars bound for concentration camps. Instead, Jews were marched to an open field where they were forced to dig trenches—men and women, children, and the elderly were all forced to dig. The Nazi death squads then forced everyone to strip naked and shot them all, even the babies. Their clothes were taken and sent to the front, where the Nazis were fighting the Russians. Jewish coats, socks, gloves, and sweaters kept

Nazis from freezing to death during the long Russian winter. The *Einsatzgruppen* stole whatever they could from helpless Jews. Wedding rings were wrenched off frozen fingers, and gold teeth were ripped out of crying mouths.

My mother's father promised her she would survive. He insisted she not follow him and the rest of the family as the Nazis had ordered. He told her that, with her blonde hair and blue eyes, she could pass for Polish. He told her to go north toward the forest. She was sixteen years old, the oldest of five children.

Alone and devastated, she wandered out of the town. She crossed a bridge, and off in the distance, she could see the killing field. She saw everyone she knew, everyone she loved, digging their own graves. She knew their fate; she also wanted to die. But her father's words echoed in her head, and she kept walking further from the town into the countryside. She kept walking away from the evil and from the greedy Poles she knew would turn her in for a few *zloty* (Polish dollars).

She finally came to a mill and there, by luck or grace, found sanctuary. A kind Pole named Jakub knew her father, Beryl. On Sundays, when the Polish taverns were closed, he and his friends visited Beryl's small cottage, which served as a tavern of sorts. Poles would come and drink, sing, and be merry. Beryl was a sweet and kind man, and made them feel welcome. The Poles paid what they could, and this money helped the family a great deal.

Jakub would have to risk his life to shelter this poor creature. But his mill was in the rural countryside, and the risk of getting caught was minuscule. It was very early in the morning when he saw her wandering aimlessly, lost in her misery. And he understood what had happened to her. He hid her in the loft of his old mill. He told her he would bring her food, but she must remain very quiet. He told her to only come out late at night and never when his wife was around. He knew his wife would turn her in, not because she hated Jews, not because of the reward, but out of fear for their lives.

Jakub brought her food when he could, but often, she went

hungry. She would eat whatever food he brought right away. If she didn't, the rats would try to take it. Sometimes, late at night, she would venture out and look at the empty landscape of her life. Often, she wished she hadn't listened to her father; at least she would be with her family in heaven.

Winter was the worst in the unheated mill. The Polish winters were brutal. Jakub gave her old sweaters and quilts. She even had a horse blanket and wore multiple pairs of socks on her feet and hands. She couldn't get warm and often shivered day and night.

The war ended about two years after she arrived at the mill, and that was when she finally saw the light of day. The Russian army freed this part of Poland well before the official end of the war. There were no Jews left in tiny Potok, so she went to the next town, Tarnogrod, and found Jews that had survived.

* * *

My father had a tailor shop in Krzeszów, not far from where my mother lived. He was a master tailor skilled at making custom-made clothes for the townspeople, Poles and Jews alike. His business was lucrative, and he owned a fine house and the store where he set up shop. He was well-liked and respected for his skill and was proud of building a successful business.

He was handsome with wavy black hair, dark eyes, and a small straight nose. He didn't look like the typical religious Jew of the town, as he never wore a yarmulke and dressed in modern clothes. This made it easier to be accepted by the Gentiles in his community. It helped that he had a great personality, was on a first-name basis with his customers, and knew the names of their children and grandchildren. He was liked and respected in his small town, and so were his wife and two children.

He had been away on a buying trip when the Nazi death squads came and slaughtered all the Jews in his town. The stench of death was still in the air when he returned, but thankfully, the Nazis had moved on, leaving devastation in its wake. He was able to go to his house, which his Polish neighbors had already ransacked; some clothes and furniture were stolen, and even dishes and cutlery were taken.

He wondered, "How long did it take after the Nazi butchers left for the Polish vultures to descend?"

He found the money he had carefully hidden for a rainy day. It was a small comfort in a world of grief, loss, and destruction. He knew he couldn't stay in this town for long. Where could he find safety now that Jews had a price on their heads?

He decided to flee to the forest to hide, think, and find a safe place to store the money. Who could he trust with his life? Who would keep him for the right price and payment each month? People knew he was a prosperous Jew. In this part of the country, most people were poor farmers who eked out a meager living by farming the poor soil.

He remembered there was a greedy man who lived on a remote road not too far from the town. He knew he had to be very clever and logical to appeal to this man's materialistic nature.

He told the man, "If you turn me in, you'll get paid once by the Nazis. If you hide me, you'll get paid every month." They came to an agreement which amounted to more than the Nazi bounty. He was hidden in a cold cellar and got watered-down soup and bread most days.

Each month, he paid, and when the month was over, he went back into the woods to retrieve a bit more of his money. He was careful to use different routes and made sure he wasn't being followed. He knew it would all be over if anyone found his stash. Each month, the Pole tried to renegotiate and ask for more money, but my father was able to work out a deal every time so he wouldn't run out of money. He stayed with that Pole for more than a year. But in the end, the Pole got too greedy, demanded too much money, and threatened to turn my father in if he didn't pay. My father said he'd come back with what the Pole wanted, but he never did. Greed grows like cancer, and he knew it was time to find a new sanctuary.

With no food and shelter, he chose to hide out with the Jewish partisans deep in the forest. He shared the freedom fighters' hatred of the Nazis and went on raids with them. Sometimes the raids killed Nazis, and sometimes they stole food from Poles. But the weather was getting cold, winter was coming, and living conditions in these makeshift camps were harsh. He had a choice: stay here and try to survive winter outdoors or find another host. He was lucky to still have enough money to bargain for a new shelter. Most partisans didn't have the money or the resolve my father had, and many died in the freezing forest.

He sweet-talked another Pole into hiding him in his dirty attic and feeding him some watered-down soup and crusts of stale bread for another month. How many more months could he go on like this? It already seemed like an eternity. Was it even worth living like this? He grieved for his old life, for his loving wife and family. He wished he hadn't gone on that buying trip and died with them instead. His life was like a game of Russian roulette; one day, he was sure a bullet would be in the chamber. But his luck didn't run out; somehow, he managed to stay alive.

Russian troops liberated Eastern Poland in the winter of 1944. The section of Poland that my father came from was one of the first liberated. He came out of hiding and found the Russians were protecting Jews. In fact, some of the Russian soldiers were Jews. The Poles' attitude toward the Jews changed immediately. It was now, "Oh, my friend, so sorry about your loss" and "The Nazis made me do it."

The survivors started to come out of hiding. In this part of Poland, they were either hiding or partisans. The death camps in central and western Poland were not yet liberated. Only a small trickle of Jewish humanity survived, less than ten percent of the original population. The survivors, now ragged and gaunt, wondered what they would find out there. Was there still something to live for?

My father went back to Krzeszów and reoccupied his house.

To his surprise, some Poles welcomed him and were kind and caring. Old friends were coming out of the woodwork to say hello. It was so strange; most of them would have turned him in to the Nazis for a bag of sugar; now, they welcomed him like a long-lost relative. Soon, his sewing machine was returned, then his supply of fine textiles and even some of his dead wife's clothes. They even started ordering clothing from him. It was crazy; it was like this nightmare had never happened. But how could he forget his suffering alone in that empty house without the love of his wife, without the laughter of his children?

One of his relatives told him about a young woman from Potok who survived but had no family left. She was in Tarnogrod, a small town not far from Krzeszów. He agreed to meet her and found a beautiful young woman who had suffered greatly. He knew he wanted to love and care for her. He was surprised that even after losing so much, after all the suffering, he could still feel a spark of love, seeds of hope, and the possibility of a future. He was fourteen years older than her, but that didn't matter to either of them.

My mother was drawn to this kind-hearted, gentle, older man, a man of experience and stability, and saw someone who could take care of her and treat her kindly. He spoke softly and sweetly and had a certain charm. He owned a house and had a good trade; surely, they could build a life together. Maybe the nightmare would finally end. She decided to take a chance on love, on life.

They traveled to Krzeszów, and sure enough, he had a nice house and a fine tailor shop. They decided to get married. It was one of the first celebrations for the Jews after the war. Many people attended, including Poles and Russians. My dad spoke Russian, and lots of merriment ensued. The Russians fired their rifles into the air after the wedding vows, the traditional glass was stomped, songs were sung, and everyone got nice and drunk.

It was hard for my father to be back in the house where his family was murdered. He tried not to show this anguish to his new bride. But he felt pain passing the room where his children once slept. He visited the cemetery where his parents and generations of relatives were buried according to Jewish tradition, but his wife and children weren't there. They were in the killing fields, commingled with hundreds of Jews he knew. How could he stay here? But where could they go? He must try to leave the past behind for the sake of his young wife.

Life was good for a few months, and then the Russians left. Once the Russians were gone, it didn't take long for the attitude of the Poles toward the Jews to change. My father said, "The Poles are worse than the Nazis. With the Nazis, you know what you're getting. With the Poles, they'll smile, be nice to you, and then stab you in the back."

One night, two Poles broke into my father's house. They grabbed my mother, held a knife to her throat, and demanded money.

My father said, "I'll give you money. Please don't hurt her. She's pregnant."

One of those hateful bastards threw my mother to the ground and began to kick her.

My father screamed, "Stop, I'll give you all the money. For God's sake, stop."

Once the money was handed over, the Pole punched my father in the stomach and said, "There's no place for you here, you dirty Jew."

My mother was curled on the floor, protecting her stomach. He went to her, picked her up, and held her. He kissed her tears away and said, "Hancha, I'm so sorry. I should have never brought you here. This place is a graveyard surrounded by Polish vultures, and they won't be satisfied until they pick our bones clean. We must leave. I'll take you somewhere safe. I'll protect you."

The next day, they packed a few things. My dad had money hidden in his shop and left for Lodz, which had a large Jewish population. Perhaps they could find peace there.

In Lodz, my father bought a nice apartment and a sewing

machine and was soon making a living. Word spread quickly that a master tailor was in town, and he was even getting Polish clientele. Soon, I was born in a hospital on August 19, 1945. I was a big, healthy baby weighing more than eight pounds.

As a male Jew, I was supposed to be circumcised on the eighth day of my life, but that didn't happen. Perhaps it was impossible to find a mohel, a ritual circumciser, or perhaps my parents were too traumatized to initiate a Jewish ritual. After what they went through, who could blame them? Circumcision is a big deal to the Jews; it's our covenant with God. Historically, the only time the Jews didn't perform ritual circumcision was during the years in the wilderness after they left Egypt. Perhaps Poland after the war was the new wilderness.

And even in Lodz, beatings and robberies of Jews were occurring. The Russian occupation kept these atrocities somewhat in check, but it was clear that most Poles hated and resented Jews. It was time to leave this heartless country now that the war was over. They heard about the Displaced Persons (DP) camps set up by the Allies to resettle the Jews and decided to relocate to one. Maybe, once there, they could even get a visa to America, *di goldena land.*

They heard about a train that went to Germany, where there were several DP camps. It wasn't a passenger train; it was a freight train. Hopping a freight train was dangerous. If they got caught, they would go to prison. But they felt it was their only chance to escape Poland, the country that was no longer the land of their forefathers. Poland was now a necropolis, full of death camps and mass graves, full of our murdered loved ones.

At the time, I was about three or four weeks old, and it took many days to get to Germany. The train made many stops, and the trip took a lot longer than they anticipated. During those stops, when the train no longer rattled along noisily, they were most at risk of getting caught. They had to keep their baby quiet. Feeding me was one way to pacify me. But, at some point during the trip, my mother's milk ran out.

She also ran out of diapers, and I developed a bad rash. When I started to cry, she put her hand over my mouth, but thankfully, only when the train stopped. When we arrived at the DP camp, I was in poor shape, dehydrated, and badly blistered. The American doctors at the camp revived me.

Maybe now my parents could feel safe. Maybe now they could find a new beginning. Perhaps now, they could rebuild their shattered lives.

Alex Ross 1909-1992

❧16❧

My parents went to the DP camp Eschwege, a former German air force base near Frankfurt in the US-occupied zone. The camp housed approximately seventeen hundred Jewish survivors of the Holocaust when it opened. It had been an air force base for the dreaded *Luftwaffe* that destroyed half of Europe. Now, it housed the wounded souls who survived the death camps, those who survived by hiding and living day and night in fear, and also the brave partisans who fought back. The largest number of survivors came from the notorious Nazi death camps Auschwitz, Bergen-Belsen, Buchenwald, and Dachau. About three million Jewish Poles—ninety-one percent of the entire Jewish population of Poland—were killed by the Nazis.

Eschwege was one of many DP camps that operated across Germany, Austria, and Italy. Two years after the war, some 850,000 people still lived in these camps. Getting a visa to emigrate was difficult. Most countries didn't want Jewish refugees and had strict quotas. With the establishment of Israel in 1948, survivors finally had a homeland, and many survivors called Israel home. As many as 170,000 Jewish displaced persons had emigrated there by 1953. But most of them wanted to go to America, which they called the Golden Land.

Displaced Persons Camps provided many services to the survivors. The camps had doctors to heal their wounds, real housing to protect them from the elements, good food to rebuild their shriveled bodies, and a community to revitalize their souls. There were many marriages, and new babies soon followed, signifying new life and hope for the future.

I was one of the first kids in that community, and everyone fussed over me. I have no memories of that time except for a few photos my parents kept, including one of me smiling bare-assed and lying on a blanket.

There are photos of me happily playing with other children in the camp. In another, I'm content in the arms of a young woman who, I imagine, longed to become a mother and hoped to one day bring a new life into the world. All Holocaust survivors dreamed of a new life and longed to leave the old wounds behind. But, in truth, they never really could, for the proof of their tortured lives was tattooed on their arms, embedded in their psyches, and seared into their souls.

It took them several months, but they got used to living at the DP camp. They made friends and attended weddings and other celebrations. Life had a certain rhythm to it until the day everything got turned upside down.

My father hurried home to his wife with the look of a man who had just seen a ghost.

"Hancha," he cried out, "My brother Herman is alive! I just heard it from Moishe, who has relatives in Belgium. Herman escaped to Belgium, where he lives with his wife and daughters. I have to go and find him. We must be reunited. It's a dream come true."

His brother was the only link to his former life, and he felt compelled to see him again. Imagine thinking everyone in your family was dead and then discovering your brother is alive. His exhilaration must have felt otherworldly. He anticipated that, with his brother's connections, he could get papers to America from Belgium. Plus, he could earn money in Belgium, which he couldn't do at the DP camp.

My mother was devastated, "Alex, how could you leave us alone? Besides, you have no papers. What if you get caught?" she cried.

He assured her that she was safe at the camp and he would arrange for us to join him in a short time. She felt abandoned and scared. She already had so much tragedy in her young life. Did she make a mistake marrying this man? He was supposed to take care of her, and now he was on a quest considered a fool's errand because so much could go wrong. Also, how did he expect her to manage taking care of her young son alone? She tried to talk him out of it, but his quest was all-consuming, and he left the following morning. We were on our own.

About a week later, a letter arrived saying he had made it to Belgium and was working on getting a visa to America, but it would take a few more weeks. My mom wrote back and announced she was pregnant. Months went by without obtaining the invaluable visa. Ironically, the visa to America my parents applied for when they first came to the camp was accepted. But my mother was not willing to go without her husband. She considered it. She was tempted. It would serve him right for leaving her. But how could she make such a trip, pregnant, with a small child and without a husband? A golden opportunity was lost. But that was not all she lost. A few days after receiving the acceptance to emigrate, she lost the child; she miscarried.

Fortunately, there was a real community in the DP camp. People looked after each other. She had friends, true friends, who helped her through this difficult time. Freda was her best friend. She was eight years older than my mother and was

My mom, dad, and me - early 1946 in the DP camp.

always available to advise and console her. Freda and others from the camp became my mother's longest and most cherished friends.

It took my father almost a year to get the papers necessary to emigrate. Though not to America as they had hoped, but to Bolivia. My aunt Sarah, Herman's wife, had a brother in Bolivia, and he kindly sponsored us. But Herman was able to get a visa to America because Sarah's other brother, who lived in America, sponsored him. But before we could go to Bolivia, my mother had to get us to Belgium to reunite with my father.

The trip to Belgium was arduous and full of stumbling blocks. My mother had to take a train to Paris and another to Antwerp, Belgium. She could pay for the fare to Paris, but the ticket agent in Paris wouldn't accept her German money for the ticket to Antwerp. She didn't speak French, couldn't communicate, didn't know where to turn for help, and was getting frantic. In the train station, an old Jewish man who realized she was alone and struggling offered assistance. He calmed her down, paid for her ticket, got her on the correct train, and refused reimbursement. She was so grateful to that man. Once again, the kindness of a stranger came at the right moment. She felt as if some higher power was looking after her.

At long last, we were reunited, finally a family again. My father had saved a good amount of money working in Belgium that past year. Together, we traveled back to Paris, booked a boat to Brazil, and took a train to La Paz, Bolivia, none of which I remember.

In Bolivia, they pretended to be Poles rather than Jews because even in this remote developing country, Jews were distrusted and looked down upon. It wasn't difficult since they didn't look Jewish and didn't have numbers tattooed on their arms. Doors that would have been closed to them as Jews were opened to them as Christian Poles.

My father opened a tailor shop and made a decent living

in La Paz. He designed and manufactured fashionable suits for the elites of Bolivia and fancy army uniforms for the military. Even the Bolivian president was a customer.

My mother gave birth to a son, Isaac. When he was seven months old, he got sick from drinking evaporated milk that may have been tainted. He was hospitalized and died. Isaac's illness could have been successfully treated if we hadn't been in a third-world country with third-rate doctors and limited medical supplies. Once again, tragedy struck. Having faced so much tragedy in their young lives, my parents must have wondered if they would ever have a life free of calamity and adversity.

My first memory of Bolivia was when I was four years old. We were in a fancy restaurant in downtown La Paz having dinner with the Brennens, fellow Polish immigrants. The Brennens had a daughter, Eva, who was my age. While our elders were deep in conversation, Eva and I wandered away and found ourselves at a large church a block from the restaurant. A large, festive wedding was taking place in the church, and we were fascinated by the spectacle, especially the bride in her beautiful white dress. Hand-in-hand, we went in to investigate. Many kids were part of the wedding party, and nobody paid us much mind. I clearly remember being awed by the beauty and majesty of the church, the high vaulted ceilings, and the beautiful stained glass. As a Jew, I'd never stepped foot into a church before that day.

When our parents realized we were gone, they became understandably alarmed and went to the police. A frantic search for two little kids followed. The possibility that we may have been kidnapped crossed everyone's mind, especially in the lawless city of La Paz.

We wandered out of the church after a while and found a hotel lobby to explore. Surprisingly, no one questioned that two little kids were walking around alone. We were getting hungry and started looking for our parents. In a short time, we were found. I was scolded for wandering off as my mother served a bowl of her famous chicken soup.

Bolivia did not have a stable government. It seemed like there was a military coup every few years. Once again, it looked like war could be a possibility. My parents feared for our safety and couldn't bear the thought of living through another war.

Again, luck or providence or grace came just in time as our relatives in America were able to sponsor us and get us a visa, the golden ticket to the promised land. My parents were so happy, and the next day, we got another letter from relatives in Canada. They were able to get us a visa, too.

Of course, my parents chose America. I was especially excited and told my friends. I remember that one of my

friends knew an English word, and I was anxious to learn it. The word was "fuck." I had no idea what it meant, but we all ran around the courtyard, yelling it. It was a fitting goodbye to Bolivia.

The plane fare to New York was expensive, but my parents had saved. My father couldn't sell the business and just left it. We were finally going to America. At long last, our

1948 in Bolivia

dream was coming true.

❧17❧

I was six when we arrived at Idlewild Airport in New York City. We got a one-bedroom apartment in a working-class neighborhood in the Bronx on 174th Street off Livingston Avenue. Relatives lent us money to help furnish it. I slept on a folding bed in the living room.

Since I spoke only one word of English, I started school in a special kindergarten class for Spanish-speaking kids at PS 50. There were lots of kids in this class, as the Bronx had many Spanish-speaking immigrants from Puerto Rico, Colombia, Ecuador, and other countries. I learned English quickly, and by the time I was in first grade, I was comfortable with my new language.

Initially, my father got a "piecemeal" job in the garment district in Manhattan. Piecemeal work meant he didn't get paid by the hour but by the number of items he completed. It was all about speed, and people often took short lunches and minimal bathroom breaks to maximize production. Even a great tailor like my father could barely eke out a living with this type of work. The challenge of survival became greater when my mother gave birth to twin girls on September 27, 1952. There was no money for cribs, so Nancy and Marion each slept in a dresser drawer for the first few months of their lives until my parents could afford cribs.

But now we had relatives we could rely on; we had family. My mother had two uncles, Louie and Joe, who also lived in the Bronx. My maternal great-grandfather had eighteen children: twelve from his first wife and, after she died, six from his second. Amazingly, of these eighteen children, there had been four sets of twins. And of the eighteen, all that remained of this family were my two uncles and an aunt in Israel. Everyone else perished in the Holocaust: both sets of grandparents, so many aunts and uncles, and dozens of cousins, all gone.

My uncle Louie loved me very much. He always took a special interest in me, taught me piano, told me stories, and delighted in everything I did. It must have been like having a grandpa. My mom said Uncle Louie looked like my grandfather and had the same loving temperament, the same inherent kindness. He was a handsome man of medium height with a square face, graying hair, kind blue eyes, and a warm smile. Uncle Louie had four grown children; three were married, and one still lived with them. Their apartment was right across the street from the Bronx Zoo, which wasn't far from our place. My uncle worked as a waiter.

I don't remember how I learned that one had to be circumcised to truly be considered Jewish. My parents never had me circumcised when I was born. But once I knew this, I begged my father to let me undergo circumcision. I was seven at the time. My father was working two jobs, my mother had my baby sisters to care for, and neither spoke much English, so I asked Uncle Louie, and he made all the arrangements.

After the operation, I felt proud to be a "real" Jew. When relatives came over, I pulled my pants down and said, "See, now I'm a Jew." Everyone had a good laugh over this, and when I was older, my parents often told the story to new friends, much to my embarrassment.

My father's talents were not a secret for long, and soon, he was working as a sample maker for a children's clothing manufacturer. When a new season began, the designers would draw the new fashion line, and my father made all the original samples for the models to wear. He was that good.

One day in 1954, he took a chance and bought a two-dollar ticket for the Irish Sweepstakes. This was a lottery based on a horse race, and the odds of winning were minuscule. He made the mistake of telling my mother about the ticket. She ranted and raved at him for having the audacity to spend two hard-earned dollars on such frivolity. "Two dollars would feed the family for many days," she said. This was when they first moved to the Bronx, and every penny counted. In the end, he relented; he had to. He then sold the ticket to one of his coworkers.

As fate would have it, the ticket was a winner. The way the sweepstakes works is that twelve tickets are chosen out of millions of entries. Each ticket represents a specific horse slotted to run in the Irish Sweepstakes race the next week. The prize money was distributed based on the results of the race, with three payouts for win, place, and show. The winning ticket holders knew which horse their ticket represented, and the bookmakers were already posting the odds. The ticket holders could wait for the race or sell the tickets before the race to gamblers. There was a good market for each ticket, and the favorites sold for a sizable sum. The coworker sold before the race and got many thousands of dollars. He quit the sweatshop, bought a brand-new Cadillac, and drove it to the shop to show it off.

My father came home infuriated. "That should have been my Cadillac," he shouted to whoever would listen. It was another tough break in a long string of them. What made matters even worse was that his horse won, and the payout was enormous. So, this drama lasted for a long time. He would bring it up during every disagreement or argument with my mom. He would fume about it when we got together with relatives. This incident simmered in his brain for years.

Money was always tight, and they couldn't afford to buy my sisters or me any toys. When I was about eleven, I went to the local supermarket and offered to help the ladies with their packages. They usually gave me a tip, and after a while, I bought roller skates with my own money. They were the kind that clamped onto your shoes. We lived on a hill, and it was fun racing down the street in my new skates. I could also buy candy or ice cream any time I wanted. I started to love the freedom and independence that money in your pocket could bring.

Being the first-born child of immigrants meant taking on a lot of responsibilities. This was especially the case when it came to communicating with anyone who didn't speak Yiddish. Handling school notices and bills and dealing with the landlord or hired help all fell on my shoulders. I didn't mind; it was what was needed. I gained confidence and learned responsibility at an early age.

After scrimping and saving for seven years, my parents had enough money for a down payment on a two-family house in Middle Village, a middle-class neighborhood in Queens, New York, with reasonably priced homes. It was probably affordable because Middle Village wasn't near the subway, and it took a long time to get to Manhattan. I didn't go with them to view the house because they needed me to babysit my sisters.

After purchasing the house in Queens, my parents bought new furniture that was scheduled for delivery. The problem was that both my parents worked and didn't want to lose a day's wages. So, they wanted me, a twelve-year-old boy, to travel to Middle Village and arrive before the delivery to pay for the furniture. I had to take a train into Manhattan, change trains for Queens, take the correct bus to Middle Village, and then find the house. The NYC subway system is complex, and it was critical that I took the right train going in the right direction to get there before the movers. It was more than a two-hour trip, and I had never taken public transportation alone. To make things more interesting, my mother had sewn more than a thousand dollars into my pants, the exact amount required to pay for the furniture. That was a bloody fortune in those days. She also gave me a list of the furniture that was supposed to arrive; I was to inspect each piece to ensure everything was in good condition. It all went smoothly. I liked our new house and was delighted I would finally have my own room.

Middle Village was lily white, primarily inhabited by Jews and Italians, and surrounded by cemeteries, which didn't faze my dad. He was fond of saying, "The dead can't hurt you; only the living can." My mother's dear friend Freda from the DP camp lived up the street, and I learned that was why we bought a house in this community.

I attended PS 87, which went from kindergarten to eighth grade; I started school there in the seventh grade. Making friends was easy. This was a safe neighborhood with nice parks. I soon found Abe's Deli and again enjoyed great knishes with mustard and Stewart's cream soda.

One of the first things I did was find a job. I started working as a stock boy at Mellmen's Grocery Store when I was twelve. When I entered Newtown High School at thirteen, I found a much better job as a delivery boy at Flatow's Fruit and Vegetable Market. These years were uneventful, but I was happy because I always had my own money, which gave me the freedom to buy clothes and cigarettes and do whatever I wanted. I had no curfew and no rules to follow.

My parents didn't hassle me since they were busy themselves. My dad had three jobs. He worked as a sample maker for a large children's clothing manufacturer, and my mom worked with him at that job. After work, he went to a local dry-cleaning shop and did alterations. He also had a workshop in our basement, and people would come to get their clothes altered, even on Sundays.

❧18❧

1962 was a tumultuous year. The United States had advisors in Vietnam, and many predicted that this was a precursor to war. The draft instituted by Kennedy hung over my head. I knew I had to attend college to avoid it, so I enrolled at City College of New York, majoring in accounting.

Tensions between the United States and the Soviet Union continued to escalate, culminating in the Cuban Missile Crisis.

Race relations were worsening, especially in the South. There were riots in Mississippi, and we became more aware of the Civil Rights Movement and the plight of Blacks in America. Some parts of New York were considered unsafe, and this was particularly true of Harlem.

In April 1962, I was faced with a dilemma. Ray Charles was performing at the Apollo Theater, and I desperately wanted to hear him.

I asked my friend Chris if he wanted to come with me.

He said, "Are you crazy? The Apollo is in Harlem. It ain't safe for two White boys to go there."

"But the first show is at 4:00 p.m. It will still be light even when the show is over. I know you love Ray's music as much as I do. Let's give it a shot." I replied.

Chris reluctantly agreed.

It took over two hours to get there from Queens. We got off the subway at 125th Street and walked a few blocks to the Apollo. It was still daytime; we were the only White people on the street and tried to look cool walking to the theater.

We bought our tickets, and to our surprise, a movie was showing. Of course, this meant the concert itself was starting later. Most of the seats were taken, and we wound up sitting in the first row, craning our necks to see the film. But when the concert began, we had primo seats. It was fantastic. Not only was Ray incredible, but his dynamic performance enthralled the entire audience.

Ray had his band and the Raelettes backing him up. He sang all his great hits: "Georgia on My Mind," "What I Say," "Ruby," "I Can't Stop Loving You," and my favorite, "Hit the Road Jack." The audience danced in the aisles. People were wild with joy, and we were having the time of our lives.

When the show was over, we thought we'd be asked to leave before the next performance, but thankfully we weren't. The next set was at 7:00 p.m., ninety minutes away, so we just had to stay. The same movie came on, and afterward, Ray took the stage again. We were so into the music we couldn't get enough.

After the second set, we considered going home. It was getting late, and the next set was at 10:00 p.m., but we couldn't drag ourselves away and had to stay for his final set. We were so happy we stayed because it was the best set of all. By the last set, we were able to free ourselves from some of our inhibitions. By now, we were so attuned to the music and the incredible atmosphere that we were able to let loose. We got up, clapped, danced, and let the joy fill our souls. There was no longer Black or White in our minds; we were just people ecstatic over this sublime music.

It was after midnight when the concert ended. The crowd streamed out of the Apollo with us in the middle. No one paid us any mind. We were happy, made it to the subway a little after midnight, and didn't get home to Middle Village until after 3:00 a.m. I was famished when I snuck into the house. I hadn't eaten supper and found my mother's famous cheesecake in the fridge. She was an amazing cook and a fabulous baker. I nearly finished the whole cake plus a container of milk, the perfect ending to a perfect day.

It was during this period that I became a pothead. Steve lived around the corner, and we often got stoned at his place. Steve had a great record collection consisting mostly of jazz, and he turned me on to the music of John Coltrane, Miles Davis, Charles Mingus, and many great artists. I have fond memories of sitting in his dark bedroom, listening to some of the finest music ever created. His parents were cool; they never bothered us or complained about the funny odor wafting through the cracks of his bedroom door.

Around this time, I started to change. My worldview expanded, and my concerns weren't limited to my small self. I wanted to be more than a suburban teenager. I wanted to belong to something greater. But to what, I didn't know. I started wearing all-black clothing. My signature look was a turtleneck sweater, pants, and desert boots. I wanted to be cool, even though I didn't know what cool was. There was so much to take in, so many different scenes: beatnik, peacenik, radical, hippie. Where did I belong? What was my scene?

In 1962, the place where we thought "IT" was happening was the Village, Greenwich Village, that is. The main drag in the Village was MacDougal Street. We walked these streets on weekends like thousands of other teenagers looking for something different, trying to fit in, trying to understand. There were dozens of night-clubs, theaters, and coffeehouses brimming with new entertainment. Bob Dylan was making his start at a club called the Bitter End, and we walked right past it without ever catching his act. But we saw many lesser acts: folk musicians, jazz artists, and poets. We were exposed to new ideas and absorbed the counterculture's values, attitudes, fashion, and spirit. We longed for freedom.

But I wasn't ready to move out of the comforts of my suburban home yet. I had determined my priorities: finish high school, buy a car, find a girlfriend, lose my virginity, and start college to avoid the draft. Freedom would have to come later.

* * *

Freedom came, and freedom went, during the five years that followed. On the day in 1967, when I was supposed to report for active duty to the Army, I flew to Montreal instead and became a landed immigrant in my new country, Canada.

❧19❧

"O Canada," what will you bring me? A new beginning was on the horizon. I hoped I could make something of my life. I hoped I could make my parents proud. I had certainly brought them enough sorrow and disappointment.

I arrived in Montreal, Canada, on May 17, 1967, looking like a respectable young man, clean-shaven with a sensible haircut. Going through customs was exactly like the folks at SUPA had explained. The customs officer was friendly, and, in no time, I had my landed immigrant card and was legal in my new country. I found my way to the bus station and, in about four hours, was in downtown Toronto.

I went to the SUPA office to inform them of my success and how easy the process was. Everyone was happy for me, and we went to a local pub to celebrate my newfound freedom.

I took the train to Cousin Harry's house. They, too, were happy for me and said I was welcome to stay as long as I wanted, but I wanted my own space. Between staying with my parents and then Harry, it had been more than a month since I had my own place.

I found an affordable apartment near the SUPA office in a predominantly Greek neighborhood off Spadina Avenue. And within a few weeks, I found a job at some government agency as a clerk. The few years of college accounting courses helped qualify me. The job didn't pay much, but it was enough to cover my minimal expenses.

My routine was simple. I worked downtown, a short trip

from my apartment, and then hung out at the SUPA office. The folks at SUPA consisted of conscientious ultra-left-wing college students and newly arrived American draft dodgers and deserters. The kids working at SUPA were constantly trying to radicalize us. Some SUPA folks were Maoists, enamored of Mao's teachings, and others were socialists. The Maoists carried Mao's Little Red Book in their pocket and revered it like a holy bible. I didn't care for the Maoists because they were preaching war and insurrection. Mao's Little Red Book, *Quotations from Chairman Mao Tse-tung*, was full of quotes justifying violence.

SUPA was a radical organization that looked down on the hippie movement as self-indulgent and blind to the world's suffering. They believed that only political action would change the inequalities in our society. The radical movement was already well established in the United States.. The war in Vietnam was raging, and many protests took place. People were angry with President Johnson for escalating the war, and the news was spreading with pictures of the terror and suffering that the Vietnamese people endured. The Civil Rights Movement was already at the forefront, and many were dissatisfied with the lack of meaningful change. The Black Panther Party was already established, holding demonstrations across America and winning support. Many hippies were embracing more radical views, and protests were turning violent.

Some of the Americans in Canada were sympathetic to the Maoists. They felt that America had let us down by engaging in an illegal war and forcing us to become killers. Many were angry, especially the deserters who went through the ordeal of basic training; some had even seen combat in Vietnam.

One of my friends was a deserter named Dick, who told us his story over beers one night. Dick was a high school graduate from a small town in Indiana who joined the Marines right after graduation. He went through basic and combat training and was about to be shipped out to Vietnam. Before shipping out, he learned from soldiers returning from the front that this war was unjust and completely immoral. He heard horrific stories of the napalming of villages, burning of children, and wanton destruction. He'd heard this from a few sources. Then, he faced a moral dilemma. After much soul-searching, he decided he couldn't be part of those atrocities. He heard of a Quaker group near where he was stationed that helped draft dodgers and deserters. This group helped him get safely to Canada.

Canada classified both draft dodgers and deserters as refugees and admitted all of them. They never asked immigrants about their military service and accepted all that applied. In Canada, there wasn't a stigma associated with being a deserter. Generally, draft dodgers were college kids from middle-class homes, while deserters were high school kids from lower-income working-class families. This was certainly the case with Dick.

The SUPA folks were passionate about their causes. Generally, they wanted to make the world a more peaceful and benevolent place for all people, especially those who are discriminated against or marginalized. They were very vocal and creative and planned many activities to promote their causes.

Shortly after I arrived, I learned a march was planned to make people aware of the horrors of the Vietnam War. The march, which was more like street theater, was held in Kingston, Ontario, about two and a half hours east of Toronto. SUPA rented a bus, and about forty of us arrived in Kingston. We were joined by a bunch of local SUPA members and had about a hundred people marching. Many of us sported costumes as bloody soldiers, ghosts, fat politicians, an ugly Uncle Sam, and bloody Vietnamese peasants. People held banners and placards; some played instruments. Many yelled slogans such as, "Make love not war," "Ship the GIs home now," and "How many more must die?" I played the part of a draft dodger carrying a suitcase and a big airline ticket to Canada. I yelled, "Thank you, Canada, home of the free."

*　*　*

About three months after my arrival, I got a letter from my father stating he was coming by bus to visit, along with his arrival info. I was happy he was coming to see me. In fact, I was deeply touched.

I met my dad at the bus depot, and we hugged. He then got his small overnight bag from beneath the bus and, to my surprise, pulled out a big square canvas satchel. It was something he had made, and I had no idea what it contained. When we got to my house, he undid the stitching, removed the padding, and lo and behold—it was my old Grundig Majestic radio.

I said, "Dad, I wanted you to have that radio; you didn't need to *schlep* it all the way to Canada."

He said, "I want you to have music in your new home." Then my dad gave me money. I was so touched that I almost cried.

We went for dinner at Harry's. It was a wonderful reunion; they hadn't seen each other since before the war in Poland. Lots of stories followed, in Yiddish, of course, which I understood. There were stories about people who survived and those who perished, stories about what those who lived were doing now, how many children they had, and how they had turned out.

I wondered to myself, what do our relatives say about me? Will I ever give my parents *naches*? Will I ever make them proud? So far, I was nothing but trouble.

I noticed that my dad gave Harry an envelope that I assumed was money. Harry tried not to accept it, but my dad insisted. We spent the night at Harry's. The next morning, we took the train back downtown. My dad caught his bus and was back in the factory sewing in New York twelve hours later. I was so touched by the visit and his love and caring. At the same time, I felt guilty because I was causing my family so much misery.

❧20❧

Apart from smoking a little weed, I stayed away from LSD. It had been more than six months since my last trip, when Florin's astral form appeared. But when I met Pete, that was about to change.

I don't remember how I met him, but I could tell he was a serious acidhead. We started talking and exchanging tales about the scenes in Toronto and the Lower East Side. Pete was impressed that I knew Timothy Leary, had lived at Millbrook, and had experienced Sandoz acid, the gold standard. Pete invited me to his apartment to continue the conversation and share experiences.

It amazed me how quickly I forgot about my bad trips, my close call with death, and my soul-sapping final month on the Lower East Side. I once again became the acid zealot, passionately regaling my many adventures. It was euphoric to relive the great experiences and the profound realizations I had during select LSD trips. And Pete's experiences were just as ecstatic. Our stories fed each other and created a natural high.

Pete was a very successful drug dealer who only sold wholesale. He had many one-ounce amber bottles with dropper caps; each contained multiple LSD trips. Filling the dropper with a few drops of LSD was plenty for a trip. Pete asked if I wanted to trip with him that night, and I quickly agreed.

He said, "I have six bottles that are nearly empty. I don't think one bottle would be enough for a trip. I'm going to take three. How many do you want to take?"

I said, "If it's okay with you, I'd like to take three as well."

He filled each bottle with water and shook it so the LSD

would be fully accessible. I chose my three bottles and drank down every last microgram. I even refilled the bottles with water to ensure I ingested it all. No sense in letting any of the holy sacrament go to waste.

What happened next was crazy. It didn't feel like a typical acid trip; it felt far more intense, like a DMT trip. I must have ingested an enormous quantity of LSD. Soon, I was totally unaware of the outside world. I became the molecules of my body, exploding with intense colors. It felt like I was floating through my bloodstream, being pumped out of the chambers of my heart and into a kaleidoscopic tunnel with bursts of intense color, bubbling images, and crazy shapes. It felt like I became my cells, hurtling at incredible speeds throughout my body. Then, I became the atoms of the cells, the electrons of the atoms. Deeper and deeper, I descended into the microcosm. I was moving at warp speed through this alien universe of intense light and surreal sounds. It was the ultimate adrenaline rush that seemed to last forever. It was like being on an unearthly roller coaster hurtling through a bizarre space through eternity. There was no mind, no thought, no separation. I was one with what was happening.

I don't know how many hours I was tripping, but when I finally awoke to the outer world, I was on a hard bench, and my body ached. It was hard to breathe, and the side of my face hurt. I looked and saw a disheveled wino lying on a bench across from me. I could clearly see his red bulbous nose and smell the piss that stained his pants. I then looked around and realized I was in a locked cell. I thought Pete was playing a trick on me. I never remembered leaving his house, so how could I be in jail?

I yelled, "Where the fuck am I? Pete, this isn't a joke; let me out of here."

The guard came over and told me to shut up. I had no shoes or shirt and was dirty, as if I had been rolling around in the gutter. I checked my pockets, and thankfully, my wallet was there, but all the money was gone, even the change. I must have been beaten and robbed and left on the street. I had absolutely no memory of this. The cops saw I was incoherent and threw me into the drunk tank.

Soon, a lady came by and told me to prepare to appear before the judge. She gave me a shirt and some old shoes, both of which were too large for me. I thought, *Shit, what did I get myself into now?* I went to the bathroom and tried to clean myself up. I washed up as best as I could, ran my fingers through my hair, and tried to look presentable.

I was charged with public intoxication. I was thankful it wasn't a drug charge. When asked how I pled, I shamefacedly said, "Guilty." The judge said that since this was my first offense, he would let me off with a warning.

He also said, "Boy, you need to learn to hold your liquor and stay out of trouble."

Suffice it to say I never saw Pete again, nor did I want to.

I went home and started thinking about my life. Another fucked-up acid trip! When would I learn? For every good trip I took, it seemed like I paid with a bunch of bad ones. Karma is a bitch. What have I learned about life since taking acid? It introduced me to realms beyond the physical, amazing vistas, closer human contact, and spiritual possibilities, but at what price? It had almost cost me my life and landed me in jail three times. Maybe I had already learned everything I needed to know from LSD. But how would I move on? Being a hippie had been my identity. Being a cool acidhead from New York was my story. If I was not that, who was I?

I felt that my time in Toronto was winding down. It was already September, and I didn't want to experience a brutal Toronto winter. I heard Vancouver was a great place with a milder climate and decided it would be my next destination.

I thought it would be a great adventure to hitchhike to Vancouver. I spoke to my friends at SUPA about my plans. My friend John was interested in coming with me. John was a tall, lanky Midwesterner with brown hair and glasses. He was a college graduate with a science degree. He was a soft-spoken, full-fledged nerd, and I liked him. He was easy to get along with, and I felt he would be a good traveling companion.

Another guy that really wanted to come was Butch, a biker from Kalamazoo, Michigan. Butch was a mini-biker, short, stout, and leather-clad. He couldn't have been more than 5'5", with a dark scruffy beard and a rat's tail hairstyle.

"What biker gang were you in, back in Kalamazoo?" I asked Butch.

"I wasn't a biker back then; I was in a frat at college."

"No shit. They let you in, dressed like that?" I asked.

"Back then, I dressed like a frat boy," he replied.

"What was your major?" John asked.

"Gettin' stoned and gettin' laid," Butch replied.

"That's a perfect recipe for getting expelled and getting drafted," John stated.

"Wow, you figured that out all by yourself?" Butch retorted.

"When did you become a biker?" I asked.

"In Toronto. I didn't look like a hippie, so I needed a costume. On Yonge Street, there's a biker store, and the rest is history," Butch said with a wry smile.

"It will be hard to get rides for three guys," John stated.

"I've got a nice-size tent that can sleep three, and I'm a fun guy," Butch said.

"Why do you want to go to Vancouver, anyway?" asked John.

"To piss in the Pacific Ocean. I already pissed in the Atlantic and the Gulf," Butch replied.

"Nice to have great ambitions," John retorted.

"Yes. I also believe in piss on Earth," Butch replied with a straight face.

"As long as you don't piss into the wind," I suggested.

We knew the trip would take longer with Butch, but it would definitely be more fun. Plus, he had a tent that could accommodate all three of us, so we decided to take him along. Now, we needed to plan.

John was very methodical and had our entire trip mapped out in no time, with a list of the supplies we would need. I knew I needed a backpack, sleeping bag, canteen, and a good pair of shoes for the journey. I accumulated these items, some of which I found at thrift stores. I sold my Grundig Majestic radio for only a hundred dollars and gave my landlord and employer notice.

We met at the SUPA office, took the train to a stop near the highway, and stuck out our thumbs, ready for a ride west.

❧21❧

Hitchhiking with three guys was tough. Cars sped up when they saw us. Our smiles didn't get us rides. So, we decided to hide Butch in the weeds while John and I hitched. Butch would come over to join us when somebody stopped. Lots of times, cars stopped but drove away once they saw Butch. But finally, we got our first ride to Sudbury, Ontario, a couple of hundred miles away.

We were stuck in Sudbury for many hours. Sudbury is a mining town famous for its nickel mines, smelting facilities, and stinking sludge ponds. We could even smell the sulfur while hitching on the town's outskirts. On this gray and drab day, we saw an enormous genuine Canadian nickel proudly displayed on a raised mound. It was the largest coin in the world, thirty feet high.

"That gray and drab nickel is what makes this gray and drab town famous," I said.

"In my town, we have statues commemorating heroes, not coins," John said.

"This town isn't worth a plugged nickel. We need to get out of here. The stink is killing me," Butch said.

After hours of watching cars speed by, one finally stopped and stayed, even when Butch miraculously appeared. The car was driven by two college kids returning from Toronto on their way home to Calgary, Alberta. The boys asked us if we could share the driving since they wanted to get home fast, and of course, we said yes, as long as we didn't have to drive through the United States. This required taking a slightly longer route, but with draft dodgers on board, it was the only option.

Sudbury to Calgary is an eighteen-hundred-mile journey that took us about thirty hours. We drove through the beautiful, forested Ontario countryside, past Lake Huron and Lake Superior, before heading into the provinces of Manitoba, Saskatchewan, and Alberta that make up the Canadian Prairies—twelve hundred miles of flat countryside, grassland, plains, and lowlands as far as the eye can see. This was big sky country, sameness for a thousand miles.

I don't remember the names of the two college kids, so let's call them Tom and Jerry. They looked like brothers, both about six feet and slender, with short blonde hair and blue eyes. These were clean-cut, wholesome, God-fearing young men who looked like the kids that joined ROTC (Reserve Officers' Training Corps), a US college program that prepares young adults to become officers in the US military. The boys were students at the University of Toronto and had never heard of SUPA or ROTC. I asked if they were brothers; they were first cousins.

Tom, the more talkative of the two, started telling us how great Alberta was, especially Calgary.

He said, "Alberta is God's country, the best province in Canada, and Calgary is its greatest city. It's like Dallas, Texas, with rodeos and oil wells, only better."

"How come it's better?" asked Butch.

"We got the great Calgary Stampede, which is the largest rodeo in the world and also the greatest outdoor show on earth," Jerry chimed in.

"The Stampede lasts for ten days, and besides rodeos, they've got parades, midways, concerts, livestock contests, chuckwagon races, and much more," added Tom.

"What the hell are chuckwagons?" Butch asked.

Jerry explained, "Them are those covered wagons that our forefathers rode out west to settle our great nation."

"Do Indians attack the chuckwagons and shoot flaming arrows at them?" asked Butch.

"No, they just race them to see who's fastest," replied Jerry.

Butch kept on asking more questions, saying, "I've always been fascinated by all this cowboy shit." He asked about six shooters and cowgirls and did cowgirls believe in free love, and he kept them talking about cowboy stuff. We got to know Butch with his sarcastic humor.

Then Butch said, "I always dreamed of being a cowboy."

Tom told him, "You need to clean up your act 'cause cowboys are wholesome folk."

We had to pinch ourselves to keep from laughing.

It was a long drive to Calgary. We stopped a few times to get gas, load up on some junk food, and take a leak. We took turns driving, and we tried to sleep, crunched up in the back seat. Mostly we were quiet, listening to crappy country music from the car's radio.

"How about some rock and roll?" I asked.

"We prefer country music, if you don't mind," one of the boys answered.

"Surely you've heard of Country Joe and the Fish?" I asked. "They're a rock band that's popular in the US. I'm surprised the country stations don't play him."

"Never heard of them," Tom answered.

"You must have heard 'Fixin to Die'?" said Butch, and we all belted out:

"And it's one, two, three, what are we fighting for?
Don't ask me, I don't give a damn, next stop is Vietnam
And it's five, six, seven, open up the pearly gates
Ain't no time to wonder why, whoopee, we're all gonna die."

"Sounds very inspired," Tom retorted.

When the boys were asleep, we tried to find a station that played rock and roll, but most of the stations played country. We'd often turn off the radio to get away from the twangy, sappy songs.

We were on the Trans-Canada Highway, which spans all ten provinces and is 4,860 miles long. The towns flew by—Thunder Bay, Winnipeg, Regina, Moose Jaw, Medicine Hat, and finally, Calgary.

The boys were dropping us off in downtown Calgary. It was getting dark, and our first experience in Calgary was almost our last.

A car going in the opposite direction took a hard right turn, cut directly in front of our car, went over the sidewalk, and smashed into the side of a brick building. We watched in horror as the drunken driver got out, cursing and walking away from his vehicle with its banged-up hood while smoke rose from the busted radiator. If that had happened a few seconds later, we would have been toast. We were all shaken up.

"God's country sure is nice," Butch said sarcastically.

"I thank God we weren't in an accident," Jerry replied.

John said, "Amen to that."

We thanked the boys. But Butch couldn't help himself and yelled out, "Happy trails to you," as they drove off.

It was Saturday night, around six o'clock. There were lots of people in the streets, most already good and drunk. The men wore ten-gallon hats and cowboy boots, and the women wore colorful frilly dresses and cowgirl boots. There seemed to be bars and honky-tonks on every corner, and country music spilled into the streets. We chose a bar, got a table, ordered a pitcher of beer, and dropped our backpacks at our feet.

Soon after our drinks were served, a big, tall guy approached our table and started talking to us. He was an enormous Indigenous Canadian, over 6'6", with broad shoulders, a narrow waist, dark and sad eyes, and a big scar on his right cheek. We invited him to join us. He went by the name Chief and turned out to be a fantastic guy. He was First Nation, wore a cowboy hat with a feather, jeans, a kidskin vest over a blue shirt with shiny white buttons, and a belt with a large turquoise and silver buckle. He was soft-spoken for a big man, and we sometimes had to ask him to repeat what he had said. We chatted for quite a while, and then Chief asked us if we had any weed; unfortunately, we did not.

Chief said, "Calgary would be a better place if people smoked more weed and drank less booze."

He told us he was full-blooded Cree and had been raised on a reservation about a hundred miles north of Calgary. He had many jobs, worked as a wrangler in a rodeo, was a boxer, and now worked in the oil fields. He told us he wanted to go to San Francisco and check out the hippie scene. I told him about the hippie scene in New York and how free the ladies are.

Chief asked, "Do you think the chicks in San Francisco would like me?"

Butch said, "Man, you would have the pick of the litter."

Chief laughed and asked if we had a place to stay. He found us a place to crash for the night and wished us a good journey.

The next morning, we were back on the highway heading west. In the distance, we could see the Rocky Mountains, and we were excited about experiencing that majestic range.

It took us a while, but we finally got a ride to Banff, a beautiful town in Banff National Park. We were now well into the Rockies at an altitude of over 4,500 feet.

The park took our breath away, with snow-capped mountains all around, crystal-clear lakes, and crisp, clean air. I had never experienced such a beautiful place. We were in no hurry to leave. We could see the enormous Banff Springs Hotel, with its many towers situated in a valley with nothing but trees and mountains, looking like a grand European castle.

We walked to town with its lovely, manicured streets and fine brick buildings. Walking down Main Street was amazing because right in front of us, off in the distance, was this magnificent snow-capped mountain taking up half the horizon. It was dusk, the golden hour, and the setting sun made this vista even more beautiful.

The stores were quaint and well-stocked. You could tell that this town catered to an affluent clientele. We stopped for food and provisions.

We decided to spend a few days in this beautiful place. In the late afternoon, we hiked into the bush and found a nice, secluded spot to camp for the night. Butch set up his tent, and we got into our sleeping bags.

In the middle of the night, I awoke to howling wolves and the screeching and squawking of animals. Clearly, the animals were alarmed, so I got out of the tent to see what was going on. It was very dark, and as I looked around, I realized we were in the middle of a lunar eclipse and it was freaking out the animals.

I got John and Butch out of the tent, and we watched as the moon became fully eclipsed. Now, the sky was ablaze with stars, more than I had ever imagined. We stood out in the cold night for a long time, watching in awe and wonder. When the eclipse ended, the howling and screeching subsided, and we went back to the tent to warm up and go back to sleep.

The next day, we decided to explore the Rockies. We started to climb up the side of the mountain to see who would get to the top. Butch and I took different routes, and John stayed at the campsite, as he wasn't into climbing.

I started my climb, and the lower part of the mountain was fairly easy to traverse. As I made the ascent, it became harder. At one point, I found myself balancing on a small outcrop of shale, trying to figure out how to continue my climb. At that point, I was halfway up the mountain, balancing on one foot and unsure how to continue my ascent. "What the fuck am I doing?" I thought. I was no athlete, and there was no sense in taking foolish chances. So, I carefully made my descent, and that was the end of my mountain-climbing career.

Butch was back at the campsite and said, "Great view from the top?"

"Bullshit, I didn't see you there," I responded with a big smile.

The next day, we continued going west. We got a short ride to Golden, British Columbia, only a hundred miles from Banff. It was a wonderful ride through magnificent countryside, and we relished the ride through the Western Rockies. We were again hitchhiking on the highway with the glorious Kicking Horse River beside us and the majestic Rockies towering all around.

We couldn't get a ride out of Golden for many hours. We didn't mind being on this beautiful road, but it was getting dark. Finally, someone stopped their car to tell us it was nearly impossible to get a ride out of Golden because a hitchhiker killed a motorist a few years back. That person was kind enough to give us a lift to the bus station, and we took a bus for the last leg (four hundred miles) of our journey. We pooled our money, and the cost of tickets nearly depleted our cash.

Even though we were on a bus, the ride to Vancouver was most enjoyable. Since the bus wasn't very full, we were each able to get window seats and gawk at the spectacular terrain. We went through Roger's Pass, with its snow-capped mountains, through the beautiful towns of Revelstoke, Salmon Arm, and Kamloops. In Hope, we marveled at all the tunnels through the Coquihalla Pass, with a raging river alongside the highway. Then, we went through a few more towns and finally arrived in Vancouver.

❧22☙

We hadn't eaten since Golden, and we were famished when we got off the bus in downtown Vancouver. We found an all-you-can-eat restaurant, had just enough money for three meals, and ate until we couldn't manage another morsel. We soon found a place to crash for the night.

The next day, we set off in different directions. Sadly, I never saw Butch or John again, though I always kept an eye out for them during my time in Vancouver. I'm sure Butch got his chance to piss in the Pacific Ocean. I made it over to Kitsilano, an area of Vancouver where hippies hang out. I met a University of British Columbia (UBC) student and stayed with him for a day. People in Vancouver were friendly and sympathetic to draft dodgers, and being one was considered a badge of courage.

I met Mary the next day. I don't remember how, but once she found out I was a draft dodger, she offered to put me up for a few days. Mary was a beautiful woman in her late twenties, with long, straight blonde hair, blue eyes, and a sweet smile. She didn't look like a hippie since she was dressed like a lawyer in a nice shirt and blazer. I was surprised she offered to put me up. Mary had a three-bedroom apartment on West 4th Avenue, and I had my own bedroom.

Mary had a beautiful younger sister, Christy, who lived with her. Christy was nineteen and a student at the university. She was 5'5" with bright blue eyes, blonde hair, a sweet smile, and a gorgeous face. Christy was a bit shy, which made her even more appealing. I was smitten from the minute I saw her. We hit it off right away. Mary wasn't particularly protective of her sister and didn't mind me spending lots of time with her. Christy showed me around the university and the wonderful beaches within walking distance of their apartment. It didn't take long for us to become lovers.

Mary was gracious and never asked me for money, but I didn't want to freeload. I wanted to contribute to household expenses and looked for opportunities to make money. A fellow I met told me about an opportunity that didn't require commuting to an office or working in some store. I earned money by distributing the *Georgia Straight*, a free underground newspaper. Each day, I went to their offices and picked up about a hundred copies. I took them to various locations, smiled while I handed them to people, and often received tips. On a good day, I could make ten bucks, most of which I gave to Mary to help with the expenses. I could have easily gotten into drug dealing, but I was adamantly against doing that. I was lucky that one time when I was arrested in Toronto and didn't want to do anything stupid in my new country.

Living in Vancouver for four months and hawking the *Georgia Straight* each day was not very fulfilling. I was falling in love with Christy, but I also was getting restless and needed a change. Since the age of twelve, I had always made money. I was independent and never liked sponging off anyone, although Mary never made me feel like a burden. The only marketable skill I had was as a bookkeeper or a clerk, and I didn't want to sit in a cubicle downtown, day after day. I heard that there were great opportunities in Whitehorse in the Yukon. Perhaps I could learn a new trade, make some real money, and find stability. As crazy as it seems now, I was excited about the possibility of becoming a miner or construction worker.

I told Christy about my plans. She became upset and said, "You can go if you want, but I may not be here waiting for you when you get back. If you get back."

I told her, "I will come back with money and a skill. I hope you wait."

"Don't count on it" was the last thing she said to me.

It was hard to leave Christy, and I hoped we could withstand the separation. I thought the break might even strengthen our relationship.

Me in Vancouver in 1968   Christy and me 1968

My friend Ken was also interested in going north, so we decided to hitchhike together. We hit the road in late March 1968 and began our fifteen-hundred-mile trek north to Whitehorse, the capital of the Yukon. Ken was a native Vancouverite who wanted to escape from a bad relationship.

It sure was easier hitching with only one other guy. I recall one ride. After hitching more than half the distance to Whitehorse, this guy pulled over in an old Buick and asked us if we knew how to drive, which we assured him we did. We could tell he was drunk and exhausted. He said he was going to Whitehorse, and we told him that was our destination, too. He told us we could start driving right now, staggered out of the car, laid down in the back seat, and immediately passed out.

I got into the driver's seat and was about to start driving when I realized this car had a manual transmission. I had never driven a stick before, and I asked Ken if he knew how, which he didn't. I knew the theory; some of my friends had cars with stick shifts. Ken was fine with me giving it a go. The car had a column shifter with a knob with a diagram of the four gears and reverse. I figured out how the gear shift and the clutch worked pretty quickly, but I ground the gears a lot in the beginning. We were fortunate the owner of the car was out cold and didn't hear the grinding or feel the jerkiness of those first few dozen miles.

By the time we got to Whitehorse, I was comfortable driving a stick shift. The guy didn't wake up until we were close to town, and then he took over the driving. He knew we had filled the car with gas and reimbursed us. He gave us twenty bucks, which was more than we had paid for gas, and told us to keep the change. We asked him about jobs, and he didn't know of any but told us where to look. He also dropped us off at a hostel where we could stay for very little money.

We started asking around about jobs and, as advertised, there were plenty of jobs, but for skilled people. We looked in the local paper and went to various businesses without any luck. We didn't have mining experience, know how to drive an eighteen-wheeler, or have any practical experience to speak of, and soon our meager funds were depleted.

Some odd jobs were available that didn't require much skill. One of those jobs was digging a grave, and reluctantly, we took it. It was backbreaking work, digging into the cold ground. Getting down to six feet took a long time. Ken and I had blisters, but it bought us a few more days of food and lodging. I didn't feel weird digging a grave. It was just a big hole in the ground. I grew up in Middle Village, which was surrounded by cemeteries. Coffins and graves held no special sway over me.

That night, sitting in my bunk in the crummy hostel with blistered hands, it finally dawned on me how stupid this journey was. I should have realized that all these high-paying jobs required skills I didn't have. "You idiot," I said to myself, "you had it good in Vancouver, and you threw it all away on a fool's errand." Now, I was fifteen hundred miles away from beautiful Christy. I was missing her and the life we had built. I was very concerned she would no longer want me back.

Finding a good job in Whitehorse seemed hopeless. We couldn't survive on odd jobs and decided to return to Vancouver. We got on the highway and stood at the side of the road with thumbs out, trying to get a ride as the big semis rolled by, kicking up dust. The highway wasn't paved because of the severe winters. We stood there for more than five hours without any luck. Soon, we were covered from head to toe with dry, arid dirt from the highway. We were miserable and hungry.

Across the street was a diner with a blinking neon sign that beckoned us to "EAT HERE." We hadn't eaten since breakfast and had run out of money. I had one lousy dime left, and Ken had even less. Standing there, it dawned on me that I was ten thousand miles away from home, a fugitive from the USA, without enough money to make a phone call. But that realization didn't depress me. I was free in this amazing country and heading back to Christy. I believed that somehow everything would turn out all right. I don't know where that optimism came from, but it sustained me on numerous occasions.

It was starting to get dark, and I could no longer resist the "EAT HERE" sign. We walked across the street to the diner, brushed the dirt off our clothes as best as we could, and tried to look presentable. We asked the man behind the counter if there was any work we could do to pay for a meal.

He said, "I'm sorry, fellas, we're about ready to close. But sit down; I'll give you some food."

He grilled a couple of hamburgers and heated up some fries. He also gave us each a hot cup of coffee. We enjoyed a wonderful meal from this kind and gracious man.

After the meal, he asked, "You boys want anything else?"

I said, "Thank you, sir, for your kindness, but if you could spare a cigarette, I'd greatly appreciate it."

He gave us a pack of cigarettes and a dozen donuts for the road.

With full stomachs, we decided to sleep on the side of the road. We didn't have a tent, just our sleeping bags. At dusk, the mosquitoes descended, mosquitoes the size of hummingbirds. We were getting eaten alive and quickly got into our sleeping bags, pulled them over our heads, and finally fell asleep.

❧ 23 ❧

The next morning, we got a ride from Reverend Joshua Phillpotts. He was a Presbyterian minister of Jamaican descent who lived in Watson Lake, Yukon, right on the border of British Columbia. We told the kind reverend about our predicament, and he put us up in his house, fed us, and, after a few days, found us lodging and jobs at a sawmill.

He took us to a reasonably priced motel where many of the millworkers lived. Even though we didn't have money, the motel owner gave us a room, trusting we would pay him when we got our first paycheck. I found people here very trusting and always looking out for each other.

Working at the sawmill was backbreaking work, but Ken and I were getting stronger, and the pay was pretty good. There wasn't any entertainment to speak of, so everyone went to the local pub after work. That's where I got to know most of the people, especially the local characters like the old prospectors and the town drunks. The folks here looked like hippies with their beards and jeans, but once we got to know them, we learned they were, in fact, very conservative.

One day, Jim, a fellow mill worker who also lived at our motel, came into the pub very upset. He announced he had lost his wedding ring and didn't understand how that could have happened. He knew it wasn't stolen since he had locked his door and window. He remembered taking the ring off and putting it on his bedside table before he took a shower. He forgot to put it back on afterward, went to sleep, and it was gone the following morning. He looked everywhere and practically tore his room apart but without luck.

Someone suggested that it may have fallen into a crack in the floor. But Jim said that he inspected the floor very carefully.

Willy, one of the older prospectors, stood up and said, "I know what happened. Someone stole your ring, and I know who."

Then someone said, "Willy, sit down before you accuse someone and make an ass of yourself."

Willy replied, "I know who it was, and it ain't no person. You got yourself a pack rat, and he took your ring. I know all about dem critters. I had to be real careful with my gold nuggets when I was prospectin'. Dem critters could cost you a week's work in a second. I have experience wit dem critters, and I know how you can get your ring back, iff'n you're interested, that is," he proclaimed.

Most of the folks in the bar were skeptical since old Willy was known for his tall tales. But the guy who lost his ring was desperate and asked, "How can I get it back"?

The old geezer said, "What you gotta do is wait for the full moon. Make sure your curtain is wide open so the light of the moon shines in. Then you gotta get some tin foil and nail it to the nightstand. You gotta make sure that the tin foil is nice and shiny in the moonlight. And the next morning, you're gonna get your ring back."

Jim was skeptical, but what did he have to lose? He had to try it. The night of the full moon was thankfully clear, and the moonlight shone brightly into the room. Jim followed the old prospector's instructions. He was able to get tin foil from the diner and nailed it to his nightstand. When he woke up the following morning, to his amazement, his ring was back, along with some coins, shiny beads, and other treasures that the pack rat had accumulated over the years.

That next day, Jim went to the pub and told everyone that he got the ring back by doing exactly what Willy said. He went over to Willy with a drink and thanked him.

"I think I deserve a bottle," Willy said.

Jim answered, "Yes, you do. In fact, I'm gonna buy you two."

Willy, who was basking in his glory, stood up and said, "I told you so. I told you, and none of you believed me. I told you he would bring it back! That's cause the pack rat couldn't carry off the tin foil, so he bought back more of his treasures, thinking that more treasure would release the shiny tin foil. The harder it is to get somethin', the more value it has to the rat. That's how his brain works."

"I learned about pack rats when I had my cabin by the creek back in '54 when I was prospecting for gold. You could pan for a week for a nice-sized nugget, and if you weren't careful, those critters would steal it right from under your nose," the old prospector concluded.

* * *

Chuck was another regular at the pub. He was a quiet man in his mid-fifties who only drank soda, or pop, as they call it, in Canada. One day, we were sitting at a table with Chuck, and I asked him why he only drank pop. He told us he was an alcoholic and had been sober for more than five years. I asked him how he managed to get sober. He told us his story.

"I came from a small town north of Calgary, was married to a good woman, and had a good job working the oil fields. But I started drinking heavily, not showing up for work, and lost my job. I found another job and lost that one, too. One day, I got so drunk I wound up in jail in the drunk tank, and my wife had to bail me out. After bailing me out a few too many times, she left me. I can hardly blame the woman," he said.

"So, I went to Calgary, continued my heavy drinking, and wound up in a rundown flop house. One day, while I was passed out on my bed, I heard heavy banging on the ceiling. That woke me up. The banging kept on getting louder, and cracks were forming in the ceiling. The banging continued, and chunks of plaster started falling. I could see the chunks all over my bed and the white plaster dust in the air. A hole started appearing in the ceiling, and it was getting bigger by the moment. Soon, I could see some black pointy thing popping out. More plaster fell, and I felt it hit me. Now I could see what that black thing was; it was a beak, a giant beak poking out of the ceiling. A big, sharp, ugly, black beak pecking and pecking like some monster woodpecker. The hole kept getting bigger and bigger, and more plaster and dust was falling. My bed was almost white with the dust, and I started coughing like crazy. I was terrified. I jumped out of bed and scrambled into the corner to protect myself. The giant beak was getting closer, and now I could see part of his ugly black head and one of his yellow eyes. Then, with one more loud bang, much of the ceiling was gone, and I could see the entire giant black head looking right at me as if I was a tasty little worm." Chuck trembled and closed his eyes for a moment.

"My God, that bird looked horrible with its menacing yellow eyes and long pointy beak. I knew that bird was going to eat me. I started screaming and screaming, no one could calm me down, and finally, the police came and took me to the hospital."

"I don't know how long I was out, but when I finally saw the doc, he told me I got the DTs (delirium tremens) and if I didn't stop drinking, I could have more hallucinations, maybe even scarier ones. He said people with the DTs could wind up in the nuthouse locked away forever. He sure put the fear of God in me. After that, I never touched another drop," he concluded.

He told me that he had driven out of Calgary as soon as he got out of the hospital and decided to head west. Somehow, he wound up in Watson Lake and, there, met the good Reverend Phillpotts.

"The reverend counseled me, and I attend his AA meetings every day. He found me a job at the sawmill, and I've been sober these last five years," Chuck explained and added, "It's by the grace of God that I'm still alive."

I asked Chuck how old he was, and I was shocked to hear

he was only thirty-five. I thought he was at least fifty.

Chuck's experience reminded me of my death trip and the hallucinations I experienced sitting on the ledge of the roof on that frightful night. I didn't know that alcohol could also cause dreadful hallucinations. It made me wonder where these horrendous images come from.

*　*　*

Another character who frequented the pub was John Kubiak, an engineer and surveyor.

One day, John asked, "Does anyone have experience as a surveyor's helper?"

I immediately announced that I did, which was true. About a month after I arrived in Vancouver, I had a job helping a surveyor in Ashcroft, BC, for a few days. The work was easy; all I had to do was carry the wooden stakes for the surveyor and bang them into the ground, where he told me. John quizzed me for a moment and was satisfied with my experience. What John required was precisely what I did in Ashcroft, which is much easier than the work I was doing in the sawmill.

It would require two weeks in the bush, and he would pay me $250 per week, which was far more than I was making at the mill. I accepted the job. I learned later that John had discovered an error in the mining claim of Cassiar Asbestos, which had a huge mining operation in the Cassiar Mountain range just south of Watson Lake.

Asbestos is highly heat resistant and was used to insulate pipes, brake pads, and many other items. Asbestos was in high demand at that time, and the Cassiar mine was one of the largest asbestos producers in the world. In fact, they built a town called Cassiar, about a hundred miles south of Watson Lake, which had a population of about fifteen hundred. This was way before asbestos' cancer-causing properties were exposed.

John discovered an error right in the middle of Cassiar's

claim, and he planned to lay a counterclaim himself. He had to be secretive about his plan. If Cassiar found out what he was up to, John was sure they would cause him harm. Fortunately, the claim was enormous, encompassing hundreds of square miles, and the chance of anyone seeing us out in the middle of the wilderness was minuscule. Of course, John never told me any of this.

John told me he would be ready to leave in three days. I gave notice at the sawmill and settled my bill at the motel.

John hired a helicopter to fly us deep into the mountains. It was a beautiful day, with crystal clear skies and hardly any wind. We flew over magnificent terrain, past snow-capped peaks and winding rivers for about an hour. I could see large herds of caribou running as we flew by. It was majestic, a pure, unspoiled landscape without any signs of civilization for most of the flight.

We landed atop a hill and set up our campsite. John was well-supplied. He had tons of food and a large, comfortable tent with cots to sleep on. Once we set up our campsite, John took sticks of dynamite and set them off all around the camp. The serene stillness was ruined by these powerful explosions. Dirt and rocks kicked up all around us. The noise was deafening. I had never heard anything so loud in my life.

John explained, "I set these off every night to keep the grizzly bears away."

"What if they come anyway?" I asked.

"They won't come. They don't like the sound and smell of dynamite."

In the early morning, John scanned the horizon with his binoculars, searching for signs of grizzlies. He was terrified of these creatures. Once he verified that the coast was clear, we ate a hearty breakfast and set out. I carried the wooden stakes. John made his calculations and found the right starting point, and I hammered the stake into the ground as John paced off the distance for the next stake. And so it went, day after day.

I did not mind this mindless work; we were deep in the mountains, perhaps where no humans had ever walked. I saw herds of caribou, wild mountain goats, wild sheep, and, thankfully, no grizzlies. Besides all the stuff I carried, John had me take a 30-06 rifle in case a grizzly crossed our path.

We were on a tight schedule. The helicopter was to come back on a specific date, and there were no cell phones back then or other methods of communication, so we had to get the work done. If we didn't finish, John's counterclaim might not be valid.

The last day came, and we weren't quite finished. So, to get the claim done, we needed to split up. John pointed me in a direction and told me to finish one section while he finished another. This was the first time I was out alone. It was nice; I didn't have to listen to John's grumbling about grizzlies or his Polish curses. I felt free in this beautiful country.

I continued in the direction that John specified. It was an absolutely glorious spring day, sunny and a bit nippy in these mountains. Every few meters, I pounded a stake into the ground. I continued this for a few hours, happy to be in true wilderness. I made it to the top of this hill on this magnificent day. At the summit was a small pond. I could see the sky's reflection, the puffy little white clouds and the surrounding mountains perfectly reflected in the pond. I remember this image very clearly to this day.

I then looked to my left and saw two beautiful bear cubs frolicking in the grass. My heart soared; it was so lovely. They played like small children, and I felt honored to see such an amazing sight. I stopped to truly savor this extraordinary moment.

Then I looked to my right, and there was the momma grizzly watching her babies. I felt terror like never before. There I was, almost right between momma and her cubs. My heart started racing. In an instant, I turned around and ran away as quickly as my feet could carry me, leaving the stakes in the ground. I was too terrified even to turn around.

As I ran, I passed a wild sheep with her baby. She took off and left the baby behind unprotected. Bad momma, I thought. Momma grizzly would never leave her cubs unprotected. Maybe the grizzly was still behind me! I continued to run, not daring to look back lest I get eaten.

After some distance, I turned around and was relieved there wasn't a grizzly in sight. It was fortunate the bear didn't smell me. Bears have poor eyesight, and I'm sure the direction of the wind saved my life. A grizzly could easily outrun me.

I made it back to the campsite as John was packing it up. I told him about the bear.

He laughed and said, "Why didn't you just shoot it? You had your rifle."

"I wasn't going to kill such a noble animal, especially a mother," I told him.

"You wouldn't think of her as noble when she's ripping out your guts," John countered.

We made it back to Watson Lake, where John paid me and said goodbye. He told me he was leaving in the morning.

I dropped off my duffel bag in my room and went to the pub. Everyone I knew was already there. Once inside, people started quizzing me about our excursion. I told my bear story and got lots of advice about how to properly confront a grizzly bear.

"You gotta carry a glass jar with pebbles and shake it; bears are scared of rattlers," an old-timer said.

"You gotta carry a small stick and whirl it in the air; it makes a sound that bears don't like," another chimed in.

I told them, "I'm glad I didn't shit my pants, 'cause I heard that grizzlies have a great sense of smell." They all laughed.

Years later, I learned that John Kubiak sold his counterclaim back to Cassiar Asbestos for a million dollars. Not a bad profit for a venture that probably cost a few thousand bucks.

Once the health risks of asbestos were made public, production at Cassiar Asbestos ceased, and the mine went bankrupt in the early 1990s. The once-thriving town of Cassiar, with its fifteen hundred residents, is now a ghost town.

* * *

I had money in my pocket. I was missing Christy and felt it was time to go home. Ken was ready as well, and we hitched back to Vancouver.

The first ride we got was with two college kids from Vancouver. They had a VW bus and were coming back from Juneau, Alaska. Perfect, we thought. First hitch, and a ride all the way home.

The boys said that they planned to stop at Liard River Hot Springs, which was about three hours south. We could continue hitching from there or join them for a dip in the hot mineral waters. We told them we wanted to join them.

Liard River Hot Springs is a British Columbia provincial park situated in a beautiful spruce forest. After walking across a long wooden boardwalk, we came to a few nice-sized hot pools with water hotter than a hundred degrees. A large cabin was next to the pools, with showers and a changing room. We were the only people enjoying these amazing pools. We luxuriated in the hot waters for about an hour and felt very relaxed and rejuvenated afterward. It was time to continue our journey south.

Once on the highway, I fell asleep in the back of the bus. Suddenly, I felt like I was floating in midair, and the world was turning all around me. Then, I felt my head hitting the roof of the VW bus. It didn't take me long to realize we had been in an accident and that the bus had rolled over.

We all got out of the bus safely, but the poor bus had rolled over into a ditch, with its wheels rotating unceremoniously in the air. One of the boys had fallen asleep at the wheel. We felt bad for them. Maybe going to the relaxing hot springs hadn't been such a good idea after all.

❧24❧

I had been gone for only two months, but it seemed much longer. I was worried that Christy might have moved on since I hadn't written or called during my absence. I headed to Mary's house with great apprehension. Mary greeted me warmly, and I could see in Christy's eyes that she was glad I was back. I was beyond happy that our relationship had survived.

I told them about my adventures and gave Mary five hundred dollars, most of the money I had saved from working up north. Mary refused to accept it, and we settled on her taking $250. We went to a nice restaurant to celebrate my return, and Mary insisted on paying.

A few days later, I met up with my friend David, who told me that a Zen Rōshi was coming to town. I've always had a fascination with Zen. I wanted to learn the Zen method of meditation called *zazen*. But mostly, I wanted a *kōan*, a paradox to meditate on. The effort to solve the *kōan* can exhaust the analytical intellect and egoistic will and ultimately lead the student to enlightenment. The *kōan* usually came as a phrase or a question. I knew of a few from my readings. One famous *kōan* was, "What was your original face before your mother was born?"

David and I went to see Rōshi Sasaki, who was speaking at the Vancouver Zen Centre. The Rōshi was a small-framed man with powerful jet-black eyes and a small mouth that seemed to sport a perpetual frown. He was wearing the traditional black robe of a Zen master. One of the things that stood out from his talk was how he described and demonstrated his morning ritual. The moment he awoke, he jumped out of bed, put his hands behind his back, expanded his chest, and let out a deep and loud "ha ha ha," which reverberated throughout the auditorium. I understood this to mean: "It's a new day! I laugh at whatever trials and tribulations you bring me." I felt he was a powerful master with a perfect attitude toward life, an attitude I wished to develop.

After his talk, we learned how to meditate using the *zazen* method. We sat in straight rows on cushions with our backs and necks straight and our eyes opened but not focused on anything. One of the younger monks sauntered up and down the rows with a long pole, monitoring each person's posture. I was getting into a nice meditative space when I got whacked across my shoulder. The stick made more noise than caused pain. It was a rude awakening. I must have slouched. Then, I made sure to sit ramrod straight. I found the meditation position very uncomfortable. My legs were cramping, but I dared not move. Finally, it was my turn to have an audience with the Rōshi.

I was nervous and excited to come before this great spiritual master. The Rōshi was sitting on a cushion, and I was directed to sit at his feet on the floor.

I looked into his clear, deep eyes and summoned the courage to say, "Rōshi, I humbly request a *kōan*."

He looked me over for a minute or two. During the silence, I was afraid he would refuse my request. But he finally said, "Where are you?"

I answered immediately, "I'm right here," not understanding the nature of his question.

He looked straight at me, shook his head, and said, "No ... No ... No ... Where are YOU?"

I then arrogantly slapped the floor with both palms and said in a louder voice, "I'M RIGHT HERE!"

He then slapped me across my face, many times in quick succession. It didn't hurt much, but it sure got my attention. He then looked deeply into my eyes and said in a louder voice, as if he was talking to an idiot, "WHERE ARE YOOOOOOOU?"

I finally understood that this was my *kōan*. So, I thanked the Rōshi and left, grateful that I now had a special weapon that would eventually lead to my enlightenment.

Although I was back with Christy and armed with my Zen arsenal, I felt stuck. I couldn't dispel my restlessness. I needed something that would provide purpose in my life, and I had no idea where to find that.

While walking with Christy up 4th Avenue, we passed the small storefront office of Blew Ointment Press. I knew the owner, Bill Bissett, an acclaimed Canadian poet. In the past, we had some quality conversations about poetry, and Bill knew of Gene Bloom and *Entrails*. I could see Bill through the front window and decided to say hello. We had a great conversation. I told him about my adventure in the Yukon and how I missed being in the wilderness. Bill then told us of a hippie community up north called Galley Bay, suggested we go there, and even gave us directions.

This opportunity sounded very promising. Christy was skeptical at first, but soon decided to give it a try. She was no longer attending classes at UBC and thought it would be fun to have an adventure together.

It was April 1968. We told Mary about our plans, and she was very supportive. She insisted on giving me back the money I had given her when I returned from the Yukon. We packed our belongings and headed out on a beautiful sunny morning. We took the bus to the Horseshoe Bay Ferry Terminal and took the ferry to Gibsons. Standing on the deck of the ferry, we watched the beautiful scenery sail by—the snow-capped mountains of Cypress Provincial Park and the lush green hills of Bowen Island. Finally, we landed at Gibsons.

We started hitchhiking on the Sunshine Coast Highway, quickly got a ride, and drove through sleepy little hamlets nestled in spring splendor. We had to take another ferry, continuing north through the lumber processing city of Powell

River, and finally got to a tiny fishing town called Lund, where the highway ended. It was now late afternoon, and we went to the docks, where we found a fisherman who took us to Galley Bay for a reasonable fee. (It was about an hour away.)

The boat ride took us through Desolation Sound, a large

Desolation Sound

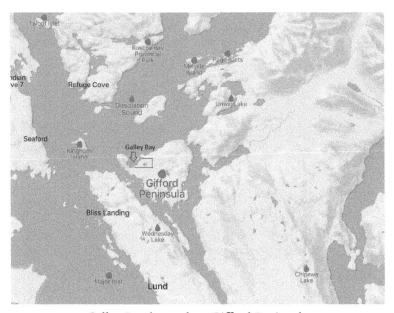

Galley Bay located on Gifford Peninsula

body of water between Vancouver Island and mainland British Columbia, with numerous clusters of islands. The sound offered spectacular views of fjords, snow-capped mountains, lush forests, rocky outcrops, and beautiful waterfalls. The coastline consisted of many peninsulas and inlets, and the golden light of late afternoon made it even more enchanting. Everywhere we looked, we saw beauty. I felt we were heading for something really special, maybe even life-changing. As we rode the little boat, I remembered the Rōshi and started reciting my *kōan* to myself, "Where are you? Where are you?" Each time I said those words, I smiled and became more enthralled with the beauty all around me. The *kōan* helped me focus on the moment and truly experience the grandeur of this magnificent place.

Finally, we navigated around Gifford Peninsula and headed into Galley Bay, a large, well-protected inlet.

❧25❧

We arrived in Galley Bay in April 1968. This hippie commune was situated in paradise. I could see a large trek of cleared land gently sloping toward a lush green forest; beyond were majestic mountains. I couldn't imagine a more beautiful location. Up the hill from us was a small A-frame cabin. As soon as we docked, a man came out to greet us. He introduced himself as Carl and asked us what we were doing there. We told him our names and said that Bill Bissett told us about the community and gave us directions to come. This satisfied Carl.

Carl was about my age, thin and muscular, of medium height, with long brown hair and brown eyes. He was a good-looking guy who spoke softly and shied away from making eye contact.

As we walked to the main house, Carl said, "My father bought this homestead in nineteen-sixty. It belonged to one family for more than fifty years. They built a fine farmhouse with a large orchard, but the kids didn't want to live such an isolated life, so they sold it to us. I've been here since sixty-six."

Carl continued, "I always wanted to go back to nature. I hate the cities with their crime and pollution. I dreamt of starting a hippie commune with people that shared my dream of living off the land—a place where we can be free of all the rules and bullshit of so-called society. But this is no fucking hippie crash pad. Everyone in the commune works for the common good."

"I also want to go back to nature," I said. "I just spent two months in the Yukon working. But the people there are super conservative. They don't understand hippie values. I'm so psyched about being here. I understand it takes work to keep the commune going and everyone needs to do their part."

"Exactly," Carl said. I could see that he was pleased that we were willing to work for the good of the commune.

I said, "I'm a draft dodger from New York, and I've been in Canada for about a year. Christy is a Vancouver girl."

"Right." He said, "I'm also a draft dodger from San Francisco. Did you get your Canadian papers?"

"Yeah," I said, "in Montreal."

"Me too, in Vancouver," he said.

Carl took us up to the main house, an impressive two-story structure with a large, covered porch that ran the length of the house. The house was painted yellow and looked in good repair. Carl explained that the property was about eighty acres. In addition to the main house, it had a big tool shed with a generator, a few acres of garden, and about a hundred mature fruit trees, mostly apple. It also had a good-sized barn that housed some goats and chickens. There was even a reservoir up the hill from the main house that provided running water. The main house had real toilets that flushed. I was amazed this property had all these amenities, being so far off the beaten track. It was incredible what the original owners had accomplished.

The property was perfect for our commune. It had a well-established farm with good living conditions, yet it was far from civilization, with no roads, no power lines, and no pollution. The closest neighbors were many miles away. It was quiet. There was just the sound of the waves, the wind rustling through trees, and the occasional call of a gull or screech from a hawk. It was a magnificent spot on a large peninsula of lush forest huddled around a deep bay, with beautiful vistas everywhere you looked.

At the main house, Carl introduced us to some of the people and showed us our room on the second floor. It was a small room, sparsely furnished with a bed and a dresser. The one window looked to the back of the property, where we could see the garden and orchard.

Once we put away our few belongings, we went downstairs to meet the rest of the community. At this point, about fifteen people were living at Galley Bay.

*   *   *

The next day, I met Carl at the dock. There were three boats at Galley Bay. One was a sailboat that Carl had sailed all the way from San Francisco called the *Bounty*, a beautiful 38-foot Tahitian Sloop, all wood with a comfortable galley. There also was an old salmon trawler and a small skiff with a little seagull engine.

Carl asked if I had ever fished, and I told him I hadn't, but I'd love to try. We got into the skiff, and Carl showed me how to start the little engine. Carl navigated the skiff to the tip of the peninsula, around a hundred yards from shore, and cut the engine. Carl informed me that this was the ideal spot to jig for red snappers. He then grabbed a reel of fishing line with its heavy silver lure and dropped it into the water. There was no need for a fishing pole, he explained. The fishing line dropped to the bottom, about fifty feet down. He then started to jerk the line up and down. Pretty soon, we had a fish. The fish gave us no fight, and when it was at the surface, I was amazed at how big it was; it must have been twenty pounds! Carl grabbed the gaff, a pole with a big sharp hook, hooked the fish, and brought the fish into the skiff. He then let me try it. It was easy, and soon I caught a fish. We now had two nice-sized red snappers for our communal dinner. It was that easy, and catching fish would soon become one of my favorite chores.

On the way back to shore, Carl told me more about the beginning of the commune. Carl was going to college in 1966 but dropped out to create a utopian hippie commune on the homestead his father had bought. Carl's father, a famous psychiatrist, had encouraged his son to achieve his dream. Carl was going out with Joanne when they sailed the *Bounty* north to Galley Bay, along with Joanne's five-year-old son. On the way up the coast, they stayed in Vancouver for a few weeks and found young people interested in living a back-to-nature communal life. Soon, people arrived; some stayed for a short period, while others were still here. Joanne had wanted privacy, so they built their own cabin, a beautiful A-frame on a slight hill overlooking the dock. It was a perfect location for securing the property.

We carried the two red snappers to the large kitchen, where one of the ladies cleaned and fileted the fish. People were already preparing our communal dinner, and soon, the fish were in frying pans, happily crackling.

We went into the dining room, which had three tables pushed together and enough chairs for everyone. The guys would sit down at the table, and the ladies brought out the plates of food—mashed potatoes, string beans, freshly baked bread, carrots, corn, cabbage, fresh salad, and pan-fried red snapper. Soon, everyone was seated, ready for a simple, nourishing meal and lively conversation.

That night, we lit kerosene lamps, built a fire in the fireplace, and settled in the living room, where Bob serenaded us with old rock, folk hits, and his original compositions. Bob had this deep, resonant, whisky-soaked voice and was an excellent guitarist. His songs invoked images of the sea and traveling and were absolutely mesmerizing. It was like having a professional musician in our community, and, in fact, we had. Some years later, Bob Carpenter cut an album on the Warner label, *Silent Passage*.

Bob was about six feet tall with a solid muscular frame, reddish brown hair, a full beard, deep-set eyes, and was in his mid-twenties. He was a great guy, jovial, funny, and big-hearted, with an aura of tragedy coming through. Bob had been born on an Indian reservation and came from a small town in northern Ontario. His mother was half-native Canadian. But Bob didn't like talking about his past. I think he got out of his hometown as quickly as he could.

Bob had two girlfriends, Ingrid and Gloria. I don't know

how he managed it, but somehow the women worked out an understanding. I think the truth was that both girls wanted him, and he couldn't accept one without hurting the other one's feelings, so he dated both. But not at the same time.

Ingrid was in her late twenties and looked a bit like Popeye's girlfriend, Olive Oyl, but not quite as thin. She was tall with long auburn hair and serious brown eyes, and she was slightly hunched over—probably because she was self-conscious of her height. She was constantly fluttering around doing something. Her primary role in the community was caring for the chickens and goats. We had four nanny goats and one billy goat named Jumbo. Ingrid milked the goats every morning and collected the eggs. She also helped with cooking and cleaning. She seemed glum when Bob was dating Gloria.

Gloria looked like a schoolgirl, probably still in her late teens. She was a perky little lass, maybe 5'2", with shoulder-length brown hair, bright blue eyes, and an easy smile. She was a natural gal who wore no makeup, didn't shave her pits, took no shit from anyone, and had a delightful laugh. Her primary role in the commune was to cook and bake. She was cheerful most of the time and didn't seem jealous when Bob was with Ingrid.

Bob dated Ingrid first; it must have been difficult for her when he started dating Gloria. Ingrid's world revolved around Bob, whom she pampered. Her mission was to make him happy and serve him like a prince. Gloria just enjoyed hanging out with Bob. She didn't make a fuss about him, which I suspected was a relief for Bob. Still, it must have been a challenge dating both girls. Bob managed to make time for himself and often disappeared for extended periods, trudging through the forest, fishing on the boat, or salvaging logs.

As we settled in, we got to know more about the people in our community. Among the earliest settlers were Harold and Delores and their young son. Soon after arriving, Harold built a fine two-story cabin. And now Delores was expecting again.

Harold and Delores also came from California. Harold was

a guy with boundless energy, always on the move. He and Carl were always working on some project. Delores was an earth mother and natural leader. She was taller than Harold, a strong-framed woman with a sharp tongue. She didn't spare anyone, especially Harold, and she wasn't someone to mess with.

Hazel, who was in her early twenties and lived in the main house, was cheerful and talkative, with a hearty laugh and an easy smile. Hazel was very attractive, with magnificent breasts, a beautiful figure, and a face to match. Hazel liked working in the garden with Christy. Hazel didn't have a boyfriend, but two guys had crushes on her.

One was Brian, who was in his late twenties and was a beat poet and aspiring writer with a deep love of jazz. Brian tried to sweet-talk Hazel with tales of Ginsberg and Kerouac. He composed poems for her, odes of love, but, alas, Hazel wasn't swayed.

Brian and I hit it off right away. I told him I was from New York, and we bonded because of our mutual love of jazz and interest in poetry, especially the beat poets. We talked about the musicians we liked, and it was clear we shared the same taste. He was glad to be in this lush wonderland. Brian lived in the hen house, and his main task was restraining Jumbo, our billy goat, so that Ingrid could milk the nanny goats. This was no mean feat since Jumbo was very strong and fond of pissing on his head. I don't know if he did that to make himself more attractive to the nanny goats or to fend off Brian.

Brian was fatalistic, with a wry sense of humor. He wasn't too upset that he wasn't making headway with Hazel. "If I'm destined to screw her, I will," he declared. "If not, I'm cool. No sense getting too obsessed over a chick."

Denny was also enamored with Hazel. He was probably in his late teens and lived outside the main house in a small shack. Denny came from the Okanagan, a region of British Columbia known for its wineries and fruit orchards. Denny's passion was taking care of the fruit trees. He taught us how to prune them and keep them healthy. Denny was a sweet, well-meaning boy, always willing to lend a hand. We all treated him like our little brother.

It was April, and the fruit trees were in full blossom; the apple trees were in regalia of white, and the cherry trees were robed in pink. Denny would bring Hazel bouquets, but he was too shy to have a real conversation with her.

One guy who wasn't after Hazel was Richard, who also lived in the main house. Richard wasn't fazed by anything. He was of Armenian descent with a bit of an accent. Richard was a strict vegetarian and practiced meditation. He never seemed to take an interest in the girls. I don't think he was gay; I think, at heart, he was an ascetic. His main work was in the garden, taking care of the composting and cleaning.

There were a few other people in the community, like Grady and Marion, but I don't remember them well. Even though Galley Bay was difficult to get to, there seemed to be a good deal of turnover. People stayed for a few weeks and then moved on, and new folks would come. Carl had a hard time turning people away despite his fondness for saying, "This is no fucking hippie crash pad."

The most mysterious guy in our community was Mac, who lived in the barn. Mac was tall and lean with grease-covered clothes. He could have been forty or fifty; it was hard to tell, and he looked like he had lived a hard life. He never smiled, rarely spoke, and never shared anything personal. In fact, he never said his name; we just called him Mac. We were glad he was there because Mac could fix anything: diesel engines, generators, and all the power tools. He kept the rifles clean and in fine working order and kept the tools—the axes, saws, and floes—sharp. Mac could also build anything, from a wooden door to a whisky still. Mac never really hung out with us and showed no interest in the girls, at least not outwardly. He kept to himself and always kept busy on some project. When he drank, he would retreat even further into himself. Mac never smoked weed with us. There were all kinds of speculations about Mac.

Was he a fugitive? Could he be a murderer? Between him, Carl, and Harold, things ran smoothly.

Although some people in our community had their own space, we always had dinner together at the main house. We still adhered to the traditional gender roles; the ladies cooked, cleaned, and served the food while the men fished, harvested oysters, salvaged logs, and did all the manual labor. The new wave of the women's liberation movementt had started but hadn't yet filtered into hippiedom. Even at Millbrook, the ladies did all the cooking and cleaning.

Soon, we got into a nice routine of helping with the various chores. Christy worked in the garden and helped with the meals. I helped with assorted tasks, but mostly, I brought home the red snappers. I loved fishing and sometimes caught more fish than we could consume. We had no freezer, but we did have an area in the big barn that served as a smokehouse, and we would smoke fish for winter consumption. It wasn't lox, but it was good.

After dinner, we would talk, tell stories, listen to Bob or Grady play guitar, and enjoy our new home with its soft light from the kerosene lamps. Sometimes, we smoked weed, but that was on special occasions, and we didn't indulge too much. Also, there was lots of work to do to survive. And Carl was fond of reminding us that this was "no fucking hippie crash pad."

I remember finding a mushroom book in the main house identifying edible and poisonous mushrooms. Christy and I wandered into the woods, searching for mushrooms where plenty were available. We carefully compared mushrooms in the book to those we found to ensure none were poisonous.

One variety of mushrooms that were plentiful in our forest was a bright red mushroom with small white dots on its cap. Our book identified it as *Amanita muscaria*, or fly agaric, and described it as hallucinogenic. The mushroom book warned that eating this will get you sick and cause vomiting. The book didn't contain any recipes for preparing these mushrooms, but it did include some fascinating details. It stated that in Siberia, indigenous tribes used these mushrooms in their religious rituals. The Shaman would eat the mushrooms, endure the sickness, and then piss in a jar. The others would then drink the piss and get high without getting sick. While reading this, I wondered how this medical marvel was first discovered.

We found many edible and delicious mushrooms: golden chanterelles, morels, oysters, porcinis, milk caps, and other varieties. That night, Christy prepared a nice mushroom stew for us to enjoy. As it turned out, our mushroom-identifying skills weren't as sharp as we thought, because some of us got stoned on the stew. Maybe a young Fly Agaric flew into the stew, or perhaps we inadvertently picked some psilocybin mushrooms. Regardless, we decided not to take any more chances. The mushrooms book identified many highly poisonous mushrooms, such as the death cap, which would kill you. Some of these poisonous mushrooms looked very much like the edible kind, so one had to be super careful.

*　*　*

One day, our dogs started barking like crazy because they heard a boat approaching. We went out on the porch and could see the dreaded Royal Canadian Mounted Police coming. They would come for only one reason: to bust us. By the time they parked their boat, we already had our little stash well hidden in the woods.

The RCMP officers rushed the house; five of them had guns drawn. When they finally arrived, they found us all relaxed in the living room with a crackling fire burning and Grady playing his guitar without a care in the world. He was playing the Buffalo Springfield song "For What It's Worth" when they rushed in—perfect timing:

"There's something happening here
But what it is ain't exactly clear

There's a man with a gun over there
A-telling me that I got to beware."

One of the cops yelled, "Stop that playing." But Grady continued with the lyrics.

"I think it's time to stop
Children, what's that sound
Everybody look what's going down"

The cop yelled, "Stop or I'll break the guitar over your fucking head."

The RCMP were extremely uptight and searched the house
from top to bottom, checking all the knapsacks and sleeping
bags. They didn't even find a roach. I don't know if they had
a search warrant; we didn't ask. We just complied with whatever they said.

One of them was a nasty SOB named Abe. He took some
of the guys into another room and made us drop our pants to
check if we hid any drugs in our asses.

"Does this turn you on?" asked Bob.

"Shut the fuck up, hippie," Abe replied.

Abe was a notorious narc from Vancouver. Why was he
here 150 miles north? Who knows? Who cares? They left with
nothing except the knowledge that it was impossible to orga-
nize a surprise raid on our community, and thankfully, they
never tried again.

❧26❧

The community wasn't fully self-sufficient, and sometimes we needed to buy various provisions. Besides what we grew ourselves, we needed fuel for our boats, kerosene for our lamps, flour, yeast, rice, beans, oil, salt, sugar, and a host of other items.

Every few weeks, we would take the *Bounty* to Lund. Carl had an old pickup truck there, and we would drive to Powell River, about twenty miles south. At the time, Powell River had the world's largest pulp and paper mills, and most of the town worked in them. Powell River was a large town with supermarkets where we bought supplies in bulk. A trip there took most of the day and required money.

When we only needed a few supplies, we would take the skiff to Refuge Cove, which was about 45 minutes away in the middle of Desolation Sound. Refuge Cove is a tiny community on West Redonda Island with about a dozen year-round inhabitants, one well-stocked general store and a post office where we would get our mail. One day, I offered to get our supplies, and the skiff got me there without a problem. Getting back, however, was a harrowing experience.

About ten minutes into my return trip, the weather turned ugly. The sky darkened, rain started to fall, the wind kicked up, and white caps began to swell. The tide was running against me, and it was hard to navigate a straight course. To get home, I had to hit the waves head-on. This action would often lift the boat practically out of the water and drench me. But I had no choice. I had to take a straight course, or I would never get home. Some of the waves almost capsized me. I was scared. The little Seagull engine barely kept me moving forward. I prayed I'd make it home safely. I would be a goner if I capsized or ran out of gas. No one was out in this weather. It took me almost two hours to get back to the dock, and I was drenched to the bone and famished. The folks were getting worried, especially Christy. She was begging Carl to look for me just as I arrived.

Christy grabbed me and gave me a big hug while sternly saying, "What the hell is wrong with you going out in this weather?"

I was touched that she was so worried about me, that she loved me.

Most people who came to live on the commune didn't have much money, so the community had to earn cash. One of the ways we made money was by salvaging logs. Carl had a license for it. With our license, we were given a sledgehammer that contained our license number. We had to hit each salvaged log with the sledgehammer so our license number was clearly visible on the ends of the log, which ensured that none of our salvaged logs were stolen.

Further up Desolation Sound were large logging operations, and each had access to a bay or inlet where thousands of logs could be stored safely. There, the logs were arranged into rafts, each holding about a hundred long, thick logs. Dozens of these rafts were chained together, creating a boom, which the tugboats towed to Powell River. Some of these booms could be more than a thousand feet long. When the water gets too choppy, logs break free. When a storm hits, whole rafts can break free, and a salvaging frenzy follows. Salvagers would rush out, braving the storm and hoping for a big payday. One raft of logs could fetch a few thousand dollars.

We weren't equipped to go out in storms. But the day after a storm, we would scour the coastline for loose logs. There were dozens of islands in the sound and hundreds of places where logs would wash up. One good-sized one could fetch fifty dollars. But the logging companies wouldn't bother buying just a few, so we needed to build a raft with at least fifty logs. It took us a while, but we built a raft that sold for more than two thousand dollars.

Our most consistent way of making money was harvesting the rich beds of oysters around our property. Desolation Sound was famous for its oysters because of the clear, cold, unpolluted waters. When the tide was low, we would fill burlap sacks with oysters and sell them to the fisherman. If we filled many sacks, we would travel to Lund and sell them for a higher price.

When salmon season came, we fired up our trawler and fished. Our trawler was a 36-foot wooden boat with two long poles, one on each side. The poles were lowered to about a 45-degree angle, and each pole had five fishing lines, giving us ten lines to catch fish. During the salmon season, we caught mostly salmon and some lingcod and dogfish. We also used our trawler to salvage logs because it had a good-sized diesel engine.

Picking salal was another profitable venture when it was in season. Salal is a waxy green plant that grew in abundance in our area. The plants are used for floral arrangements, especially wreaths. The demand was highest before Christmas.

One day, Carl and I went searching for logs to salvage. Since we had no luck in our area, we ventured further north but couldn't find any. It had been a long day, and we were coming home at night. Fortunately, Carl knew these waters like the back of his hand. I was sitting at the back of the boat, amazed by a river of glowing bright green lights behind us. It was surreal. I called Carl. He came and looked, cut the engine, and dropped the anchor. Once we stopped moving, the light faded.

Carl told me to dive into the water with my eyes open. I asked why, and he said, "You'll see."

I dove into an explosion of bright fluorescent green light. It was unbelievable. It was like something you might experience on acid, but this was real; it was in nature. Carl also dove in, and we splashed and laughed while playing with the light. Every time we splashed, the sea around us lit up. Every time we were still, it stopped. When we lifted our hands, we could see the tiny creatures glowing and then darkening.

Carl explained, "That's phosphorescent algae. When they are disturbed, they light up."

"Wow, I've never seen anything like this. It's amazing, so incredible. Does it happen often?" I asked.

"No, it's pretty rare," he replied.

We got back to Galley Bay rather late. We were naturally high and headed up to the main house, and happily, there was plenty of dinner left.

❧27❧

Summer finally arrived, and word about the Galley Bay commune had started spreading. New people would come every few days, and by the height of the summer, we had over fifty people in the community, far more than it could handle. The house was overflowing, and people were sleeping in the tool shed, tents, and even the barn. The main house had about thirty people crashing in every nook and cranny. The house had two toilets, but people soon were shitting in the woods. We didn't have enough food or dishes for everyone. Carl's nightmare came true—Galley Bay became a fucking hippie crash pad.

At the beginning of the summer, Carl found it hard to turn people away. People would beg to stay for a day or two, but would inevitably stay for a week or more. But soon, he had to intercept the boats coming in and not allow people to even dock. He also needed to hound people to leave, which was very uncomfortable for him. Carl was miserable that summer.

People brought drugs with them, and lots of stoned hippies were smoking dope or dropping acid, frolicking naked in the summer breeze. Respectful lusting soon turned to pure lust. There were people fucking in the apple orchard, screwing in the meadow, or humping in the bay right off the dock. Free love was in the air again. I had opportunities and was tempted, but I stayed true to Christy. I loved her, and I wanted to be in a committed relationship.

Hazel found a lover, a big hunk from sunny California. After a few weeks, they left together. Brian and Denny weren't too devastated since they had found lovers of their own.

Soon, the townsfolk heard that the Galley Bay hippies were walking around naked and started coming in their boats to gawk at us. We didn't pay them any mind. One time, a couple of ladies in our commune wanted to have some fun, so they swam out naked to a boat full of young guys, probably high schoolers. They swam around the boat on their backs so the boys could get a good look. It was likely the first time they saw boobs and pussy up close.

One of the boys in the boat got brave and said, "Hey, honey, you want to party with us?"

"What have you got to party with?" the girl asked.

"Beer," they answered.

"Come back when you've got some good dope," she taunted.

Then the girls bummed a pack of cigarettes from the guys and swam back laughing. The young guys came back the next day with a carton of cigarettes to see our mermaids. But this time, the women didn't swim out to the boat; they just waved and laughed from the shore.

The community wasn't equipped to handle so many people. People stayed for a week or two or even a month. Our food supply dwindled. Thank God for the abundance of fish, oysters, and apples.

In late July, we had a bountiful apple harvest from our hundred trees, most of them Gravenstein apples. We picked tons of apples. Our apples were perfect; none of them had blight or worms. The cool sea air was a natural fungicide.

Gravensteins were good for eating, and we sold plenty of crates of them in Powell River. But they didn't keep well, so we concentrated on preserving them. We had an old wooden apple press and made lots of apple juice. We also made apple sauce, apple butter, pie, jelly, jam, dried apples, and our favorite, applejack. Mac built a still in Denny's tiny cabin, and Denny nurtured it until we had some fine apple whisky.

Mac found an old jug, and Denny filled it with his special brew.

"This is some good shit," proclaimed Bob as he took a gulp.

"Yeah," said Carl, "this will get you stoned and could also clean the rust off anything."

"Yeah, my old pipe needs cleaning," said Denny.

"Your old pipe needs dipping, and there are sure to be some fine honeys here to choose from," said Harold.

"You better keep your pipe in your pocket, or Delores will cut it off," Denny retorted, and we all laughed.

Our community was run very loosely since Carl wasn't a natural leader. There were no rigid rules or laws to follow, and people did as they chose. Some people were conscientious and worked for the community, tending the garden, pruning the fruit trees, milking the goats, fixing things up, and cooking for the community, while others just hung out.

Most of the new people didn't help because they were too stoned or lazy, or nobody had shown them what to do. Carl was busy trying to keep people out, so there wasn't anyone designated to assign tasks and responsibilities to the new people. But when things got out of hand, Carl asked people to leave, and he asked many to leave. As summer ended, the community was back to a manageable size.

One day, we heard that Delores was going into labor. She was adamant about giving birth naturally in Galley Bay. She reminded us she had already birthed one baby naturally and didn't need a doctor. There was no point arguing, but we were worried. What if something went wrong? Getting her to Powell River Hospital would take at least two hours. Carl got the *Bounty* ready, just in case. Harold paced and tried not to look nervous.

All the women came to the cabin to help Delores. They would breathe with her, get clean sheets, hot water, and anything else she might need. None of them had any experience with childbirth, so Delores directed them during her delivery. After about six hours, we added another member to our community, a healthy baby girl.

❧28❧

Now that the throngs of hippies were gone from Galley Bay, we started to feel like a commune again. Autumn was just beginning, and everyone was happily busy.

One day, Carl announced that if anyone wanted to continue living at Galley Bay, they had to build their own cabin. We were about twenty people at that time. Christy and I discussed it. We really wanted to remain a part of the commune, so we found a nice spot overlooking the bay and claimed it for our new home.

Carl was experienced at cabin building and was happy to guide us. Carl helped us design a modified A-frame. He learned a lot from his experience building his cabin and helped us develop a great design. In a short time, we had a detailed plan and a good understanding of what we needed.

Suddenly, we found ourselves building our first home, our love nest, which had a euphoric effect on us. This was a giant step in the evolution of our relationship. We now had a common project. We were working on building something just for the two of us. It would be part of the commune, but it was also all ours, which made a huge difference. We discussed the design, labored over every detail, and couldn't have been happier. And the commune was there to help make this dream come true.

The first thing we needed was suitable wood, and we found most of it in our rich forest. Carl told us to find tall, straight pine trees and remove a small band of bark from around the entire circumference of the trunk. Then, when I chopped them down in a few weeks, it was easy to strip off the bark. Peeling the bark off logs increases the longevity of the wood because bark provides a home for damaging insects and a place for moisture to collect, which can ultimately lead to rot. Soon, we had lots of beautiful logs to serve as posts and beams for our cabin.

We also needed roofing shingles, which were easy to make since there was an abundance of large cedar logs, many already cut to the right size for making shingles. Then, with a froe and mallet, I made cedar shingles just as Harold had shown me. When done correctly, they pop right out. An extra benefit was experiencing the wonderful fragrance of freshly cut cedar. I was rewarded with that earthy, woody aroma when each shingle popped off the log.

The barn had a second level that contained lots of useful stuff. We found an old door, a window with its frame, and an old wood-burning stove and claimed them. We had all we needed to build a house except for nails and plywood for the floor and loft.

Carl and I went to Powell River on a supplies trip for the commune, and I found the rest of the things we needed for our cabin—sheets of D-grade plywood and nails. My entire purchase was under $25; that's what it cost to build our house.

I loved wandering the forest, searching for wood for the cabin, or dead trees for firewood. Sometimes, while working in the forest, I would remember Rōshi and start repeating, "Where are you? Where are you?" This had a grounding effect. I loved being close to nature. I truly appreciated this gorgeous country with its jagged coastline and majestic mountains. The air was clean and crisp, and I often saw eagles and ospreys gliding by in the sky.

Now, there were no strangers among us. There were only the core members of our commune, and I loved them all. Everyone was happy to lend a hand. Life was good again now that summer was over, and there was no drama or conflicts.

Once we had all the materials, the community came and helped us dig holes for the foundation and set logs. Soon, the frame was up. We didn't have cement, so we packed boulders and clay around each footing. We then covered the entire house with cedar shingles.

One of the men from Quebec knew how to build a fireplace out of stone and said he would do that for us. We gathered stones and clay, and he expertly laid the stones. The fireplace was starting to take shape. It was hard work dragging the rocks up the hill, and when we were less than a quarter done, he left the community without a word. We tried to finish it ourselves, but it never looked right. We wasted so much time on that lousy fireplace. In the end, all we had was a stone wall. We placed the stove in front of it and ran the stove pipe up through the roof.

The land the house stood on was on a slope, and the back of the house was three feet lower than the front. We used the drop in elevation to our favor. We made the floor level for the first twelve feet and built a big step down, making for a sunken kitchen. The step made a perfect seat, so we never needed chairs. We put a trap door on the vertical part of the step for storing food in the cool area under the cabin.

Since it was a modified A-frame, the walls were almost vertical, and the wall beams were spaced about a foot apart. Those beams were a built-in ladder to the loft. The loft was not very high. We couldn't stand up tall, but it was easy to crawl into bed.

It turned out to be a practical and efficient design, small but functional. Christy and I were very comfortable in our new home until it got cold. Fortunately, no rain got in, but the wind sure did. The thin shingles didn't provide enough insulation. We tried to caulk the house with anything we could find; cardboard and old rags were stuffed or nailed in most nooks and crannies. This helped a bit, but it still wasn't enough as winter approached. Fortunately, we secured a small stove that we installed at the entrance, and with two stoves, we were warm and snug. However, two stoves required a great deal of firewood.

We built an outhouse near the cabin. It was another

A-frame, a short distance into the woods. We dug a deep pit and cut a nice hole for the seat, a perfect fit. I didn't bother putting a door on it; the bushes protected us, and ours was the last house in the commune, so there was no through traffic. We found a fat old *Hudson Bay* catalog, perfect for toilet paper. I watched eagles fly by while I sat on the toilet.

Bob was the only other person who took up Carl's challenge to build a cabin. Bob was an incredibly hard worker. Rather than relying on shingles to complete his house, he built a log cabin and only used shingles for the roof, which took much longer. Each log had to be cut to size and notched so he could place the logs onto one another. Once done, he caulked the logs with clay and had a nice, cozy, warm cabin that only required one small stove and a hell of a lot less firewood in the winter.

❧29❧

Feeding two stoves required lots of wood. I spent five to six hours each day hauling dead trees out of the woods, cutting them to length with a bow saw, and chopping them up for firewood. This provided me with a good opportunity to practice my *kōan*: "Where are you?"

The cabin's roof extended out an extra two feet on one side. This overhang was part of Carl's great design, which allowed us to stack lots of firewood and keep it dry. By November, I had a big stack of cut, dry firewood.

I was developing muscles I had never known I had. I felt stronger, more vibrant, and healthier than ever. I loved providing for our home, but this left very little time to work for the commune. Firewood was an absolute necessity, and I was always afraid we might run out.

By November, we pretty much stopped having communal meals. Some people still lived in the big house, but the entire community didn't eat dinner as before, especially when the autumn rains came. It rained most days, a bone-chilling rain. This area gets over a hundred inches of rain annually, which is great for the trees and ducks.

Christy had a lot of chores that kept her busy for most of the day. We didn't have running water, so she would have to take a few trips to the spring each day, about a hundred yards away, and haul five-gallon buckets of water back to the house. She prepared delicious meals every day and made sure we were well-supplied with food. We accumulated a good stock of rice, beans, flour, and many other provisions, which we stored under our cabin, which was like a root cellar. Mostly, we followed a vegetarian diet.

Cleaning our clothes was a challenge. The most practical way was to boil them in a big basin and hang them up to dry on ropes in the cabin. It was challenging to navigate with clothes hanging everywhere. Over time, all our clothes became dull shades of gray.

Bathing in the autumn and winter was something I looked forward to. We fired up both stoves, making the cabin nice and toasty, like a sauna. We would strip and lather each other up inside the house, then run outside and pour warm water all over ourselves. The temperature outside was somewhere around freezing. Once we were free of suds and shivering profusely, we would rush back into the cabin to dry off. Then, we would climb up to the loft and make love.

We had lots of blankets and old sleeping bags in the loft, and we were snug and cozy up there. In the winter, before we went to sleep, we would make sure the big kettle was boiling and both stoves were on with wood full to the brim. In the morning, I was the one that dragged my ass out of bed while my princess stayed warm. Sometimes, there was ice in the kettle. It took eight hours for the water in the kettle to go from boiling to ice. That's how cold the cabin got.

One evening, we heard scratching and yowling under our floor. We figured some wild animal had gotten in since we kept our provisions there: potatoes, carrots, onions, and a tub of lard. The howling and crying then turned into barking. We opened the trap door, and there were our dogs, Pearl and Gordon, looking very guilty.

I took the little dogs out and noticed their stomachs were quite distended. Those little fuckers dug their way under our cabin and ate all the lard. There must have been five pounds of lard in that tub. Now, they were too fat to get out. I scolded them and put them outside.

❧30❧

One day, a flock of mallards graced our bay. While viewing these beautiful birds, I started envisioning Peking duck. My mouth was already watering for a tasty meal. I went to Carl's cabin, borrowed a rifle, and shot one of the ducks. The blast scurried the flock, and I got into the skiff to get my prize.

I carried the duck back to our place and gave it to Christy to prepare.

She said, "I don't want to do this. I've been a vegetarian for a month, and this will make me puke."

I said, "Do it," and left to get firewood for the stove.

When I returned, I could see that she was clearly upset while plucking feathers. Next, she cut it open and cleaned out the guts, heart, liver, and intestines. Christy was almost retching. I watched and became more disgusted with myself for killing that beautiful mallard and for making Christy prepare it. Once the duck started to broil, our cabin filled with a horrible smell—this was clearly a foul fowl.

When the duck was cooked, I started eating, and it tasted horrible. It tasted fishy; unlike the grain-fed ducks I had eaten in New York. This whole ordeal disgusted me; I killed this beautiful animal for nothing. I had plenty of healthy, nourishing food to eat. *Do I need meat to survive?* Richard had been a vegetarian for many years and was very healthy. And right then and there, I decided to become a vegetarian.

* * *

One of the books I brought to Galley Bay was *Zen Macrobiotics.* We were already eating lots of rice and vegetables, so transitioning to vegetarianism was easy. The book recommended a ten-day fast, in which you only eat brown rice. The purpose was to cleanse the body and regain balance. The theory was that every food was either yin or yang. According to macrobiotics theory, food varies in its degree of yin or yang. Fruit was yin, and sugar was more yin. Brown rice was slightly yang, and meat was very yang. The bodies of people new to macrobiotics are usually very yin. Since brown rice is yang, eating it for ten days is supposed to get you back in balance.

Also, it was highly recommended that we chew each mouthful fifty times, which we did. Eating this way was quite tiring, but we didn't have much else to do in the dead of winter. There wasn't much to talk about, so we sat together, counting our chews, rolling our eyes, and making funny faces. It wasn't the tedium of chewing so much that drove us crazy; it was eating the same thing day in and day out for breakfast, lunch, and dinner. After about five or six days, we had to get some variation in our diet, or we would go stir crazy. So, we finally stirred some delicious veggies into the brown rice and added soy sauce. That hit the spot.

Winter was the perfect time to read and study. I read spiritual books, started to practice my *zazen* meditation regularly, and remembered to repeat my *kōan* more often. We liked visiting Bob and Richard, who were interested in spirituality. Richard asked if I was interested in finding a guru.

I thought back to Ravi and the Rōshi and said, "I never want to follow a guru. I can learn everything I need from books."

One of my favorite books on Zen, *Zen Flesh, Zen Bones,* compiled by Paul Reps (Knopf Doubleday Publishing, 1960), contained "Ten Ox Herding Pictures." Those pictures and their commentary explained the entire spiritual path from ignorance to enlightenment. The ox herder is us, and the ox represents our true self or soul. The ten pictures represent each stage of the journey. Below is a basic interpretation of each stage based on studying the book:

1. **Searching.** We feel that there is something more to life, that something is missing.

2. **Seeing the Footprints.** We embark upon a wisdom path. We have a glimmer of the proper understanding.

3. **Perceiving.** We gain a taste of our true selves. It's fleeting but real.

4. **Catching.** We begin the work in earnest. We need discipline and regularity.

5. **Taming.** We start realizing success. We gain compassion and wisdom. We start to understand our true nature.

6. **Riding Home.** We gain mastery over the mind.

7. **Transcending the Other.** The mind is now totally under our control. We are free of the cares and worries of the world. Nothing is relevant, and everything is relevant.

8. **Transcending the Self and Other.** There is no self, no true nature, no delusion, no wisdom, no seeking, no finding.

9. **The Source.** Out of emptiness comes form. We are now in our true abode. Everything is as it should be; everything is as it always was.

10. **Returning.** We return to the world in bliss with care and compassion. Now, before us, even dead trees become alive. This is enlightenment.

While studying this book, I couldn't help but wonder about my spiritual progress. At which stage was I? Here, in the dead of winter, I had plenty of time to review my life. I've experienced so much and had loads of amazing adventures, but what have I learned?

I knew I was searching for the meaning of my life, the purpose of my existence. A spark was ignited by my conversations with Florin back in 1963. My first LSD trip gave me a glimpse of my true self and perhaps even a fleeting experience of The Source. But I knew LSD wasn't wasn't the answer. I'd seen too many fucked-up people stuck in the psychedelic world, especially at Millbrook. And even Timothy Leary, with his brilliant mind, who took a thousand trips, was far from being a master, far from being enlightened.

I'd seen the footprints many times. Had I embarked on a path in earnest? Was Zen *my* path? I resolved to become more disciplined in my practices. I decided I needed to sit in *zazen* for longer periods. But I found it a challenge. The posture wasn't the problem; my mind was the problem. Within a few minutes, I would get distracted. Remembering my *kōan* was easier. Remembering my *kōan* would bring what I was doing into focus. If it was snowing, thinking of my *kōan* made me aware of the wonder of each snowflake, but it didn't stop my chattering mind. I couldn't see how my simple *kōan* could provide the breakthrough needed to attain enlightenment.

The snow was different than it was in New York. Mostly, it was a dusting that beautified everything. I wandered the community, always amazed at its splendor. I hadn't tired of this place, even in the dead of winter. Although life wasn't easy, it was fulfilling. I never felt so free, healthy, and strong.

We often visited our neighbors. We looked in on Harold, Delores, and the new baby and always offered to help with anything they needed. We would sit with them, enjoy a cup of hot tea, and share stories. We saw Carl and Joanne and learned what new projects were in the works. But mostly, we hung out with Bob and Richard, since they shared similar spiritual aspirations.

Some nights, we would congregate at the main house to catch up with other friends and listen to Bob play. There weren't many people left in the main house.

Bob told us Gloria had left, but he still had Ingrid and was okay with that.

Shortly before Christmas, Christy decided to go back to Vancouver. I chose to stay behind. When she returned, she came back on a seaplane. It was quite a sight seeing it steer to our dock. Christy came with her good friend Red, who stayed with us for about a week. I was jealous of Red, but Christy assured me that Red was only interested in Mary.

Christmas Day was special. The whole community gathered at the main house. Many of us worked all day preparing a special feast. We ate, sang songs, and were merry in this magic kingdom by the sea. We celebrated with some of Denny's applejack.

Replenishing our firewood was a constant concern. Dead trees were harder to find as the winter dragged on. I had to venture even deeper into the woods, which meant more work for less firewood. But we never ran out of wood and were cozy and warm, except in the early morning.

Finally, spring came, flowers bloomed, the rain came less often, and people were out and about. With the fine weather came more work. The garden needed planting, the fruit trees needed pruning, and many small repairs were awaiting us. But at least we needed less firewood.

It was nice to feel the sun on our faces and the sweet fragrances in the air. One day, I decided to go on a seven-day fast, drinking only water. I don't know what prompted me to make such a radical decision. I read about the benefits that were not only physical but spiritual as well. The first three days were the hardest, but after that, it became easier.

I remember, during the middle of the fast, taking a deep breath and hearing a pop from inside my lungs. It was weird; I felt air entering a new section of my lungs. Could it be that a part of my lung had collapsed? It sure felt that way. I thought about how I had abused my lungs since I started smoking cigarettes at thirteen. I had only stopped smoking a few months earlier when I ran out of tobacco in the middle of winter. In the past, I had also smoked lots of DMT and DET, which didn't help. It now seemed that my lungs could hold more air. I could breathe more deeply. It felt great, and I was happy to be cleansing my body.

I also found that the fast enhanced my awareness almost in proportion to the weakening of my body. I was slow to rise; my steps were labored, but my senses were super keen. Also, my meditations were better than ever. I had deep discussions about spirituality with Richard. He had done many fasts and encouraged me to continue right to the end. He also advised me to break my fast slowly. Fittingly, I broke it first with warm water and lemon juice and later with Gravenstein apple sauce from the Galley Bay orchard.

In late March, Carl became paranoid about another influx of hippies descending on the community. He announced that he had decided to tear down the beautiful old main house. I was stunned by his decision.

"Carl, isn't that a bit extreme?" I asked. "You could always tell people no."

He replied, "I want to make it clear to everyone that there is no room here for people to just pop in. There's no way I want to go through another summer like the last one."

I knew he had a hard time saying no, especially with a big old farmhouse nearly empty. What a shame! A fine old farm that stood for more than forty years was being torn down to keep people away.

After an awkward pause, he said, "You know, I think you and Christy need to leave as well."

I was shocked and said, "What ... are you serious?"

He answered, "Yes. I thought about it very carefully. I'm sorry, but you and Christy must leave."

"But Carl, we built a cabin, and you said that anyone who builds a cabin can stay."

He said, "Yes, but once we tear down the main house, we will need that space. I only want ten people in the commune."

"Carl, you promised us. That space is our home. Why are you going back on your word? Why do you want us to leave?"

It was hard for him to answer, but he finally revealed the truth. "Bernie, I like you a lot, but you guys have changed. You really weren't part of the commune most of the winter. I think you have a different set of values than when you came."

What could I say? He was right. We had changed. I didn't feel a strong connection to the commune like I did before. I felt like progress on my spiritual journey had become a greater priority. I was grateful for this incredible experience, but it seemed like the right time to move on.

With a tear in my eye, I said, "Shit, Carl, I hope you're not making a mistake. We had a good community here after the summer. You're right, our values have changed, but that could be a good thing for an open and growing community."

Carl replied, "I don't want an open and growing community. I want a small, closed community."

"Okay, man. I'm fucking disappointed, but I wish you good luck."

Carl said nothing. He only shook his head and walked away.

Christy was furious. Once Carl was out of sight, she let it all out. She felt that Carl lied to us and that we shouldn't let him step all over us. He promised we could stay if we built a cabin, and now he was going back on his word. We should sue him. We should fight. She thought I was weak for giving in so quickly. She ranted and raved all the way back to the cabin.

I finally convinced her that if we fought and stayed, we would never be able to regain the peaceful life we had before. It would turn negative and ugly, and it wasn't worth it. I told her that I was grateful for our Galley Bay experience, that we had both grown as individuals in the past eleven months, and that our relationship was deeper and stronger than ever. It was time to move on to our next adventure.

It turned out that Carl also asked Bob, Richard, and a few others to leave. He wanted the community to consist of only ten people. Knowing we weren't singled out helped us accept the inevitable.

The folks from the main house staying were Bill, Jen, Ingrid, and Mary. Once the main house was demolished, they would relocate to Bob's and our cabins. The rest of the folks that were staying already had houses. Carl and Joanne were in the A-frame; Harold and Delores had their cabin, as did Mac and Denny.

We knew that Carl would tell us when we were supposed to leave. Now that our days at Galley Bay were ending, the weather became beautiful. The long winter had ended with glorious days of bright sunshine. Christy said that the weather god was mocking us for leaving. We cherished each day. We kept to ourselves, nestled in our little cabin in the woods, until Carl announced he would take us back to Lund the following day.

* * *

Over the years, I have heard news of the Galley Bay community. Carl tore down the old farmhouse right after we left, which made his father furious. The group of ten that Carl envisioned as the core group unraveled soon after we left. The new crop of people in 1969 were mostly druggies. Carl kept the group small, but that didn't make it a functioning commune. What began as a hippie dream turned into a hippie nightmare. The new commune had lots of acid, drama, fights, partner swapping, and bruised egos. One of the 1969 group, Paul Williams, wrote about his experiences in a book called *Apple Bay*.[3]

I was shocked after reading it. I couldn't believe how quickly

---

3 Paul Williams, *Apple Bay: Or Life on the Planet* (Glen Ellen, California: Entwhistle Books, 1999).

that glorious paradise turned into a bad trip. It looked like the commune ended in 1970, and only Carl, Joanne, and her son, plus Harold, Delores, and their two kids, were left. At some point, Carl and Harold started feuding, and Harold's family also left. It's difficult to have a successful commune without strong leadership, fair distribution of duties, and clear values. We had been lucky to be there when it was still paradise.

The property still belongs to the Bloom family, and I heard some luxury summer homes might be there now.

BOOK 2
THE DISCIPLE

There is a candle in your heart, ready to be kindled.
There is a void in your soul, ready to be filled.
You feel it, don't you?

-Rumi

❧1❧

It was a beautiful, crisp day at the end of March 1969 when we left Galley Bay to return to Vancouver. Carl gave the evicted members of the commune a lift to Lund aboard the *Bounty*. Surprisingly, we were all cheerful as we enjoyed the magnificent scenery and each other's company on our final boat ride.

Carl didn't say much. He was quite glum, offering no eye contact. I couldn't help but wonder if he was having second thoughts about his decision to evict us from paradise. He docked the boat at the pier and left us as we gathered our few belongings. We yelled goodbye, but Carl didn't respond. He walked away, presumably to get his truck for a supply run in Powell River. Bob suggested we split up to make hitching easier.

Christy and I hitched a ride, and once we got past Powell River and the massive papermill and its stinking air, the ride became beautiful. The highway runs along the jagged coastline, past lovely little towns. We stopped in Saltery Bay to catch a ferry to Earls Cove and onward past charming little hamlets like Sechelt, Secret Cove, and Halfmoon Bay. At Langdale, we caught a forty-minute ferry to Vancouver. We watched the gorgeous landscape slowly become urban sprawl. Beautiful Vancouver, with its mountains and beaches, looked too congested, too busy, too dirty. That's what eleven months in the bush did to my perspective.

We arrived at Christy's sister Mary's place in the late afternoon. Mary was delighted to see us.

Mary said, "My God, you're back. It's so good to see you. You guys look so healthy. You're both glowing. Come on in."

177

Mary insisted we stay with her; our old room was still available. I told Mary I wanted to help with the rent, and she said we could discuss that later. Joan, Christy's other sister, came over with her husband, Bob. We caught up on the lives of our friends and shared some of our adventures at Galley Bay.

That night, I wondered what to do with my life. At Galley Bay, there was always an array of tasks and activities to choose from. Something always needed to get done. My life had purpose. Now, I had no idea what to do. I didn't even know where to start. I could find a job as an accounting clerk downtown, but I wasn't ready to be cooped up in a cubicle making a meager wage. I certainly didn't want to return to my hippie lifestyle, giving away free newspapers and hoping for a handout. That night, I yearned to return to Galley Bay, but I knew that was impossible. I shared my concerns with Christy and Mary as we talked late into the night.

A few days later, we met up with Brian, our friend from Galley Bay, and brought him up to date. Brian said, "I'm not surprised that Carl is tearing down the farmhouse and kicking people out. The summer was a shitstorm. I couldn't take it, and I'm sure Carl doesn't want a repeat next year." Brian told us about a new vegetarian restaurant that just opened on West 4th called the Golden Lotus. Christy and I decided to go for lunch the next day.

The Golden Lotus was a small establishment with about a dozen tables in the Kitsilano section of Vancouver on the corner of 4th Avenue and Balsam. When we arrived, it was nearly empty, and we took a table by a window. The restaurant was decorated with Indian sheets, and soft Indian music was playing. There was also a counter at the front of the restaurant with four or five stools and a small section by the bay window well stocked with health foods and spiritual books.

It didn't take long for our waitress to provide menus. Once we placed our order, it took quite a while for the food to come. I was getting a bit impatient, but Christy reminded me to relax and enjoy the atmosphere. Our food finally arrived. I ordered a fruit salad, and what I got was a work of art. They had arranged the fruit on the plate like a mandala, and it was absolutely beautiful and delicious. I savored every morsel. Eating the meal felt like meditation.

Everyone working in the restaurant was young, friendly, and relaxed. When we finished our meal, I went to the counter and paid. As I walked out, I noticed a black-and-white photograph displayed in a beautiful wooden frame on the far wall. I walked up to it. It was a portrait of a man with a white beard and turban. I was intrigued by the photograph.

I stood before the photo and looked at this man's incredible eyes and benevolent smile. I stood there transfixed for a time, and suddenly, the man in the picture came alive. I was no longer looking at a picture; I was seeing a being of light with

Sant Kirpal Singh Ji Maharaj
1894-1974

magnificent rays of golden light radiating all around him. His long white beard sparkled, and his eyes were iridescent blue. I had no fear when this happened; it was natural and wonderful. Waves of love and compassion flowed from his eyes and enthralled me. I looked deeply into his eyes, and it was like being dipped in an ocean of pure love. I felt like he knew me, like he had always been with me. The love and joy spread through my body. I was drenched in love like never before. Those magnificent, loving eyes welcomed me like a prodigal son. I felt like I finally found my true home after being lost for eons.

I was transformed, standing in front of this being of light. It was more than a realization or an epiphany; it was a total transformation. I was reborn to a new life and new possibilities. I felt safe and loved. I don't know how long I stood there.

It seemed timeless. I realized that my whole life's journey, with all my experiences, was in preparation for this moment to finally meet my guru. I didn't know his name, but I knew he was alive and was my future.

I had no idea what it meant to follow a guru. I had no notion of what was required. I was always skeptical of organized religion and turned off by the folks who shaved their heads, donned orange robes, and chanted endlessly. I was leery of people who professed to have found the truth and claimed to know what I needed. I never wanted a guru. I never wanted to be anyone's disciple. But that all changed in an instant. It never was a matter of the intellect; it was always a matter of the heart. I walked away from that picture in love with this man, whoever he may be. I was ready to take the next step, whatever that might require. I knew the road to love and wisdom lay at his door and I would follow it.

My hippie persona instantly fell by the wayside like soiled clothing. I realized the next phase of my development had already started. I was sure I had just taken my first steps as a disciple. While I didn't know what that entailed, I was anxious to find out. I was brimming with profound happiness.

This was a seminal moment in my life.

This was the picture I saw on that blessed day.

One of the Golden Lotus workers came over, and I said, "I have never seen anyone so beautiful in all my life. Is he your guru? Is he alive?"

Mischa, who happened to manage the restaurant, said, "Yes, he is my guru, and yes, he is alive. His name is Sant Kirpal Singh Ji Maharaj, and he has an ashram in Delhi, India."

He also said that most people referred to him as Kirpal, and most people working at the restaurant were either initiated and already on his path or interested in learning about his teachings.

I told Mischa about my experience looking at his picture and that I wanted to learn about initiation. He wasn't surprised.

He said, "Many people get interested in the path after seeing a picture of Kirpal or reading one of his books. Why don't you come to our meeting tonight to find out more about these teachings?"

Mischa was a man of medium height in his mid-twenties, with an unruly mop of dark hair, a trimmed beard, and friendly brown eyes. He impressed me as an introspective person who spoke softly and carefully.

I was so excited. I told Christy about my experience and how I couldn't wait to attend the gathering that night. She didn't feel what I felt, but was open to what could happen.

That evening, we went to the gathering above the restaurant. Christy and I went upstairs to an apartment with a large living room and four small bedrooms where some Golden Lotus workers slept. About a dozen people were seated, mostly on floor cushions. Everyone was young and looked like spiritual hippies.

Mischa read from one of Kirpal's books for about thirty minutes and then read the meditation instructions. This meditation was very different from the zazen I had practiced for the past year. The center of attention in zazen is the hara, located at the abdomen, also known as the third chakra. Kirpal's meditation focused on the third eye, located slightly above and between the eyes. In yogic studies, this is the sixth chakra. This type of meditation aims to focus attention at that center with the eyes closed. One can experience inner light if done correctly and with focused attention. The third eye is considered the gateway to the higher spiritual regions.

Mischa told us that the biggest obstacle to making progress in meditation was the mind, with its endless desires and ceaseless activity. With the help of a mantra—a repetitive word or phrase—we can control the mind and intensify our focus on the third eye. At the time of initiation, Kirpal would give us our mantra, but for now, we could repeat a word or short phrase with spiritual significance, like a name for God. I chose *Adonai Eloheinu* from the Jewish scriptures, which translates as "The Lord is our God." The entire prayer is *Shema Yisrael Adonai Eloheinu Adonai Echad*, which translates to: Hear, O Israel, the

Lord is our God, the Lord is one.

We sat in meditation for about thirty minutes. I had dif-ficulty focusing on the third eye since I was accustomed to meditating at the *hara*. It was a struggle, but I was determined to embrace this method and leave *zazen* behind. After the meditation, we had a chance to speak with Mischa about the requirements for initiation.

He said, "I recommend you take your time before applying for initiation. This is a big decision that shouldn't be taken lightly. There is so much to this path. Take your time. Be sure before you proceed."

"I know this is my path," I said. "I know Kirpal is my guru. It became perfectly clear to me while I was looking at the picture."

"That's wonderful," Mischa said. "Some do come knowing."

He then explained that we needed to be on a strict vege-tarian diet for at least three months prior to initiation. We also need to understand the basic principles of the path. He then gave us an application form.

Once accepted, he explained, "One of Kirpal's regional representatives will provide all the details of the path and give you the mantra. It's the Master Power that initiates, not the representative. We get the same initiation results as we would from going to India to get initiated by the guru."

He also gave us two booklets written by Kirpal: *Man! Know Thyself* and *Seven Paths to Perfection*.

I had already been a vegetarian at Galley Bay for more than three months, but not to the standards of this path since I had still eaten eggs. That meant I would need to wait three more months before getting initiated. For some reason, I felt an urgency to get initiated. I wanted this very badly. I wanted Kirpal as my guru and could hardly wait for it to happen.

After reading the two pamphlets, I was even more con-vinced this was the right path for me. Spirituality is a science, Kirpal said, not mere theoretical discussion, and if done cor-rectly, the results are guaranteed, just like an experiment done in a laboratory. This path doesn't require blind faith or promises of spiritual experience after death. This path didn't need me to renounce the world or my religion or take on a new name or mode of dress. On this path, one could be a productive member of society and still succeed in spiritual development.

The teachings are very straightforward. Kirpal states there is a God, who is the controlling power in the universe, and our soul is a part of God. The pity is that our soul is under the control of the mind, and the mind is under the control of our senses. We are engrossed in the world and have no idea how to free our souls. Through meditation on the inner light and sound, we can rise above the body and contact the astral or radiant form of the guru, who becomes our inner guide. He then takes us through the various planes of creation, ultimately uniting our souls with God.

I felt like I had some of these experiences already. My first LSD trip gave me an inkling of the interconnectedness of all things. I felt like I was seeing with my soul and seeing the soul of all things during that incredible trip. I also experienced Florin's astral form, which spoke to me. Therefore, connecting with the guru's astral form during meditation wasn't an alien concept.

My only concern was that this path placed a strong emphasis on ethical living, on living a moral life. I had been living a very free life and enjoying sensual pleasures. Kirpal spoke about the importance of developing the qualities of truthfulness, non-violence, chastity, and a loving humility, not only in our actions but in our thoughts and words. The emphasis on chastity worried me. Horny was practically my middle name.

The next day, I spoke to Mischa about my concerns. He explained that to control our minds, we would need to gain mastery over all our desires, which takes years.

Mischa said, "All the Master is asking is for you to work on overcoming your desires. He's not asking you to take a vow of chastity. In fact, many of the disciples are married and have children. The only real requirements are to be a strict vegetarian, to meditate daily, and to work on leading an ethical life."

"Okay, that seals the deal for me," I said.

Many of the disciples referred to Kirpal as Master, and this struck me as a more intimate way of referring to him. Generally, non-initiates refer to him as Kirpal.

Christy and I discussed it that night. She asked, "Shouldn't we wait and learn more before jumping into initiation? Let's read more of his books and get a better understanding of these teachings."

I told her, "I had such a powerful experience looking at Kirpal's picture. I know there is still a lot to learn, but I'm sure he's my guru, and I really don't want to wait any longer before I apply for initiation. Also, I can apply on my own, and you can wait and see if you want to later."

In the end, she decided to give it a try. For the application, we needed to write a letter about ourselves and why we should be accepted. I visualized Kirpal and felt like I was writing to him. I wrote a bit about my history and how I had been searching for my life's purpose for many years. Now, I knew that spiritual enlightenment was my goal. I wrote about my extraordinary experience seeing his picture and how I was sure he was my guru.

I'm not sure what Christy wrote, but the next day, we handed Mischa our initiation applications to send to Kirpal. We also asked him if there was any work we could do at the Lotus. We were both hired on the spot. I started working as a dishwasher, and Christy worked as a server. We stayed with Mary, who insisted we didn't need to pay rent.

❧ 2 ❧

We found our new commune at the Golden Lotus. The scenery wasn't as spectacular as Galley Bay, but the people were great, and the food was much better. Most everyone working there had left the hippie druggy scene behind. There was harmony, and a peaceful vibe filled the atmosphere. The staff wanted to embrace spirituality as taught by Kirpal and worked on being open, loving, and authentic.

The Golden Lotus wasn't making much money, but we got free meals and a meager wage. I loved working at the restaurant, and as time passed, I learned new skills and took on more responsibility. I learned how to turn a fifty-pound bag of whole wheat flour into gluten, the main ingredient of our yummy veggie steaks. Christy loved taking care of the tiny health food section. She watched what sold best and made sure to reorder before we ran out. This little section of the restaurant soon became very profitable under her watchful eyes.

Mischa was laid back, and there was hardly any pressure on the staff. People took on responsibilities, and everything got done eventually. Some customers complained about the slow service, but most accepted it because the food was great, and the Lotus radiated peace and harmony.

To my delight, my old friend David worked at the Lotus. He and I had gone to see the Zen Rōshi a year earlier. I didn't notice him at first. He was quiet and unassuming, almost floating through the restaurant, creating a peaceful mood with the right music. David didn't like being in the limelight. He was responsible for the book section, which had a good selection of spiritual books, in addition to Kirpal's writings. David was already initiated and knowledgeable about Kirpal's teaching as well as many other wisdom paths. He was the person that could explain the finer differences between the various spiritual disciplines.

David told us about how he found Kirpal. He was walking on Fourth Avenue and saw a vision in the sky of a man with a turban and white beard sitting cross-legged. It disappeared when he stood in front of the Golden Lotus. He decided to enter the restaurant and was drawn to Kirpal's photo, the same one that changed my life. His vision was of the same man in the picture, and he knew he had found his guru.

Victor was another fixture at the Golden Lotus. He was a classically trained pianist turned ascetic with short red hair, a thick red beard, and a strong frame of medium height. He looked like a giant leprechaun; he was only missing green clothes. Victor could build anything. He even built himself a coffin where he slept at night. The casket was made of fine, highly polished wood, with a satin lining and storage drawers beneath for his clothes. It was a beautiful coffin, the purpose of which was to always remind him of life's impermanence. Victor had a wry sense of humor, and even though he sometimes poked fun at the whole guru experience, he was very devoted. He was our handyman extraordinaire and available to do whatever needed doing: washing dishes, waiting tables, or building more shelves in the health food section. He was a hard worker and always available to lend a hand.

About a dozen people worked at the Lotus, including Christy and me. Linda, a tiny ball of energy, was our head server. She made the customers feel at home and often chatted with them while they patiently waited for their meals.

LeeAnn, a tall and serious young woman, ran the kitchen. She did her best to keep things moving and wasn't hard on anyone. Amazing culinary delights came out of that kitchen, the meals artfully displayed. She was dedicated and loved feeding people.

Mrs. Nagra, an elderly Indian lady, came in once a week to

cook an enormous pot of her fabulous chana, an Indian dish of curried chickpeas. She and her husband were devoted disciples of Kirpal. Chana was one of the most popular dishes on our menu. I loved putting hot chana atop a salad. As far as I was concerned, it was the perfect salad dressing. Other people also started enjoying this dish, and someone suggested putting it on the menu and asked me to name it. I came up with "Mountain Man Special" in honor of Galley Bay.

There was a lot of turnover at the restaurant. Most people stayed for a month or two and moved on. What was fascinating was that when someone left, their replacement magically appeared, and we were never short of staff.

The other thing that made this a great community was our customers. It reminded me of when I first moved to the East Village and felt strongly connected to everyone. There was a buzz in the air. People were interested in spirituality. Most had concluded that enlightenment doesn't come from a pill but from following spiritual teachings.

Vancouver was a hub for seekers of spirituality; there was the Zen Centre, yoga groups, a Hare Krishna center, and several groups following various gurus. And now, the Golden Lotus seemed like a spiritual vortex that drew seekers to Kirpal. When Kirpal finally visited Vancouver in 1972, thousands would come to his talks and hundreds would be initiated.

❧ 3 ❧

As a newly minted spiritual seeker, I entered a new phase in my life with the objectives of love, honesty, and commitment. It had been about a year and a half since Christy and I began our relationship. I knew I was in love and wanted to spend the rest of my life with her. I felt it was the right time to ask Christy to marry me. But how should I propose? This was a big step. I wanted it to be meaningful and for her to accept. I had no money for an engagement ring. What should I say? When should I ask?

I was so excited about proposing that I just couldn't keep it in. It felt so right on every level. So, as we walked back to Mary's, I stopped, faced Christy, and said, "Christy, I have loved you from the day we met, and I love you even more now. I know you are my soulmate, and I want to marry you."

I don't think Christy was expecting this, but after a short pause, she replied, "I love you too, and I want us to be married."

I was so happy that I felt like jumping up and down. I then said, "Sorry. I forgot to get down on one knee."

She laughed and said, "You still can." Which I did, right there on 4th Avenue, repeating my proposal. People walked around us and smiled, knowing full well what was going on.

I was so happy she felt the same and was ready for marriage. We arrived at Mary's and blurted out the great news the moment she opened the door. She was thrilled. We laughed and hugged, brimming with excitement. Then Mary suggested we go to their mom's house to let her know. This made me nervous since I thought her mom didn't like me.

Christy's mom, Elizabeth, was a very proper English woman, and I was sure she disapproved of my relationship with her daughter. To her mind, we were living in sin, and I was a useless bum who might never amount to anything.

We told her the good news, and she could see we were both thrilled. She was also glad we were back in Vancouver and working.

Elizabeth then looked at me and said, "For the last two years, I didn't know what to call you, but now you will be my son-in-law. I can see that you make Christy happy, and I hope you can provide for her properly."

I said, "I love Christy very much, and I want you to know that I will do my very best to be a good husband and a good provider."

She asked if we wanted a church wedding. Christy said, "But, Mum, Bernie is Jewish." So, it was decided we would have a wedding officiated by a justice of the peace. Mum wasn't totally pleased. Finally, her daughter would no longer live in sin, but she was worried about her future.

We got our marriage license and were wed about a week later with Mum and Christy's two sisters, Mary and Joan, as witnesses. We dressed up as best we could. I found a suit in a thrift shop, and Christy wore a cream-colored suit with a lovely little hat. There was no white wedding dress, no tux, and, unfortunately, no photos of the joyous occasion. Now, we were husband and wife. I couldn't have been happier.

I let my parents know in a letter. I'm sure my parents surmised that Christy was not of the Jewish faith, but they never complained about it. I suspect they were happy I was working and finally married. Maybe I would turn out to be a *mensch* after all. Kirpal taught us that living an honest and ethical life was essential to the spiritual path. And being married and having children was not a roadblock to spirituality. In fact, this path emphasized living a regular life, earning an honest living, and serving others.

After our wedding, we returned to the Lotus. Everyone was happy for us. David mixed up a batch of smoothies, and all had a drink to our health and happiness. Several people were in relationships at the Lotus, but we were the first to take the plunge.

❧4❧

Kirpal had written around a dozen books on various aspects of the spiritual path. He wrote brilliantly and was highly educated—not only in Eastern religious thought but also in Western teachings. He presented his teachings with quotes from all the great wisdom paths—Eastern and Western. He explained that God is within us, and we could directly experience God through meditation with a competent spiritual teacher. He stated that a perfect master could provide an actual inner experience at initiation and ultimately guide us through all the planes of creation. I didn't doubt this was possible. After all, my experience while looking at Kirpal's picture was extraordinary.

I learned that Kirpal's path was known as the Path of the Masters. This path goes back more than five hundred years to the great spiritual Master Kabir and the first Sikh guru, Nanak. The mantle of guruship flows from master to disciple. I learned there has always been a living master on Earth who is best equipped to teach spirituality. This path was primarily in India until recently, and Kirpal was the first of his line of gurus to come to the West. He had two previous world tours in 1955 and 1963. He also established hundreds of centers throughout the world. The world was now ready for his teaching of love and light. The world was now ready to learn the great benefits of meditation. The West was hungry for the secrets of the East.

It was common practice among Kirpal's disciples to refer to him as Master. After all, he comes from a long line of spiritual Masters.

Kirpal's teachings were straightforward. The goal was the same as with most spiritual disciplines. To gain enlightenment, you must master your meditation practice, which requires mastering your mind. But Kirpal added two additional requirements: ethical living and service to others.

Kirpal was able to encapsulate the entire spiritual path with six words:

BE GOOD. DO GOOD. BE ONE.

BE GOOD is to lead an ethical life of non-violence, truthfulness, purity, and humility.

DO GOOD is to serve others selflessly.

BE ONE is to master our meditation practices.

Most of us who worked at the Lotus were serious in our devotion to the path and tried our best to be good disciples. When things were slow, we took meditation breaks upstairs in the quiet meditation room. Kirpal recommended we devote at least ten percent of each day to meditation, about two and a half hours. In the beginning, it was challenging to sit for long periods. So, many of us would meditate four or five times daily for thirty minutes at a time.

It was wonderful having this community with good values and shared principles. We would encourage each other to follow the precepts of the path. We also had access to the books that Kirpal wrote, plus Mischa and David, who were great at explaining the finer points. Our understanding of the path grew, and each day, we longed for that letter accepting us for initiation.

One day, we received a very sweet letter from Kirpal accepting us as initiates and telling us we could receive instructions from a local representative after we completed our three months as vegetarians. Arran was the regional representative for Canada and wasn't due back from India for months. I didn't want to wait; I couldn't bear to wait. So, getting initiated sooner required going back to the United States, where there were several authorized representatives. My three months as a vegetarian would be complete in a couple of weeks, so I needed to make arrangements.

SIPPING SUNLIGHT: A MEMOIR

Shortly after Kirpal's letter, I got a letter from my parents with my new draft card reclassifying me from 1-A to 1-Y. This meant I wasn't a draft dodger anymore. Only 1-As were getting called up. Was this an example of some special grace or a coincidence? At this point in my discipleship, I didn't ascribe any event to divine grace. Later, I experienced that grace many times and learned to trust what life offered me.

I could now travel using my own name. I was no longer a fugitive. This was incredible. But why was my status changed after almost two years in Canada? I became suspicious. I didn't trust the US government.

"I bet this is a trick," I told Christy. "Once I cross the border, they will say, 'Sorry, that form was sent in error, or maybe it was a typo.' Maybe 1-Y wasn't even a legitimate classification." There was no easy way to verify. Checking the internet was decades away.

Christy devised a solution: "Why not use someone else's ID?" She asked a friend from school to lend me his Canadian ID so I could sneak across the border.

It made sense to go to New York since Kirpal's representative and my folks were there. Perhaps it was time for Christy to meet my parents. I called my parents about coming for a visit. They were delighted and offered to pay for our airfare. I arranged for a flight from Seattle to New York.

Christy also found someone to drive us across the US border and to Seattle, a three-hour drive. We made it across the border without a hitch. After seeing three sets of Canadian IDs, the border guard didn't look at mine. He waved us on, and I felt good about not having to lie.

❧ 5 ❧

We got to Seattle with plenty of time to catch our flight. After an uneventful six hours, we landed at JFK Airport, where my parents met us. Seeing them was wonderful. When I had left two years earlier, I doubted I would ever return.

It felt strange being back. My hippie journey had started with such great expectations. When I had first left New York, I was lost and depressed. Now, I was joyous and elated. In a few days, I would be an initiate of the great spiritual Master, Sant Kirpal Singh.

Our house was the same as when I left, with one major exception. My bedroom was now a dining room. Clearly, my parents didn't expect me to move back. But a nice guest room on the second floor served us just fine.

My parents liked Christy, but it was hard for them to accept our vegetarian diet. We were adamant about not eating anything that contained meat, fish, or eggs. My mother had made her famous chicken soup for my homecoming, and I knew she was disappointed that I wouldn't even taste it. But she accepted our decision and served us only vegetarian food.

My twin sisters, Nancy and Marion, had just finished their junior year of high school and were both beautiful young ladies. They always looked up to their big brother and were happy I was married to such a beautiful woman. Christy was only a few years older than them, and they liked each other immediately. They wanted to know all about our lives in Vancouver and asked Christy lots of questions. They especially enjoyed hearing about Galley Bay.

While awaiting our initiation, we attended various spiritual meetings called *Satsangs* that focused on Kirpal's teachings. The leader of the New York City *Satsang* was an older gentleman named Ben, who represented the entire Northeast and was responsible for conducting initiations.

Ben was a big, strong man with a sweet disposition who looked more like a longshoreman than the spiritual representative of an Indian guru. But when he spoke about the path in his strong Philly accent, his great love for Kirpal was clear.

Ben lived in Philadelphia, and we traveled to his house on June 29, 1969, to receive our initiation. This was exactly three months from the date I saw Kirpal's picture. Ben lived in a small one-family house in a working-class neighborhood. His home was comfortable, with many beautiful photos of Kirpal displayed. Ben had been initiated during Kirpal's first world tour in 1955.

Initiation signifies acceptance into the Master's school. Kirpal taught that a competent teacher is required to truly understand any topic. This is especially true for spiritual seekers. Furthermore, a spiritual teacher can guide you only to the level they attained. Only a *Sant Satguru*, or perfect master, is competent enough to take someone to the highest region, the pure spiritual plane.

During the initiation ceremony, we received the teaching in detail and the mantra of the five names of God. The names come from Sanskrit and are the names of God in each of the five regions or planes of creation: the physical, astral, causal,[4] super-causal,[5] and pure spiritual.[6] These regions are the universes that the soul must traverse on its journey toward union

---

4 The planes of creation are defined by the Sant Mat Masters. The causal plane is the plane of the "Universal Mind," through which the Supreme Lord has created the cosmic universes. However, the Supreme Lord is not that Universal Mind.

5 The super-causal plane is the "Realm of Ecstasy," where the word is enrapturing. Everything created here is marvelously strange and beyond description.

6 The pure spiritual plane is unchanging and eternal. It is all joy and bliss, all wisdom and love, and the abode of God. Here, in ineffable wonder, dwell the perfected spiritual beings and the supreme saints of all time.

with God. The five names themselves have no power; it's the master's attention or charge that makes them effective.

One of the signs of a perfect master is that he can give each seeker a spiritual experience at their initiation. We sat for about a half-hour during the inner light portion, and I had a wonderful experience of bright lights. It was my best meditation so far.

We also received a second type of meditation on the inner sound. All major religions have references to the sacred sound, also known as the Word, Shabd, Naam, the Voice of Silence, and many other names.

During this sitting, we focused on listening to an inner sound coming from the right, and I heard the enchanting sound of bells. During this sitting, we did not repeat our mantra. This was a new meditation practice for me, and it was blissful.

We were asked to split the meditation time equally between the two practices. During the day, when we weren't meditating, we were encouraged to repeat our mantra. This practice is called *simran* and provides sweet remembrance of the Master and offers protection.

The final part of our initiation was devoted to the self-introspective diary forms that help us weed out our imperfections and gain control of our thoughts, words, and deeds. Kirpal said an ethical life is the foundation for building spiritual progress.

Ben said, "I encourage you to fill out your diary forms every day. This will record your progress. You can send the forms to Kirpal every three months. If you have questions, you can write to him. He will respond, and you will treasure those letters. I have many letters from him. Each of us has a direct relationship with our Master. This is a great blessing."

The Master also urged us to practice selfless service—service without expecting recognition or a reward. This is the highest form of service because it's free of ego and karma. Any chance to help someone in need or a worthy cause is an opportunity to serve.

The entire mission was built on selfless service. No one working for the mission got paid—not even Kirpal, who lived on his pension. There's never a charge for attending *Satsang*, getting initiated, or visiting the ashram in India. The Master said that spirituality and meditation are gifts from God and should always be free, like air, sunshine, and water. Our path was funded through donations made only by initiates who could afford it. Donations were never required.

Now that I was initiated, I understood how perfect this path was. It wasn't about ostentatious rites and rituals. This path was a superhighway leading to enlightenment. And the beauty of it was that it doesn't require you to renounce the world or be sequestered in a monastery away from family. On this path, you could be a good member of society, have a family, rise in your chosen profession, be a good friend and neighbor, and still attain perfection.

On this path, you do not need to leave your religion or faith. All the various religions developed rites and rituals for major events in life, like births, marriages, and deaths. The path doesn't have outer ceremonies and rituals since it focuses on our inner beings. So, as an initiate, you can celebrate the major events of your faith with your family and friends.

We took the train back from Philadelphia and repeated our mantra as much as possible to remember it. I was so happy. Initiation was an amazing experience, and I was now a disciple of a great spiritual master. I was officially on "the Path."

The various *Satsangs* in the area were attended by people of all ages, races, and means. It wasn't like the Vancouver one, which was predominantly young people. Many of these people had been initiated for years. Kirpal visited Europe, North America, and South America during his 1955 and 1963 world tours and had over a hundred thousand disciples and more than a hundred centers around the world.

We loved going to these *Satsangs*, where the atmosphere was charged with divine radiation. At *Satsang*, I felt a deep peace settle over me and found my concentration was more focused and my meditations better than at home. Also, many group leaders who ran the *Satsangs* were dynamic and powerful. Their love for the Master poured out of them, and their knowledge of the path was tremendous. I was especially fond of Ruth, who ran the Long Island *Satsang*. She was a powerhouse of love and devotion. Her love was infectious; you couldn't help but smile around her.

After a few days, we decided to return to Vancouver. I learned about an agency that delivers cars to people who don't want to deal with a long drive. This agency had cars that needed drivers from New York to Seattle. The agency didn't pay us. We were responsible for gas and tolls, but it offered the least expensive way to get to Seattle without hitchhiking.

We had a directory of *Satsang* group leaders in the centers across the United States. I charted our course and found we traveled through many cities with centers. Many group leaders were happy to welcome us into their homes, feed us, and even give us a bed for the night. Each person we visited was kind and gracious and shared their experiences. Kirpal had a tremendous impact on their lives, and our love and appreciation for Kirpal grew.

One story was from an older woman living near Chicago. She said she was reading the scriptures one night and came across a passage about a comforter sent by the Father and prayed to God to please send her one.[7] That night, she had a vivid dream and saw a man dressed all in white with a turban and glowing light around him. She felt deep comfort from seeing him.

The next day, a friend called her and told her that a guru from India was going to speak in her area that very day. She went, parked her car, and, as she was walking to the lecture hall, a car pulled up. A man dressed all in white with a turban stepped out of the vehicle. It was the same man she had seen in her dream. She told him, "I saw you in my dream last night." And

---

7 See John 15:26, "But I will send you the Comforter from the Father. When he comes, he will give evidence about me. He is the Spirit of truth who comes from the Father," *Free Bible Version*.

he replied, "I know." That's how she met Master Kirpal. Shortly after that meeting, she was initiated.

We finally got back to Vancouver after being away for a few weeks.

❧ 6 ❧

The Golden Lotus was just as we had left it. It still had that unique charm we felt on our first visit. It felt like home, and I was excited about returning to productive work after my hiatus in New York. Mischa was still in charge, although some of the staff had left and been replaced with new folks. We quickly slipped into our old routine.

Arran, the restaurant owner, returned from India after a month with Ratana, his beautiful Indian bride. Arran was handsome, wore a white turban, and was articulate, super-knowledgeable, and clearly a devoted and advanced follower. He regaled us with stories of the Master and life in India. His beautiful remembrances and exceptional tales made us all long to be at the feet of the gracious Master Kirpal.

After Arran arrived, Mischa left to finish his education. He went to Emerson College in England to become a Waldorf teacher.

As the owner and manager, Arran wanted to run the Lotus in an organized and disciplined manner. However, the Lotus had been run loosely for the past eight months, and people were accustomed to being asked to do things. If something wasn't done one day, it could wait until the next. Almost everyone working at the Lotus had never met Arran until his return. Arran was the boss, would tell people what to do, and expected it to be taken care of promptly. This caused friction and resentment. After all, most of these people were paid a low wage and didn't want to be ordered about, yet they loved working at the Lotus.

After several months of bickering and complaining, we all met and decided that something needed to be done. We devised a plan to buy out Arran and run the Golden Lotus as a cooperative. If Arran disagreed, there was a chance many people would leave, and the restaurant would have to close. Arran understood the situation and accepted our offer. But I suspected this rebellion had hurt him. He was a proud man, but never really showed his disappointment.

There was great rejoicing at the Lotus once the business was ours. We hung a sign saying we were under new management. People loved that we were a cooperative rather than some capitalist venture. On our first day, we did a brisk business. Everyone was so happy.

The next morning, when I arrived at work, I found the cash register empty. I assumed someone emptied it and perhaps deposited the money in our bank. I asked everyone who worked at the Lotus, and nobody admitted to taking the money out of the till after closing. Clearly, someone stole our money. Could it be one of our own people? I couldn't imagine one of our staff, interested in spirituality, being a thief. Was it possible? Maybe the Lotus wasn't locked securely that night, I rationalized.

I was distraught and concerned we wouldn't be able to pay Arran at the end of the month as promised. At that point, I took responsibility for the money, revenue, and expenses and set up a proper bookkeeping system. I put everything I had learned at college about accounting into practice. This was a perfect opportunity to try my hand at running a business. Not only did I handle the accounting, but I became the manager and found I was pretty good at it. My management style was somewhat like Mischa's, caring and respectful of the employees. I made sure everyone's duties were clearly defined and everyone had easy access to me. I was also very aware of costs and found ways to save. In a short time, the Lotus was running smoothly despite the turnover. The theft turned out to be a blessing.

When I took over the management, the restaurant had

bought most of its food at supermarkets and paid retail. I found wholesale outlets, which saved us a lot of money. Soon, we purchased an old International Harvester panel truck, making it much easier to buy in bulk.

The restaurant became more popular, and our lunch and dinner service soon were busy. With the increase in sales and decrease in costs, we increased wages. People kept track of their hours, and we paid them at the end of each week. Even though I was the manager, my wages were the same as everyone else's.

Soon, Christy and I found an apartment and even started a savings account. Our expenses were meager. We only spent money on rent and a few clothes we bought at the thrift shop. We worked at the Lotus ten to twelve hours per day, practically every day.

Even with increased wages, turnover was still a problem. People stayed for a few months and moved on, and we had to continually train new people. One day, we had a meeting. Most of the members weren't even there when we had started running the restaurant. We asked who would commit to the Lotus for a year. Anyone willing to do so could be an owner, but only David, Christy, and I were willing. So, we were now the owners, and surprisingly, the rest of the folks didn't care. Nothing really changed; it was business as usual. What mattered was that we ran the business honestly and fairly, and people were treated with respect.

This was a wonderful opportunity. It was the foundation of my management style, which served me well for years. People enjoyed working at the Golden Lotus. Our business grew, and our staff of fifteen became more stable as we paid our employees a better wage. And so, the year went by.

*   *   *

Due to our crazy work schedule, the only way that Christy's sister Mary could see us was by coming to the Lotus. One day, when Christy wasn't around, Mary told me about her work as a special education teacher. She was part of a new program to help school children with dyslexia. When she described the symptoms, I almost fell off my chair.

"Oh my God, that is exactly what happens to me. In school, I was terrified that the teacher would ask me to read aloud. While reading, letters got jumbled, or sometimes I interjected a word that wasn't in the sentence. I also had problems with spelling and comprehension. I thought I just wasn't smart and never applied myself at school." I stated.

Mary explained that dyslexia has nothing to do with intelligence and that some brilliant people suffer from this disorder. She even gave me an IQ test without the distraction of a time limit. I was very surprised to learn my score was in the bright range. It was a tremendous relief hearing this. The shame and insecurity I felt for most of my life started to fade away.

One Sunday, Christy and I were driving our old truck in Surrey, a rural section about 45 minutes from Vancouver. We were on a two-lane road going about forty miles per hour. Suddenly, I saw a car coming from the opposite direction, veering into our lane. It was happening so fast that I didn't have time to react. I felt certain we would be in a head-on collision. Then, just as suddenly, the car wasn't there. I looked in my side mirror and saw the car behind us turning out of our lane and back into its lane. It seemed we had dematerialized for a second and then rematerialized once the car was behind us. But more likely, the car turned onto the shoulder on our side of the road and went around us; still no easy feat with two vehicles zooming toward each other. I pulled over to the side of the road. We were so badly shaken that we needed time to regain our center. Christy looked terrified, and my heart was racing like crazy.

"What just happened?" she asked.

"Did you think that the car was going to hit us?" I asked.

"I felt certain it would. It's a miracle we weren't hurt or killed," she said.

We silently thanked Kirpal. We sat there for a while doing our *simran* until our shaking stopped.

I experienced some near miracles in my life, like missing a car crash in Calgary by a few seconds and surviving an LSD death trip on the roof in the East Village. But this was truly a terrifying event. We were sure the Master's grace had saved us.

* * *

In Vancouver, many of the folks who became interested in Kirpal's teachings were hippies. For some, following this spiritual path was a short-lived experiment, and many returned to their old ways. I could understand the challenges this path presented to hippies. The idea of total freedom was alluring. The ethical principles of this path seemed like Sunday school or the values our parents possessed, which were precisely what we had rebelled against. But many embraced this path and understood the drug culture was a dangerous emotional roller coaster.

The ones that stayed tried living up to the virtues prescribed by Kirpal, but it was a challenge. There was lots of drama, hurt feelings, and wounded pride. Christy and I were often asked for advice or to try to shed some light on difficulties. We were young and inexperienced, but we tried our best to help. Quoting Kirpal helped resolve disputes and heal hurt feelings. Reminding people about the practice of *simran*—the repeating of our mantra—was another way to prevent conflicts from occurring.

The important thing was to listen with love and compassion. Often, all that was required to help someone was friendly, non-judgmental talk.

Anyone sincerely interested in progressing on this path longed to go to India to be with Kirpal, and various people from our community went. When they returned, we could see a significant change. They were more focused, more loving, humbler, and more patient. They seemed to have grown tremendously. They shared their experiences with the community, and some even had 8 mm videos of Kirpal. Those special evening talks were filled with love, devotion, and appreciation for the Master. They fueled our longing to go to India.

After managing the Lotus for thirteen months, I felt a strong urge to see the Master in India, provided Kirpal approved it. My partner David had just returned from India, and I told him how I longed to go. David was sympathetic but felt he couldn't manage the restaurant by himself. I came up with the idea of selling my shares in the restaurant to someone who could be David's new partner. This would get us some much-needed funds and provide David with a dedicated person to count on. But before we could do anything, we needed the Master's permission to come.

❧ 7 ❧

With longing in my heart and a prayer on my lips, I sent Kirpal a telegram in September 1970, asking for permission to come to India. The days waiting for his response were tense. If he said no, what would we do? But he most graciously gave us permission. Next, we needed to find a suitable partner compatible with David, capable of doing the work, and able to pay for our shares. We interviewed several people and found two people willing to buy our shares. I didn't get much money, but every little bit helped.

But now Christy was having second thoughts about going. The Master was planning his next world tour, and the rumor was that he would come to America in eight or nine months. Christy argued, "Why travel to India when he would be here soon?" We could travel with him around Canada and the United States and continue saving money by working at the Lotus.

I told Christy, "I can't wait that long. I yearn to see his face. I long to be in his holy presence. I have to go now." I added, "If you don't want to go, you can run the Lotus with David, and I'll go alone."

She finally agreed to go to India.

The next challenge was getting a passport and a visa. I went to the US Consulate in Vancouver, and with faith in the Master, I prayed that my draft classification would hold up, which it did. I was able to get a passport in a few days.

I still don't know why my draft status was changed from 1-A to 1-Y. If it hadn't, I wouldn't have been able to travel to India. (Eventually, in 1977, President Jimmy Carter pardoned the hundreds of thousands of Vietnam War draft dodgers.)

Next, I researched cheap flights and bought tickets from Seattle to London on a questionable charter and from London to Delhi on Kuwait Airways, which we would learn was inexpensive for a good reason.

I hoped to get a visa to India for six months. Canadians were automatically granted visas for up to six months because both countries were Commonwealth nations. Americans could get a visa for three months. Since I was married to a Canadian, however, there was a chance we both could get six-month visas, but that required a special application. Unfortunately, our visa application wasn't approved before our flight left, so we would have to reapply in London.

In London, we stayed with Sant and his wonderful family while waiting for our visa. Sant was Kirpal's representative for Great Britain and a devoted follower. He also was most gracious and kind, the perfect host.

Sant was very disciplined and ensured we didn't forget our meditation practices amid the frenzy of getting our visas and tickets to India. His home, Kirpal Bavan (Home of Kirpal), radiated peace and love. We felt the Master's presence as soon as we entered. Shortly after arriving and exchanging pleasantries, we sat for an extended meditation, a great blessing with many good inner experiences.

The following day, we went to the Indian Consulate to apply for our visa. We filled out the application and were advised we'd have an interview with a consulate officer soon and should call back each day to see when it was scheduled.

The visa drama dragged on, and every day brought more delays. My nerves were getting frayed, and Christy and I started to argue. We had a few shouting matches followed by tearful reconciliations. I realized when it was my fault since I tend to barrel along and get impatient. Sant felt the tension and asked if we knew anyone else in London (we didn't). He sat us down and spoke about how it was to be with the Master at the ashram, and his talk brought tears to my eyes and hope to my heart. If only we could get our visas. It had already been four or five days of trying and getting nowhere.

We finally got an appointment to meet with the consular officer at India House. We sat in a small cubicle before a short, bespectacled man in a beige suit with a Nehru collar. He carefully reviewed our application.

He looked up and said, "I'm sorry, but under these circumstances, we can't grant your visa application. You will need to go back to Canada and apply there." He didn't say why.

We were distraught. Our dreams were shattered, and I was close to tears. We had already been in London for nearly a week, and our situation seemed hopeless. We also had a non-refundable ticket to Delhi and very little cash. We remained seated in that little cubicle. I closed my eyes and prayed.

The consular officer didn't know what to do. He could see our distress and that we weren't voluntarily leaving. He finally said, "Let me take this to the high commissioner for further consideration."

We sat in the tiny cubicle for what seemed an eternity, praying and meditating.

When he finally returned, he said, "I am very surprised. The High Commissioner has approved your visa. I don't understand why. This is most unusual."

I couldn't believe my ears. This huge burden that hung around our necks for a week had suddenly disappeared. My emotions instantly went from despair to elation. I remembered what Kirpal wrote in one of his books: "When all human efforts fail, prayer succeeds." I felt this was a miracle, and I silently thanked the Master. I then thanked the consular officer, and we left as quickly as possible.

I later learned we could have avoided this entire visa nightmare if I had applied for the three-month visa and Christy for the six-month visa in Vancouver. Once in India, I could have had my visa extended with a simple application form. But my distrustful and stubborn nature insisted it needed to be done my way. If

I had taken the time to get all the facts and had more trust, we could have already been in Kirpal's sweet presence for a week.

Next, I went to Kuwait Airlines to finalize our trip to Delhi. There was a flight the next day. Perfect, I thought; things are finally looking up. But, as the agent reviewed the flight status, he said he was sorry, the flight was fully booked, and we could secure a flight next week. More disappointment. Once again, when we were almost home free, another obstacle was thrown in our path. Dejected, I prayed to Kirpal again. Then, while still at the counter, the agent said in a surprised tone, "Wait a second, two seats just opened. How unusual."

This day was truly incredible. I was elated but exhausted. Now for my happiest chore, sending a telegram to the ashram with our arrival date.

The next morning, we thanked Sant for his most gracious hospitality and took a taxi to the airport. From London, we flew to Abu Dhabi for our connecting flight to Delhi. Unfortunately, we missed the flight because a thick fog descended at the airport, and it took a lot of extra time before we finally landed.

Christy said, "Another obstacle. When will things go smoothly?"

I said, "I don't know, but we are getting closer, and we'll have six full months once we get there."

We disembarked on the runway and had to walk through thick yellowish fog to get to the terminal. It was surreal. We could barely see one foot in front of us. Once we were in the terminal, the police separated the men from the women. There was even a policeman guarding the room designated for women.

Once Christy was situated with the other women, I felt the urge to meditate. I wandered into a foggy field and was suddenly greeted by the most intoxicating aroma of roses. I sat there enraptured and had a wonderful meditation shrouded in fog. It was like being on another planet.

Unfortunately, Christy was stuck with all the women in overcrowded conditions, with crying babies and one smelly bathroom. She couldn't sleep and was miserable when we finally reunited.

The next flight to Delhi wasn't for a week, and the only arrangement we could make was a flight to Karachi with an overnight stay, followed by a flight to Delhi. Kuwait Airlines was trying to book us into some second-rate hotel, but thanks to a German businessman's insistence, we got to stay at the InterContinental, a five-star hotel. That luxurious hotel almost made up for the miserable night Christy had cloistered with the women in Abu Dhabi. We had room service, ate on a balcony overlooking the city, and slept in a fine bed.

The next morning, we took a taxi to the airport and landed in Delhi two hours later. From there, we got another taxi and finally arrived at Sawan Ashram on Sunday, November 8, 1970, after more than a week of travel.

The ashram was in a densely populated area of Delhi called Shakti Nagar. The entrance had a wrought-iron gate, and once we entered, we felt like we had arrived at an oasis of peace and tranquility. We were welcomed by a woman named Khuku, dressed all in white, with a white scarf on her head. She asked someone to take care of our bags and chatted as she walked us to our room.

I asked Khuku when we could see the Master.

She replied, "The Master is up north at Manev Kendra and is not due back for four days."

I was very disappointed. After this long and arduous journey, we were told to wait longer. At every step, it seemed we were met with obstacles, and now that we had finally arrived, we encountered another. I asked Khuku if someone could arrange a taxi to take us north to see the Master.

Khuku said, "I know you are anxious to see him, but I suggest you stay in the ashram until he returns. Look at this as a golden opportunity to prepare to meet the Master. The ashram is charged with his presence, and you can spend lots of time in meditation. This will still your mind, cleanse your soul, and make you more receptive when you are in his presence."

I thought about what she said and told Khuku this made perfect sense. I realized we would be here for six glorious months.

We needed to cleanse the grime and dust from our minds and prepare ourselves to meet our guru. I now was looking forward to spending the maximum amount of time in meditation.

Khuku showed us around the ashram, which was a few acres in size. It had a large open space with a raised dais in the center where the weekly *Satsangs* were held. To the right was a row of small rooms with a medical dispensary, laundry, and offices. To the left was the Master's small two-story house with a large, covered veranda and balcony. Right in the middle of the structure was a big, beautiful tree. Kirpal wouldn't allow the tree to be cut when the house was built, so his residence was built around the tree, and it now provided shade when sitting on the second-story balcony. Just behind the ashram walls was a canal and, beyond that, railroad tracks.

Past the *Satsang* area was the small two-story western quarter with a kitchen, dining room, meditation hall, and about a dozen small bedrooms on the second level. There were a few bathrooms scattered among the rooms, but no showers. Each bathroom had a Western-style toilet and a small water heater with a bucket and cup for bathing. The accommodations were spartan. Only about a dozen Westerners were there, and we got acquainted quickly. Most were young, and they all beamed when they spoke of Kirpal.

Now that I was here, how would I prepare to meet the Master? I felt elation and fear. I knew the guru was perfect and seeing him in person would fulfill my deepest desire. But what about him seeing me? He would see my innumerable faults and how woefully inadequate I was. I was good at hiding these faults, pretending to be more loving and spiritual than I truly was, but there was no place to hide from him.

We were excited because the Master was scheduled to return the next day.

❧ 8 ❧

"The Masters see more in a brick than you do in a mirror.
They were bathing in the Divine Bounty before
the world existed.
They lived for lifetimes before bodies were born.
They saw the harvest while the wheat was still seed.
They understood the meaning when it was unformed.
They found the pearl before there was an ocean."

- Rumi

Sant Kirpal Singh Ji Maharaj

Finally, Kirpal arrived. The old dust-covered Ambassador auto stopped in front of his residence. We Westerners lined up as he walked to his house, patiently awaiting his *darshan*, or loving glance. We stood with our palms folded together next to our hearts, the traditional Indian greeting.

Seeing him for the first time was like a bolt of lightning hitting me square on. Here was my heart's desire, the pinnacle of my longing, much more magnificent than I could have imagined. I anxiously awaited my first glance. My heart raced as he approached. But alas, he walked right past.

A few moments later, we were asked to join him on the veranda, where he was seated in his white and red wicker chair. About fifteen or twenty of us sat on the floor near him. Now he looked lovingly at me; now I felt seen and welcomed. Looking into his eyes when he looked directly at you was the personification of bliss; there are no words to describe it. He looked at me many times, and my heart filled with joy and deep gratitude. After the meeting, I floated into my room and sat in meditation for a long time. His beautiful image filled me with love.

The next morning, we once again met with him on the veranda. He asked me about my trip and the *Satsang* in Vancouver. I couldn't keep eye contact while answering him. If I had, I don't think I could have spoken. I would have been lost in his loving gaze. I remember fumbling out something about how much his presence is needed in the West. I felt so ashamed of the inadequacy of my response. He was loving and accepting, regardless of my deficiencies.

That evening, I tried to summarize in my diary what Kirpal had said earlier:

"We are triply blessed: we have the body, the mind, and the spirit. We must develop all three, or else we are not complete people. We must maintain the body with good food and exercise. The mind must be kept constantly engaged. At work, sweet remembrance should be kept. We should be fully aware of our thoughts, words, and deeds. We must evict wicked thoughts from our minds. For the spirit, the bread of life is needed. For the time being, forget the past and the future. Devote yourself to a minimum of five to six hours of meditation. What you can accomplish here in weeks would take years in your homes. Make the best use of your time. My love and best wishes are with you all."

So, there it was, all I needed to know. I must keep my mind constantly engaged in sweet remembrance of God and not on my myriad hopes and desires. I shouldn't dwell on the past or the future but live in the present moment. And I needed to put serious time into meditation. This was a tall order, but I knew that I would try my best.

We had no work assigned to us. Food was prepared. We were there to grow spiritually. We were there to perfect our meditations and rise above bodily consciousness. We were there to gain self-knowledge and, ultimately, to realize God.

Most mornings and evenings, we met with the Master. He would sit in his old white-and-red wicker chair, and we would sit on the ground around him. He would talk to us about an aspect of the spiritual path, answer our endless questions, and lovingly glance at each of us.

Master's *darshan* (glance of love) was the highlight of my day. Usually, I woke at 4:00 or 5:00 a.m. and meditated for a couple of hours. Next, I had breakfast and meditated before the Master arrived. This usually lasted about an hour. After the *darshan*, around 10:00 a.m., I would sit in meditation for another couple of hours. Then, it was lunchtime. At this point in the day, I'd already meditated for about five hours. After lunch, there was free time to read, exercise, or shop, and I would sit again for an hour before dinner. Then, we all meditated for an hour or two while waiting for Kirpal's evening *darshan*. That would give me seven or eight hours per day. After *darshan*, I would return to my room and work on my diaries for an hour or more. Such was my typical day.

Friday, November 13 of that year, was the 501st anniversary of Guru Nanak's birth. Guru Nanak was the first Sikh guru, and Master Kirpal's line of succession went back to him. That day, the ashram was festively arranged with garlands of flowers and strings of colored lights. This was to be a special *Satsang* commemorating Guru Nanak and celebrating the marriage of a very devoted couple.

The Master was very jolly, and I couldn't keep my eyes off him. This was my third day in his presence, and now I'd had the opportunity to observe him for many hours on end. I tried to be close to him but kept a respectful distance, sometimes hidden behind a post. I had never seen anyone so beautiful, so natural, so magnanimous. A golden glow enveloped him, and his eyes shone like beacons of love. His walk was effortless as he seemed to glide across the threshold. His focus was solely on whomever he spoke to, and the faces of those he spoke with glowed with love and appreciation. Several dignitaries tried to place a garland of flowers around his neck, but he would always bless the garland and place it around that person's neck. The Master never accepted anything for himself.

His magnificent white beard was especially lovely in the late afternoon light, and I couldn't help but think, "Oh, what I wouldn't give for one hair of that magnificent beard." I knew this was a silly thought and quickly moved on to another wonder of his persona that delighted my heart.

After the celebration, I stayed behind to be alone with my thoughts. I was intoxicated. I didn't want to lose this incredible euphoria, this all-encompassing love flowing through the core of my being. It was getting dark, and I was alone. I walked over to the dais, covered with many colorful flower petals. I stood before it and remembered the Master sitting there earlier in the day and majestically showering everyone with divine love. I pictured him and scooped up a handful of flower petals: bright red and pink roses and yellow and orange marigolds. When I looked at the treasure nestled in my palm, I saw among the colorful petals a long white hair, which I felt certain was from the Master's beard. Tears of gratitude filled my eyes as I remembered my wish.

I found a newspaper and carefully wrapped my treasure. I was beaming with joy and love. I thought, what an amazing gift, what a gracious and kind Master you are. I knew I needed to rush to my room and meditate immediately. I was sure this gift would be rocket fuel to propel me into the beyond.

One of the most common phases in our group is "Master's grace." Whenever something fortuitous or wished for occurred, we attributed it to the Master's grace. Of course, I don't believe that Kirpal orchestrates every little thing personally, but there is no doubt that it happened by coincidence, accident, or divine intervention. But I believe attributing these events to grace is a very positive response. Gratitude is the antidote to entitlement and egotism. Gratitude opens the heart to God, Master, universal consciousness, a higher power, or whatever else you call it.

Gratitude and a fervent desire for God, for a union with the divine, are the keys to attaining oneness, the mortar for enlightenment. And the highest form of gratitude is when we attain the state where everything is grace, when every breath is "sweet is thy will." In that state, we eliminate disappointment, anger, jealousy, hate, and all the other thieves of our soul. In that state, the universe is perfect, and we are one with it.

❧ 9 ❧

Kirpal was building a major center called Manav Kendra, which translates to Man-Making Center. Manav Kendra was situated near Dehra Dun in the foothills of the Himalayas, about six hours north of Delhi. This center was designed to offer free services to the community with a hospital for the sick and needy, a home for the elderly poor who had no one to care for them, a library for the study of all religions, a school for the children of disadvantaged families, a shared kitchen, and a beautiful open stage for *Satsang*. It also would have a large holy body of water called a *mansarovar*, where people could sit and meditate.

Master was spending a lot of time building this center and was often away from the ashram. One day, toward the end of November, he announced we were all moving close to Manav Kendra so he could spend more time with us. All fifteen or twenty of us piled into a few taxis and relocated to Rajpur, near Manav Kendra. We departed dusty, noisy, congested Delhi. We drove north into the lush mountain country, past a beautiful tiger preserve, and into the foothills of the Himalayas to Kirpal's private residence, his sweet, secluded bungalow at 207 Rajpur Road. Some of us stayed at his home, while others stayed at a house down the road.

Heaven just got better. Now, in this quiet setting, with its cool nights and sweet air, we could sit undisturbed for long periods of meditation. Each morning, the Master would meet us in the mango grove and give us heart-to-heart talks. He addressed every aspect of spirituality and answered every question. Then, he'd leave for Manav Kendra to supervise the work. When he returned in the evening, he would give another talk. Sometimes, he arrived very late but always gave us his *darshan* before eating.

Every morning, seven days a week, Kirpal would go to Manav Kendra. A large hole was being dug for the *mansarovar*. There were more than a hundred volunteers, mostly Indian, carrying dirt from the ditch with buckets. Master would sit in his wicker chair and watch as the work proceeded. The volunteers walked past Kirpal many times, got his blessing, and were grateful for this opportunity.

One of the very wealthy initiates told the Master he would be happy to provide a bulldozer to dig the *mansarovar* in a few days. Kirpal said no, since that would deprive hundreds of volunteers of the opportunity to serve. Selfless service was an important tenet of the teaching, which meant helping others with love and no desire for reward or recognition. The entire mission was built on selfless service.

One day, we were invited to Manav Kendra, about a half-hour away from Rajpur. We arrived in time for lunch. Everyone was seated on the ground atop burlap and lined up in rows facing each other. We took our seats with the workers. *Sevadars* or volunteers handed out plates made of banyan leaves and

Master Kirpal at Manav Kendra in 1971; I'm second from the left, munching away. Christy is at the end, shading her eyes.

gave everyone *chapatis* (flat bread). Then more *sevadars* came with buckets and ladles and scooped out meals, usually a bean dish, chickpeas, or lentils. We used the *chapatis* as spoons, and soon, everyone was fed and happy. The leaf plates were given to the cows, who happily ate them, creating no waste. Some Westerners volunteered to work on the *mansarovar*, but the Master encouraged us to focus on our meditation.

*   *   *

On the site was a magnificent and massive old tree that was five different types of trees fused together. The banyan part was predominant, but one could tell that other tree types were present by seeing the different kinds of leaves in the canopy. The Master explained that Guru Gobind Singh, the tenth guru of the Sikh tradition, sat under this tree about three hundred years earlier. After working for a few hours in the hot sun, I sat under the shade of this incredible tree and had a beautiful meditation.

One initiate told me she had one of her best meditations under that tree while wrapped in her meditation shawl. When she exited meditation, she noticed that her red shawl was nearly white and completely covered with bird droppings, but not one drop was on her body. She laughed and silently thanked the Master for his all-pervading protection, which includes protection from being dumped on from up high.

*   *   *

One evening, the Master returned late from Manav Kendra. We were all in the meditation hall awaiting him. He came in, sat down, and didn't say a word. He lovingly and deeply looked at each one of us. No one spoke, and no questions were asked. His loving glance was all we wanted, and he dispensed divine love freely. After a short time, I heard the inner sound,

the holy word reverberating loudly. It was melodic, enchanting, and divine. It was the perfect accompaniment to his gaze
of love.

The Master then said, "Hear the ringing radiance." It was
clear that every person in that room was enraptured by the Holy
Word. My focus was on the beloved. Along with the sacred sound
current, I became aware of the Master's breathing, each breath
in ... and out. I focused on his compassionate eyes, and then suddenly, the light around Kirpal exploded into columns of bright
golden light. All that existed at that moment was the Holy Word
and divine radiance. There was no sense of self, no observer, no
object of observation, no me, no you, no separation. There was
nothing to analyze, nothing to explain. It was all pure love in
that magic moment. And it was all His grace.

I don't know how long this *darshan* lasted, but it filled
me with love and understanding beyond words. It gave me a
glimpse of what was required to progress on this path back to
God. The Masters say the path is narrow, like a razor's edge. Two
cannot walk on it. We need to become one to traverse this path.
We need to conquer the ego. We need to master our minds. We
need laser-focused attention and grace to merge into the divine
light. What we all experienced during this *darshan* was love, true
love—love that flowed into our souls and filled us with divine
bliss. And all this came from gazing into the Master's eyes. The
Master says that two-thirds of the teachings come through the
eyes. Where else could you experience such deep love? No book
could give you this. The scriptures may talk about love, but can
they give you a firsthand experience of love? That is why a living master is needed. He is not the body. He is a channel for
God's love, and his mission is to teach us how to realize our true
selves and, ultimately, God.

Once we progress on this path, we experience the inner
Master and can gaze into his eyes even when thousands of miles
away. We can have his *darshan* even when his earthly work is
done. Once we are initiated, the beloved Master is within us. To

see him, we just need to fervently want him and put serious time into our meditations.

The next morning, Kirpal continued his discourse on love. The most important of all gifts is love itself. If we had everything in life on a material level but lacked love, we would be the poorest of the poor. Without love, life is meaningless.

Excerpts from the Master's talk:

"Put one ounce of love in all your affairs, even the mundane affairs; you'll have your happiness. All these strifes are going on for want of love. And the main thing is love knows giving. Love knows service. Love knows sacrifice. If we learn that subject, everything comes in.

"So, love is a great blessing. We have developed love for our own self. Now, help one another. If you live for others, only then, not otherwise, can you truly be called a man—in the terminology of the saints. Learn that lesson; we are already blessed. Everything will be beautified. Love beautifies everything. Love knows service and sacrifice."

(*Note:* During this era, the word "man" was used to connote any human being.)

Master also said, "Love cannot be bought. It cannot be taught; it can only be caught from one that is overflowing with the love of God."

After the morning talks, we would meditate for a few more hours. This was our golden time. We were freshly inspired, floating on the memory of his beloved *darshan,* and ready for a plunge into the beyond.

Each day after lunch, we each had four or five hours to read, exercise, or shop. During these times, I would sometimes shop. If I needed food, I would walk up Rajpur Road; if I needed other items, I could take the bus or scooter into Dehra Dun.

One glorious day, a few devotees sat in the mango grove after lunch, discussing the amazing *darshan* we'd just had with the Master.

One of the brothers said, "We are so fortunate. Here we are, just a few initiates all alone with the Master, and we get his *darshan* twice a day. What did we do to deserve such blessings?"

Another said, "It must be some special good karma."

We were all feeling especially lucky, incredibly fortunate, and a bit proud to have been chosen to be here in the lap of the divine.

A few hours later, at that very evening's *darshan*, the Master started his talk with a question, "If two men came to see a doctor, and one had a minor ailment, and the other had a major wound, which one would the doctor see first?"

We all said, "The one with the major wound, of course."

The Master replied, "Yes, the doctor would see the emergency case first." Then he looked around the room and said, "Some of you are my emergency cases."

We then all realized that we were indeed there because of special grace, not because of merit on our part. And this put everything in the proper perspective; nobody earned the right to be with the Master. It was all his grace. *Kirpal* means compassion in Hindi, and he was truly the lord of compassion. We weren't surprised that he was responding to a conversation we had earlier that day. Time and again, the Master showed that he knew what we were thinking and doing.

We could only do our best and pray for guidance and forgiveness. That's why Kirpal placed so much emphasis on filling out our diaries. The diaries recorded our failings in thought, word, and deed related to the five virtues (truth, compassion, contentment, humility, and love). If we fail ten times by being untruthful, we should endeavor to fail less the next day. We needed to analyze what caused us to fail, resolve not to repeat the mistake, and pray for forgiveness. Once we mark it down, it is forgiven, and we should forget it. We need not dwell on those failures again. We need to love God and live in the present moment. We also record the time we spent in meditation and our inner experiences in our diaries to help gauge our progress.

The Master would often ask us how our meditations were going. If we were not making progress, he would say, "See to your diaries." Sometimes, he asked us to bring our diaries to him to examine.

❧10❧

It was getting very late, and the Master had not yet arrived from Manav Kendra. We were told he wasn't coming for many hours and to get some sleep. I returned to my room and did my diaries but couldn't fall asleep. Perhaps having warm milk would help, so I went to the kitchen. Just as I got there, the Master arrived and went into his bedroom. One of the attendees told me I could see him if I wanted to. My heart leaped at the opportunity.

I entered his small, dimly lit room containing a single bed. He was seated on the bed, reading correspondence. This was the first time I was alone with the Master, and I was elated and scared at the same time. Master Kirpal gave me a loving glance and asked me how I was progressing with my meditations. I told him what I saw inside and that sometimes I had difficulty concentrating. He asked to see my diaries the following day. Then he said that Shri Raghuvacharya had died and his cremation was the next day; he asked if I wanted to go. I said I would love to. With that, I left the room elated.

The next morning, most of the initiates took taxis to Rishikesh to attend the cremation. Raghuvacharya was a renowned yogi and spiritual head of Darshana Mahavidyala Ashram on the banks of the Ganges River; he was 115 years old when he died.

Rishikesh is a holy city with many ashrams. In 1947, Kirpal spent six months in seclusion here after the death of his Master, Hazur Baba Sawan Singh. There, he met Raghuvacharya, who, who saw Kirpal's greatness and took initiation from him.

The view from the ashram was quite beautiful. We had a

clear view of the Ganges, which flowed wide and strong in this section as it cut through the foothills of the Himalayas. Dozens upon dozens of ashrams were on both sides of the river. Yogis and renunciates filled the streets; many gathered to pay their their final respects to the great yoga master. Some were singing a beautiful *bhajan*—a spiritual.

I entered the room where the corpse of this great yogi was seated in a chair, erect and completely at peace. It was hard to believe that life was no longer in this body. He looked so beautiful, so still and peaceful. His features were sharp, distinct, and refined. His face was hardly wrinkled and quite beautiful to look at. His frame was small and slight. I couldn't believe he had lived for 115 years. He was adorned with garlands of flowers. It looked like he was in deep meditation; the only thing that betrayed this was his eyelids didn't flicker when a fly walked on them.

I looked at his body for a long time. This was the first time I'd seen a dead man. It was hard to believe I would die someday and that every living thing must undergo the same physical-to-spiritual transformation. I hoped I would be at peace like Shri Raghuvacharya when I died..

The Master arrived and said,

"Raghuvacharya is gone. What you see here is just an empty shell. The body is a useless machine once that power leaves it.

"In 1948, after the death of my Master, I came here to renounce the world. I came for six months, living on the other side of the river. This is when I met Raghuvacharya. He was developed in Ashtanga Yoga and could rise above body consciousness at will. I saw this in him, and he saw this in me as well, and he greeted me very warmly. He had much love for me. He would clap his hands and hug me whenever I came here.

"So, the important thing is to rise above body consciousness. You will not die until it's your karmic time. The silver cord will not be broken. You must do this while alive."

We left the room so the body could be washed and prepared for cremation. After a while, some yogis carried him out and seated him on a special wooden platform decorated with flowers. Four yogis picked up the platform, put it on their shoulders, and marched it through the town and toward the Ganges. A procession followed the body. A band played, conches blown, gongs and drums beaten. As the procession passed, many people threw flowers, food, and money.

This was a happy procession, not somber like many in the West. The band's music was very similar to that played at weddings. All these folks believed in the soul's immortality and celebrated the great yogi's return to the spirit. Finally, we got to the river, where a wooden pyre was ready for the body. The body was placed atop the pyre, and more wood was put over it, making him barely visible. Then, the pyre was lit, and the flames consumed everything. I didn't feel fear or sadness. I watched the flames rise to the heavens and the dark smoke billowing upward. I realized that death is the natural end to life and nothing to fear.

All the yogis and swamis had great respect for the Master. They all greeted him reverently. Many knew him because he was President of the World Fellowship of Religions (WFR), which was created in 1957 and held its initial conference that year in Delhi. Sant Kirpal Singh was elected president and served for fourteen years. Four WFR conferences were held in India, and several regional ones in Iran, France, and Germany followed. These conferences brought many prominent religious leaders together. Hindus, Christians, Muslims, Jains, Buddhists, Jews, and others sat together as brothers and sisters. In 1962, he received the Order of St. John of Jerusalem, Knights of Malta, for his ecumenical work. He was the first non-Christian to be honored with this appointment.

In 1974, the Master shifted his focus from the WFR toward the Unity of Man conferences. He stated, "We are children of God, born the same way, with the same privileges from God. Soul being the same essence as that of God, we are all brothers and sisters in God, and the same One Power whom we worship is called by different names."

Kirpal's successors continued these conferences under the name Human Unity; they occur annually at different locations worldwide around Kirpal's birthday.

❧11❧

The Master permitted us to record his talks, which were so illuminating and inspiring. I had a tape recorder, as did a few other disciples. However, there were only a limited number of cassette tapes, so we took turns taping the talks.

We also started transcribing the tapes since everyone wanted copies. Without access to photocopy machines, the talks would circulate, and people would write them out by hand. Eighty-one of these talks were eventually published in two volumes, *Heart to Heart Talks*.[8]

Transcribing these talks was a wonderful service that I was involved with, and it helped me delve more deeply into the teachings. We spent most of our afternoons sitting in the mango grove, reliving the most recent talk.

Darshan summary:

The cause of every failure comes from thinking we are the body. All these things—lust, anger, jealousy, pride, and attachment—are all because we are identified with the body. We think of ourselves as separate beings.

When we rise above bodily consciousness, our whole angle of vision will change. We will see that we are not the body, and a higher power is controlling us in the body. That same power is controlling the whole creation; IT is in us, and we are in IT, and IT is in everyone. It is everything, and we see that we are all one.

---

8 Kirpal Singh, Heart to Heart Talks (India: Ruhani Satsang, 1975).

So, we are conscious entities. It is we who give life to the mind, the body, and the outgoing faculties. The pity is we ourselves are slaves in our own house. After our long association with the mind, we become identified with it and forget that we are the soul. With the grace of the Satguru, we regain our Godhead and see who we really are.

The guru's method gives us the right understanding and inner experiences. He weans us from the world, makes us masters of our own house, and brings us to the lap of God himself. He never leaves us; his love goes beyond the portals of death. Can any earthly love compare with this love?

As the months went by, my meditations improved, and the failures in my self-introspection diaries lessened. I still had failures but wasn't beating myself up like before. My diaries were full of prayers and poems to the Master.

On a few occasions during *darshan*, Kirpal would mention a disciple by name. Once, in the middle of a talk, I couldn't help but think, "How sweet it would be if the Master called my name." A few minutes later, he smiled at me and said, "Yes, Bernie." I happily answered, "I have no questions, Master." This experience filled my heart with such joy and happiness. I felt acknowledged, and my deep love for him expanded further.

One day, Mounti Baba arrived at the ashram. He was a man of about 65 with a shaved head and a toothless smile, wearing an orange robe. He was a *sadhu* (monk) renunciate who took a vow of silence 25 years earlier and communicated by writing on a handheld chalkboard. He came to the Master about fifteen years earlier when his practice with Ashtanga yoga awakened his *kundalini* (energy center), and his whole body felt like it was on fire day and night. Nobody would help him until he came to Kirpal. During initiation, the Master put his hand on Mounti's head and took him inside. The fire stopped immediately, never to return, and he had a great inner experience.

As a renunciate, Mounti was used to living off alms. As an initiate, he had to live off his own honest work. He told Kirpal that the only thing he knew was palmistry, and the Master told him it was okay to have that as his livelihood.

Mounti was a jovial character with his animated facial expressions and chalkboard writings. Many of us had our palms read. He did the basic reading for free, but if we wanted an in-depth reading, he charged a few rupees and would write everything in a small notebook. Christy and I both had readings done, but unfortunately, I lost the book and don't remember what my future predictions were.

During *darshan,* when the Master asked Mounti a question, he would answer with his raspy voice. He never spoke to anyone but Kirpal.

With interest bubbling up about palmistry, Master spoke about astrology and palmistry in the next *darshan.* He said they are both valid sciences when properly done. However, they were only effective in the astral plane, and, as initiates, we were not bound by these laws. He said a world-famous palmist examined his hand when he was a young man and said his lifeline ended and he would die in 1947. That year, he and some initiates were looking for land for his ashram. They were near a large dam, and as he walked on the dam's wall, his foot slipped, and he went headlong into the waters below. He said that while falling, he experienced falling into a great light. The initiates were frantic. How could someone survive a fall from a large dam? But the Master emerged unscathed and said that Hazur (Kirpal's Master) still had work for him to do.

❧12❧

My March 23, 1971, diary entry:

What is my goal in life? I have this one life. What am I
going to do with it? I want to know myself, and I want to
know God if it is His will. What greater thing can there
be than this? I know that the Master is more than a man,
and I have faith in Him.

In his presence, my mind is still. He captures my
attention, and I experience deep calm and peace. In
his presence, I hear the ringing radiance, the divine
Shabd, the Holy Word. His loving glances fill my heart
with such joy that I forget everything. I'm drunk from
even one sweet glance, and all worldly woes are forgotten. Looking at him, I see radiant golden rays dancing around him, and his eyes are like bright blue suns
filled with all wisdom and compassion.

He knows my heart and sometimes answers my
prayers. He shows me beautiful visions during my meditations. He comes with me when I remember him. He
protects me from those who would harm me outside
and inside. He's my best friend, the best Master I could
ever hope for. And I can't help but sometimes swell
with love and bubble over with happiness. Those are
my cherished moments. In joy or woe, he is with me.
But the most precious moments are when I remember him with a grateful heart. When I ask for nothing.

When what's best for my spiritual advancement has already been given.

But when I forget him, I get lost in the world of desire, fantasy, and delusion. Unfortunately, forgetfulness is way too easy, and I can get lost in that gray mist for far too long. But the pain in my heart brings me back; the sweet remembrance of his eyes restores me. I pray I will never forget him, not even for a moment.

It was April 1971, and we'd been at the ashram for more than five glorious months, mostly in beautiful, tranquil Rajpur. In the last month, the weather got appreciably hotter. Even here in the foothills of the Himalayas, the afternoons sometimes became sweltering. One afternoon, Christy and I were pouring water over our heads behind the bungalow, trying to cool off.

Christy said, "Bernie, I can't take this heat. I think it's time to go home. It's only April, and it's bound to get even hotter."

I asked, "Do you mean we should plan our return over the next week or two?"

She replied, "No, let's make the arrangements now. We've been here for five wonderful months. I'm ready to go home."

That afternoon, we told Khuku of our plans, and she jokingly said, "So soon, didn't you just get here?"

Khuku helped us arrange a flight later that week. The plans were made so quickly and efficiently that we faced the prospect of leaving for Delhi in two days. At this point, I had trepidation. I hoped our leaving could be dragged out a few more days; I wanted a long goodbye. After all, our visa was good for a few more weeks. I meditated with a heavy heart later that afternoon. It was hard to believe we would say goodbye to Kirpal that night.

That night (Sunday), Christy and I had a private meeting with the Master in his bedroom.

He said to us, "You're going? You may leave, but your memory will never leave."

He brought out a beautiful meditation blanket and placed it on my head. I touched his holy feet in gratitude (an Indian custom). He also had a meditation shawl for Christy. He gave us lots of *prashad*—food he had blessed—to bring back to Vancouver. He was incredibly cheerful and loving. I don't remember everything he said, but I remember telling him how grateful I was. He filled me with so much love that I wasn't feeling the pangs of separation. I was bubbling over with bliss.

Monday, we had his *darshan* as he was leaving for Manav Kendra and when he returned. That evening was to be the last *Satsang* with our dear Master.

Tuesday was a difficult day. We were all packed up, and this was the morning we would leave Rajpur. To our delight, Kirpal called us in for one more meeting. He spoke sweetly and gave each of us a red rose. His kind, luminous eyes filled us with love. We were in bliss, and the pain of leaving vanished.

A few hours later, our taxi arrived. With heavy hearts, we climbed in and said our silent goodbyes to Rajpur, our blessed paradise for the last four months. On our way to Delhi, we were passing Manav Kendra when I asked the taxi driver to stop. We went to the Master's room and saw he was very busy with correspondence and had people waiting for him. But he took the time to see us off again. He walked us to the taxi and showered us with love that sustained us through the long drive to Delhi.

We arrived in Delhi late afternoon. The ashram is a sacred sanctuary in the middle of tumultuous Delhi, but we missed the quiet of Rajpur. We were now hundreds of miles away from our guru and flying home the following day.

I said to Christy, "I wonder when we will see him again. Hopefully, the world tour he is planning will happen soon. I already miss him."

Then, to our amazement and delight, we heard the Master was returning to Delhi that evening. What a wonderful surprise. We eagerly awaited his return. Around midnight, we were blessed with his *darshan* once more.

Wednesday morning, we got to see him yet again. He gave us a message for the dear ones back home in Vancouver: "You convey my love to each and every one of them. Tell them to go on with their meditations with special emphasis on the self-introspection diaries. That's my only message."

On Wednesday afternoon, we had our final *darshan* before departing. He took my hands in his. His touch was soft; I could barely feel it. I looked at his sweet face, the face of love that filled my heart with joy, and said, "I hope I will see you soon." He said, "When we come, this time, God willing, Bimla will come too." Then, a few more words of encouragement and a final glimpse of those eyes.

So, it turned out I got my wish for a long goodbye. Once we decided to leave, we got his *darshan* eight times and met with him privately on five occasions. I could not have hoped for more. Each time we thought it was our last meeting, another opportunity arose. To our delight, the Master kept giving and giving. He often said, "As long as you live, give, give, give."

❧13❧

On April 8, 1971, we flew from Delhi to London. It was hard to imagine I wouldn't have the Master's *darshan* that night or see him physically for a long time. Now, I had to live by his teachings in the real world with its myriad temptations. The bliss the Master filled me with was still overflowing, and I felt at peace.

We arrived at Sant's home and were greeted warmly. We shared stories of the Master, talking late into the night. Sant regaled us with his experiences at the ashram. He recalled the wonderful expressions Kirpal uses and all the little things that lovers of the Master delight in. The more we shared, the more intoxicated we became. Each story is like a glass of fine wine from a bottomless decanter. With each story, we became more intoxicated by His love.

We were different people compared to the frazzled couple we were five months ago. We enjoyed a few wonderful days with Sant and his family as we awaited funds from my father for our plane fare back to New York.

One afternoon, while awaiting funds, I felt my first pangs of separation from the Master. It was agonizing. I felt depressed and longed to be back in his company. With tears in my eyes, I jumped into meditation, which helped considerably. I resolved to keep his sweet remembrance more often during the day and not get sucked into the world. Sant's home was like an ashram; being there helped immensely.

* * *

We arrived in New York and saw my parents for the first time in almost two years. My mother was concerned the moment she saw me.

She said, "Bernie, you look terrible; you're all skin and bones! You need to eat some meat."

I told her, "Mom, I'm fine, and I would rather eat a stone than meat."

But my mother was right about how I looked. Since she saw me last, I must have lost more than 20 pounds and now weighed 138. I was having digestive problems and eating like a sumo wrestler. The Master always said to eat a morsel less, but I tend to eat a few helpings more. I finally relented, went to the doctor, and discovered I had intestinal parasites, which explained a lot. After a short while, I started to feel better and gained weight.

I didn't want to mooch off my parents continually, so we tried to get jobs to earn enough money to return to Vancouver. Christy immediately got a job at a perfume factory, but there was no job for me. So, most of my days were spent meditating or wandering around town.

On certain evenings, we attended one of three local *Satsangs*. We were greeted like celebrities since we just returned from being with Kirpal. We worked hard at not letting this go to our heads and made sure not to engage in too much socializing. I learned too well how quickly lots of chit-chat dissipated our little store of spiritual bliss. Each *Satsang* coordinator asks us to talk about our time in India. We shared many stories and felt His loving presence when we remembered Him.

Christy and I went to the East Village to visit some of my other friends. It was great seeing Perry. He was warm and wonderful, like he always was, and we had a great reunion. He offered us some weed, which we politely refused. He wasn't surprised that we had been in an ashram in India for five months. We caught up on what was happening with some old friends. I was sad to learn my dear friend Andy was then hooked on heroin. He no longer lived across the street, and

Perry didn't know where he lived. Steve Tintweiss was touring Europe with the great jazz artist Albert Ayler. Howie was a sound engineer touring with a rock and roll band, and Gene Bloom was in prison. Mac, who lived downstairs from Perry, had moved away, and Ravi hadn't been around for years.

Thousands of hippies had moved into the East Village, and many squatted in abandoned buildings. Relations between the hippies and locals had gone from bad to worse. Perry explained that the Summer of Love in 1967 (a few months after I left) was particularly violent in the East Village. Two hundred police had broken up a scene at Tompkins Square Park and made dozens of arrests.

Perry told me that Florin was now living in Harlem and had become a spiritual leader with a following. She now went by the name Ishvara, meaning "supreme soul." I got her address and planned to see her.

I didn't want to visit Eric since I was no longer interested in the acid scene. As we wandered around the old neighborhood, a little black kitten decided to adopt us. We were smitten by her, named her Blacky, and decided to bring her home.

On the day that Christy was working, I decided to visit Ishvara in Harlem. She was much the same as I remembered her from Millbrook. Her golden gown was beautiful, ornate with intricate beadwork. She sat on a magnificent, large, wooden throne chair with a beautifully embroidered back. A few of her followers were with her. When she saw me, she came right over, smiled, and said, "Bernie, it's so nice to see you, and I see you have a great, great Master." This was before I told her anything about Kirpal. Once again, she amazed me with her psychic abilities.

Ishvara showed me around her temple, an upstairs office decorated with African fabric, African sculpture, lots of pillows on the shiny oak floor, and an atmosphere infused with the sweet smell of incense. All her followers were African American and mostly women. She told me friends had encouraged her to start the temple shortly after her Millbrook trip.

"My friends found the location and rented the property

for me. Once I agreed to head this temple, I knew I had to change my name. Florin was a nice old lady that people sometimes listened to. Ishvara is a spiritual teacher that they fear and respect and is someone they come to for guidance. But I'm the same person you met eight years ago."

I told her about my guru, how I came to him, and my time in India. I explained the type of meditation I was practicing. She again told me that my guru was a very high Master. She knew about meditating on the third eye. She said that she focused on chanting and spiritual dancing at her temple.

I thanked her for starting me on my spiritual journey.

She said, "You were already on your spiritual journey; I just added some water."

I thanked her again for everything she did for me and told her I was glad that people now saw her light and love. We hugged, and I left with a lump in my throat. Who would have thought this older woman, whom I tried to sell a Bible to on the day President Kennedy was assassinated, would be a catalyst on my spiritual journey.

* * *

It didn't take long before worldly complications started to invade our spiritual calm. Christy and I were having problems. Every so often, our marital issues would bubble up to the surface. This had been happening since we first met. At the ashram, it didn't happen at all, but once we were back in the world, our relationship problems cropped up again. I was happy being in New York, and she was miserable at her job and my parents' home. I was headstrong, and she needed to confront me to be heard. I had to learn to listen better and be more loving. We agreed it was time to return to Vancouver.

After a few weeks, we had enough money for a drive-away to Seattle and the bus fare to Vancouver. Once again, I had to say goodbye to my dear family. My mother was particularly sad. Who knew how many more years would pass before I would see them again?

Before we left, we called various *Satsang* group leaders in cities en route to see if they would accommodate us for a night. In almost every instance, they were happy to have us stay. We were welcomed and fed, and we shared stories of the Master. Since our hosts knew we were just back from being with Kirpal in India, many people came to see us. Seeing the range of old and young devotees of various ethnicities, religions, and social statuses was wonderful. Clearly, the Master loves all.

Once we got to Seattle, we learned pets were not allowed on the bus. We couldn't leave our dear Blacky behind, so we decided to smuggle her into Canada. She was a good girl and didn't give us away. We sat at the back of the bus, and she slept the entire time.

ᢒ14ᢒ

It was good to be back in Vancouver. The *Satsang* community was strong and offered much support to keep the fires of love for the Master alive. We had many wonderful opportunities to share our experiences with the *Satsangis* and enjoyed catching up with our old friends.

The entrepreneurial spirit was thriving in our community. The Golden Lotus had been closed, and its assets had been sold to the Naam, a vegetarian restaurant about a block south of the Lotus and owned by initiates. David was now called Kolin and had opened a spiritual bookstore called Banyen Books. Arran had a health food store called Lifestream Natural Foods, and Victor had a restaurant called Nature's Path, situated behind Lifestream. It seemed like the *Satsang* community was doing well financially and spiritually.

Every Sunday, we would attend *Satsang*. This activity helped keep the Master's teaching at the forefront. Maintaining a spiritual focus was made easier because of our wonderfully supportive community. The *Satsang* was growing rapidly and decided to acquire land in Surrey to build a meditation center. Arran was our group leader, and I was asked to be treasurer, which I happily accepted.

Ever the visionary, Arran decided to expand Lifestream to include a wholesale division and asked me to be the comptroller for some fortuitous reason. I knew how to set up a bookkeeping system based on generally accepted accounting principles but knew nothing about being a comptroller. Arran said not to worry; I would learn on the job.

When I started, Lifestream had a few employees, all initi-ates. The business began to grow in leaps and bounds. I decided I wanted to be a real comptroller and registered at the University of British Columbia for a course that would provide a profes-sional certification; it entailed an intense night school program that would take four to five years to complete. Once I gradu-ated, I would be an RIA, Registered Industrial Accountant, a certification equivalent to a Chartered Accountant designation. I chose the RIA program because it emphasized comptroller-ship and cost accounting rather than the auditing that was the emphasis of the Chartered Accountant program.

In my first year with Lifestream, sales increased by about three hundred percent, which required more people in the ware-house and additional accounting help. Soon, I needed more assis-tants. I was able to quickly incorporate my classroom learning into my work. I couldn't have imagined a better situation. If a good financial control presented itself from my studies, I would discuss its benefits with Arran; he would usually approve it, and I would implement it. Thus, we grew every year.

The people working at Lifestream were wonderful. They were more than employees; they were family. Victor, the guy who slept in a casket and was mentioned previously, was our main handy-man and a warehouse worker. Arran told me a great Victor story. One evening, Arran was working late and heard a commotion from the warehouse. Victor was yelling, and Arran rushed over to see what was happening. Victor was standing on a wooden platform, jumping up and down. What Arran saw was Victor as a gnome. He looked four feet tall with red rubber boots and red suspenders matching his red beard. He was yelling in a high-pitched voice and acting quite gnomish. Victor really looked the part with his colorful clothes and mannerisms.

What Victor had done was build a platform with holes for his feet. He then cut holes in the rubber boots so that when he stood on the platform, he looked four feet tall. It took a lot of work to create this illusion, but it sure gave us a great laugh. That was Victor, full of surprises. I only wish that a Super 8 video camera had recorded it.

Some other notable Lifestreamers were the Montagues. There were eight Montague kids, six of whom were initiates; most worked at Lifestream. Marion worked with me in accounting, three of the boys worked in the warehouse, and a couple worked at the health food store. Peter was a gifted cartoonist, and every month, he would come up with "The Lifestream Funnies." These were hilarious. Peter spared no one, and Arran and I were often the butt of his jokes. Arran was atop his desk in one issue, stuck in an impossible yoga pose, begging for help. We enjoyed laughing at ourselves.

The eldest Montague daughter, Liz, was fond of saying, "My brothers and sisters follow Kirpal; I follow my nose."

Part of the Lifestream crew in 1972. That's Arran wearing the turban. I'm way to the right in the third row.

Kolin, née David, my partner at the Golden Lotus, had taken his share of the proceeds from the sale of the Golden Lotus, opened a New Age bookstore, and was doing extremely well. I asked him why he had changed his name. He said he was studying numerology, and his old name wasn't balanced. He felt that people didn't take him seriously and he would never be a success. His new name helped give him the courage to invest in his bookstore.

I asked Kolin about my name. He analyzed the letters and said Bernie wasn't a great name, but Bernard was perfectly balanced, and so was Ross. To get the most out of my name, he suggested adding the middle initial H. So, I gave it a shot and was then Bernard H. Ross.

One day in 1972, we heard the Rolling Stones were coming to the Pacific Coliseum in Vancouver, and we could purchase a concession stand for the concert. Christy thought we would do very well selling brownies. We paid for the concession stand and hired a bakery to bake thousands of brownies without eggs. The venture was a great success. Everyone hoped they were hash brownies, and all we said was, "I'm sure you'll enjoy them." Christy stayed at the concession stand, and I walked up and down the aisles with a tray. We ran out of brownies about halfway through the show. We could have sold a thousand more. But we were very happy. We heard some great music and made a lot of money.

Christy was very enterprising. My courses were expensive, and we wanted to save money for a house, so she started a side business selling Christy's Carob Kisses. She would make up fresh batches every couple of days and make the rounds to the health food stores to sell them. Her venture was almost a full-time job. Everyone loved Christy's Kisses, and it was a nice supplement to my salary.

❧15❧

In August 1972, Master Kirpal began his third world tour. Lifestream was doing well, and our staff had about thirty people, almost all initiates. Everyone wanted to see the Master the minute he arrived in the United States, but that would have destroyed Lifestream. We all met and prepared vacation schedules so people could have time off to see Kirpal and not hurt the business. Arran, the Canadian representative, would attend the entire tour. I would see the Master during the West Coast portion, which began November 8.

When he arrived, I was among the hundreds of people at the Vancouver airport. Many initiates had never seen him before, and their excitement was profound. The noisy airport suddenly became as silent as a church when he passed through the glass doors. Kirpal walked through the crowd, which included many there just by chance, and blessed us all. A throng of people followed him as he got into Arran's car. As he drove away, many people stayed behind for a while, just standing there in awe.

The Master gave two major talks in Vancouver, both well-attended. In fact, at each event, the auditoriums were overflowing, and many people sat in the aisles. Over twelve hundred people attended each talk. On the last day of his visit, 222 people received initiation, the largest group of any on this North American tour.

*   *   *

Christy and I were now free to follow the Master on the California section of the tour. He spent four days in San Francisco, four in San Jose, and ten glorious days in Los Angeles. It was great seeing him and hearing his voice.

At every talk, I longed for his *darshan*, for the intense connection I enjoyed in India, but I didn't get it for some reason. Sometimes, I would arrive at his talks early to get a seat near him. Even though I was close to him, I didn't feel the intoxication I had felt previously. I wondered if it was because of the multitudes. But I knew his love was infinite, and it didn't matter if there were ten or ten thousand in the audience; he could fill us all with divine love. And this was especially true for initiates who had experienced it before. I saw many of them intoxicated, brimming over with love.

Why was I not getting his love? I was afraid of the question. Every time it arose, I pushed it to the back of my mind. I couldn't face being out of favor with the Master. I didn't understand why I wasn't basking in his love. I was very devoted. I did my daily meditations and diaries, was treasurer of the *Satsang*, and attended *Satsang* every Sunday. I knew I let him down at times. I knew I made mistakes. But he must have known that I was trying my very best. He must have known that I needed a boost, that I needed his love now. Why was I not getting it? Not getting it when he was a few feet away from me was almost unbearable.

With a heavy heart, I kept repeating, "Sweet is thy will" and "This is for my greater good." But during the tour and for years afterward, this experience occupied the back of my mind, especially at weaker moments. I felt a resentment I was afraid to face, so I buried it. And as it happened, there was a good reason for him to turn off the divine juice, which I would not discover until many years later.

After the tour, I threw myself back into my work and study. Lifestream was quickly growing, and I instituted various financial controls.

During my studies, I learned about the power of computers and thought computerization would greatly benefit

Lifestream. This was in 1973, way before personal computers. Only mini-computers and mainframes were available, and they were expensive. Somehow, I talked Arran into buying a Wang 2200 minicomputer with multiple terminals and a high-speed printer. This required a considerable investment, but I convinced him it would soon pay for itself by making us more efficient and providing better controls.

Having a sound inventory control system is vital to the success of any wholesale operation, and once we computerized it, it turned out to be a blessing. Now, we had sales and purchasing figures for every one of the thousand items we sold. While reviewing the massive printout, I noticed a huge discrepancy in one of the health bars we sold. As it turned out, one of our suppliers was cheating us big time. He was a "friend" who had supplied us from the very beginning of our operation. He had personally delivered his health bars and stacked them in our warehouse. Because he was a long-time supplier, our workers trusted him and signed his packing slip, never verifying the count like they were supposed to. The fraud was significant. We had no idea how many years it had gone on—just a few months of computerization had brought it to light. I was upset and wanted to call the police, but Arran said we should just not deal with him anymore.

I felt fulfilled during this stage of my life. Work was rewarding, my studies were progressing nicely, and I meditated regularly. Then, to my delight, Christy announced she was pregnant. This was a dream come true. I had always wanted a family. We started talking about buying a house, and, as it turned out, Kolin's mother's house was for sale. I called my parents with the great news that they would soon have their first grandchild. We also talked to them about buying a house. My parents offered us a substantial gift to use as a down payment. I then applied for a mortgage, which the bank approved. When I told my father how much interest the bank would charge, he said he would give us the mortgage money at the same interest rate. I was so touched by their generosity and their faith in me. They weren't wealthy people, and this repre-sented a significant part of their savings.

So now we had a lovely house in a beautiful community only a few blocks from Arran's home. The house had three bedrooms and a finished basement. With a little work and a small investment, we turned the basement into a suite and rented it to a pleasant young couple. The backyard had a large area that we turned into a garden. Christy worked her magic and grew lots of veggies. She was once again a happy gardener. We picked our salad each evening after work and had tasty fresh vegetables for most of the year.

On September 14, 1973, our dear daughter, Natania, was born. We were so happy; she was so perfect, such a joy. My parents were thrilled and wanted to come, so we arranged for their upcoming visit. Soon, they arrived, and seeing them with their first grandchild was a delight. This represented for them the second generation after the Holocaust.

Me and Natania in 1973, when she was one month old.

It was a pleasant visit, except Christy wouldn't let my mother prepare food in her kitchen. My mother did all the cooking when we visited them in New York and was always careful to ensure our food was purely vegetarian. Preparing food for her family was a big part of my mom's persona, and not being allowed to even cook something for my father hurt her deeply. But my mom held her tongue and didn't make a fuss. Christy was stubborn, and this was her kitchen, end of story. Other than that, we had a lovely visit.

Suburban life suited us just fine. We settled in nicely in our new community. Many young families were in the neighborhood, and Arran's wife, Ratana, had a baby daughter and was only a few blocks away. There was also a community center within walking distance with many programs for new moms. Christy's sister, Barbara, also had a couple of young children, so we then entered the parenting stage of our incredible journey. To celebrate, we bought our first-ever new car, a golden-yellow Toyota, the least expensive model.

❧16❧

Natania was growing nicely. We loved our new home, work was good, and our health and finances were all in check. But on August 21, 1974, our world fell apart when we learned that our beloved Master had died. I remember being at work when we got the news. We were all in shock and deeply saddened. How could he leave us? He was the light of our lives, the love in our hearts. It was a sad day, and no one could work anymore. We closed for the day.

Arran was frantically arranging to go to India for the funeral. I wondered how he could do that. Wouldn't it tear his heart apart? I knew I couldn't go; I only wanted to curl up into a ball and cry. But even in his grief, Arran understood that the mission of Kirpal would continue, and a successor would emerge. Surely, he would bring news of a successor who would help heal the wounds of separation and guide us onward on this holy quest.

There were many tears over the next few weeks, and slowly, things started to somewhat return to normal. Most of us carried on, but the pain of losing my Master did not subside. After several months, Arran returned with news that there was a successor, and he would come to Vancouver shortly. Perhaps the successor would help heal our broken hearts.

The successor that Arran found was Ajaib Singh. We also heard from other sources that two others claimed to be Kirpal's successors, Thakar Singh and Darshan Singh, Kirpal's son. However, we trusted Arran and awaited our meeting with Ajaib Singh.

I discounted Darshan Singh. When we were at the ashram, he had promised to send us some of his poetry, which never happened. To my mind, that meant that he couldn't be the one. How could a true master not keep his word?

After a few months, Ajaib came to Vancouver, and most of the initiates accepted him as the successor. For some unknown reason, I had a strong aversion to him. I don't understand why. I wanted a successor to guide me. I needed the solace and healing a successor purported to bring to a disciple. But as hard as I tried, I couldn't accept him, and Christy felt the same.

Of course, we all wanted Kirpal, and we knew the successor was a different person with their own unique personality. However hard I tried to accept him, I couldn't. Something was missing when I looked into his eyes. In my limited vision, the *darshan* wasn't true, and the intoxication wasn't there. I understood that perhaps my limitations kept me from accepting him. But the reality was that I didn't feel the love or connection I felt with Kirpal. I continued to go to *Satsang*, but something had changed; something was broken.

We needed a break from the entire scene and decided to visit my parents. Natania was a year old, and my parents had not seen her for almost a year. They had recently sold the house in Middle Village and bought a beautiful North Miami Beach condo a block from the ocean. We visited them and had a lovely time in sunny Florida. Of course, my mother wouldn't let Christy cook in her kitchen. But Christy didn't mind.

The condo was on the fourteenth floor and had a large balcony overlooking the Atlantic Ocean. Christy was terrified that Natania could stick her head through the rails. No amount of measuring would dissuade her from the danger. So, I went to the store, bought some fishnet, and tied it all around the balcony. Then Natania could play there without causing Christy undue concern.

Natania was my parents' pride and joy. All their friends and relatives came to visit and dote over her. We swam most days at the large pool that was part of the condo complex or in the ocean. The week flew by, and soon it was time to return to Vancouver.

Once back, I returned to my old routine. My days consisted of morning meditation, work at Lifestream, a bit of family time, night school, lots of homework, and a bit of sleep. The final year of my program was exceptionally tough. Passing any course in the RIA program not only required a minimum grade of seventy percent but also required that you were in the top seventy percent of your class. In other words, at least thirty percent of the students failed regardless of what grade they got. Fortunately, I never failed a course and graduated in September 1976 after four years of a five-year program. It was a great honor to earn that degree.

I learned so much from the RIA program. Working at Lifestream was a double blessing since I could implement the many things I learned; theory immediately became practice.

However, there was still much to learn about comptrollership, and I needed a teacher to truly master this profession. It was like meditation; you could only learn so much from books. So, I had a long talk with Arran, and he was sad to see me go, but understood my needs. I told him I wouldn't leave him until I found a suitable replacement and trained them thoroughly. It took six months to find the right candidate, a chartered accountant and initiate. It took another couple of months to train him.

I found a great job as a comptroller for Great West Steel (GWS), reporting to a VP of Finance, Ron, a perfect mentor. The company manufactured steel and installed the joists they fabricated. Cost accounting was challenging, but I mastered it, and since GWS was a public company, the accounting records had to be meticulous for the auditors. Ron taught me a lot. He was a great, big, jovial guy, fun to work for, and enjoyed mentoring me.

It had been more than five years since I came to Canada, and I considered it my permanent home, so I became a Canadian citizen. I had no regrets about no longer being an American. My life was here, or so I thought.

Around this time, things started to get worse in our marriage. More fights, more arguments, more screaming, more broken dishes, more tearful making-up. The previous few years had been tough on our marriage. Between work, school, and homework that often required me to study into the wee hours of the night, I wasn't around much. I didn't make time to be available to my family, and Christy was having trouble coping. I admit I was stubborn and a know-it-all, so my lack of understanding had surely contributed to our problems. We needed help, but the Canadian health service required extreme circumstances before you could see a therapist. Screaming matches and broken dishes weren't considered extreme enough.

During this time, we heard that Thakar Singh was coming to Vancouver. Some of the initiates embraced him as the successor to Kirpal. Christy and I had stopped going to the Ajaib *Satsang* and hoped that meeting the true successor would help heal us. We were invited to see Thakar in his suite at a local hotel and had a private interview. He was a big, handsome Sikh with a long white beard. We sat in front of him on the floor, and he was very loving and kind to us. He spoke lovingly of Kirpal and the need for healing. We were getting some charging from him and starting to like him. But as I sat there, I couldn't help but smell an unpleasant odor from him. It was similar to the scent of our Galley Bay goat, though much less intense. At that moment, I remembered Kirpal's talk about thoughts having colors and odors, and this particular odor is associated with lust. We thanked Thakar for his kindness and never returned. We were saved by a nose.

I had one private accounting client from my Lifestream years—my good friend Ron, a dentist who lived in Victoria. I bartered accounting services for dentistry, and each year, I would go to Victoria and have my teeth taken care of. I also did Ron's books and prepared his tax return. There were several initiates in Victoria, and most of them followed Darshan Singh. I attended a *Satsang* while there and felt a similar charge to what I got from Kirpal. I had a good meditation, the best in a long time. I learned that most of the old Kirpal initiates across the United States and India had accepted Darshan. But I also learned that another faction didn't believe there was a successor and continued to have *Satsang* in Kirpal's name. So, our family was now in four camps, each adamant they were right. Even after my great meditation, I still didn't accept Darshan. I figured I was destined to be an orphan.

We started hanging out with a group of initiates who also didn't accept any of the successors. We began having regular *Satsangs*. We also had parties and meals and supported each other through these trying times.

At first, we would console each other, meditate together, and try to stay true to the precepts of the path. But slowly, things began to unravel. It started with little things like no longer filling out our diaries or eating a cookie we knew was made with eggs. Then, we began to skip our meditations. Things were breaking down.

The Master used to say that we were like young saplings and needed a strong protective hedge while we grew—once we were well-grounded in the path, not even a bulldozer could unearth us. But we were still young saplings, and a world of desires was cutting down our protective hedge like a weed whacker, quickly loosening us from our spiritual foundation.

Having this group was a blessing and a curse. Alone, we may have held it together, but the group encouraged irreverent behavior. It was fun rebelling, and it became easier as time went by. Also, we truly liked our group. We had known them for years and had fun together; we laughed again, which helped us forget our great loss. Ironically, it also helped us forget Kirpal.

❧17❧

Our marital problems went from bad to worse. Christy and I were fighting a lot. Bad feelings hung in the air like a putrid odor. For some inexplicable reason, we were incapable of making up. By then, we rarely made love, and it wasn't fulfilling when we did. This was my reality. It was demeaning for both of us. After a while, we stopped trying.

Also, Natania was not an easy baby, and Christy was the principal caregiver. She often didn't get enough sleep, and I was too self-absorbed to help. At this point, I forgot what Kirpal had always said: "Love knows giving; love knows service and sacrifice."

Christy insisted that now was her time. She had sacrificed so much to help me get my degree; now, she wanted to return to school to get hers. She wanted me to stay home with Natania and be a househusband. I told her this was impossible; what money would we live on? I was the principal breadwinner; if I quit, we wouldn't last more than a few months on our savings.

She wouldn't have any of it. More fights, more broken dishes. I didn't know how to solve this. I couldn't see beyond her words. I didn't see her wounds, her disappointments. I was trying to be logical and forgot to be compassionate.

We talked about marital counseling. Clearly, we needed help if we were to save our marriage. We inquired about getting a therapist and were told it would take months before we could get an appointment through Canada's healthcare program. We could have hired a private therapist, but we couldn't afford that, or so I believed.

My job at Great West Steel had become boring. I learned a lot from my VP of Finance, but after two years on the job, I had too much free time. The challenging cost-accounting work required only one week per month. The rest of the staff handled the day-to-day operations of billing and collections. So, I had tons of time to wallow in my misery. I started writing poetry, which began to fly out of me.

What was astounding was realizing that our marriage, which I had thought was so strong, could be dying so abruptly, so completely, so coldly. I felt a great deal of pain and anger over this. I still felt some love for Christy, but I was sure she didn't love me anymore. And there was no one to talk to about the pain. Writing poetry became my therapy.

I had more than fifty completed poems and dozens of fragments in a short time. Many were self-indulgent, but I thought a few were pretty good. I put the best ones together in a volume, *Wedlocks and Half Nelsons*. "Half Nelson" is a wrestling term. The title was better than most of my poems. Here's one from that collection:

Suspension

Yesterday was blight
On the face of love
No words succeeded
No tenderness eradicated
The canker of despair.

Hanging suspended
Between glittering reflections
And jagged stones,
My bridge of love
Could not span your errant river.

My foundation weakened
By the rifts of anger,
My cable frayed
By the rust of doubt,
I tried to call out to you.

Unreachable,
Immersed in a secret bog
Lost in your own mist
Silent as a rainbow
Your colors fading.

My vision failing
My grasp slipping,
This bridge crumbling,
And I, wondering,
Will the river be merciful?

I was now sleeping upstairs in a small bedroom. I felt like a stranger in my own home. I was resentful, and we'd fight whenever I tried to discuss our situation—more angry responses, more slammed doors, more fodder for my poetry.

No Longer Just Friends

Tonight, I lost a friend
She wiped me off
Her crystal heart
As if I were some lint

She heard my tactless words
Adding fire to her tongue
Ignited, we both raged
Anger razed our fragile cage

256

That cage once held our love
Was emptied into the wind
That howled with our lies
That whimpered in demise

Too proud to hear beyond the words
Too arrogant to let up
We spun the mirrored sword of blame
Like a pointer in a childish game

Yesterday I lost a love
Today I lost a friend
I never thought she'd feel
Indifference in the end.

By that point, we weren't talking much. I was eating out, and when I came home, I went to my room like a boarder. So, when a friend told me he was planning a trip to California, I asked if I could come along. I told Christy about my plans, and she didn't seem to care.

It was great getting away from all the drama. I spent a week sleeping in a tent by the beach and hanging out with pleasant college folks in San Jose. I had a good time and managed to forget my troubles back home. After a week, I came home hoping to make things better. Perhaps the absence would give us a new perspective, a chance to reassess our relationship.

I got to my house and noticed the door was locked. I tried my key, but it didn't work. "Fuck, she changed the locks on me," I thought. I banged on the door, but no one answered. I was furious. I went to her mother's house and found that Christy and Natania were there. The mother wouldn't let me in. She wouldn't let me speak to Christy. It seemed hopeless. It seemed more than likely the marriage was over.

What was I supposed to do now? I didn't have a place to stay. I thought of going to a hotel. Then I remembered that Kolin had a macrobiotic house. Perhaps I could spend a few days with him until I could find my own place. Kolin was sympathetic to my situation, and I rented a room in his house. This was an ideal situation since the rent included room and board. So, I moved in, but it took about a week to get all my stuff.

It took a while to find out why Christy was so angry. After I left, a stalker started coming around and frightening Christy and our basement tenant. Both women were alone, each with a young child. The stalker kept getting bolder and started coming up to the window. Christy called the police, but of course, he wasn't around when they came. Finally, Christy moved to her mom's apartment. Christy couldn't forgive me for not being there or even calling. That was the breaking point for her. I was already established in my new macrobiotic house when I learned this.

One of our housemates, Melanie, was our macrobiotic cook. She was very devoted to macrobiotic living and all things Japanese. Dinners at the house were incredibly delicious and perfectly prepared. I loved her cooking, and soon we became lovers. It sure was nice being in a new relationship without all the drama.

Melanie was the glue that kept our household together. Each day, she prepared splendid meals that we ate together. The members of our home were devoted to macrobiotic philosophy, and I was learning a lot. Contentment and harmony radiated in our household, which was exactly what I needed after being tossed out of my home. Four guys lived in the house, and all wished to win Melanie's heart. But I was the lucky one.

I continued to pay the mortgage and provided Christy with money. I hoped we could resolve our differences, but temptation killed that. I was having an affair with Melanie, and Christy was probably involved with someone new. She had taken a job at a Greek restaurant, and it was rumored she was seeing a coworker. Just like that, our marriage was over.

We had been together for ten incredible years. I sat on my futon and recalled our amazing experiences—Galley Bay, our five blessed months with Kirpal in India, building a life together, buying a home, seven years on a wonderful, fulfilling spiritual path, and having a beautiful daughter. Then, it was all over, and regrettably, we were no longer friends. It hurt. And I had thought our love would last forever.

Here I was, still pining over Christy, my lost worldly love, and completely forgetting about the divine love I had for Kirpal. How could I be blind to it? How could I forget all my spiritual experiences and all the wisdom he gave me? How could I forget the peace I felt every day as a disciple? Right then, I was lost in the misery of my life, trying to make the best of it. But one day, I hoped to understand. One day, this mystery would be solved, or so I hoped.

Life in the macrobiotic house turned out great. I really liked the people. I enjoyed coming home to a happy place, and Melanie was a sweet and caring lover. But I wasn't over Christy and didn't treat Melanie like she deserved. After a few months, we ended the relationship but remained friends.

Some of my housemates wanted to try a ten-day brown rice fast. I hadn't been successful when I tried it in Galley Bay, but perhaps it would turn out differently this time. Melanie made perfect short-grain brown rice, just the right consistency, every time. With a bunch of us supporting each other's efforts, we made it to day eight in no time. We were feeling quite good, and after our evening dinner, the topic of beer came up. One of our crew said that he thought beer should be part of the fast since it was made of hops, a grain. Melanie was aghast and said drinking beer during a macrobiotic fast would be sacrilegious.

"Beer is yin and will cause significant imbalance," Melanie stated.

At first, we were joking to get a rise out of Melanie, but soon, one of our team got a six-pack. Surely, one beer wouldn't hurt. So, we drank and got seriously buzzed. This was the first time I had had alcohol since the moonshine in Galley Bay nine years prior. One of the guys remembered the *Star Wars* movie was having a special showing at midnight. So we all piled into Kolin's car and went. The movie blew our minds—it was the original one, released in 1977.

*   *   *

Christy and I finally sat down and talked about the future. Our house had appreciated over the last few years, and if we sold it, we would both have a nice nest egg. We discussed our finances, and we agreed on the alimony payment. We put the house on the market and went our separate ways. Christy was great about allowing me to see Natania, and we worked out a schedule where I had her every other weekend. I very much wanted to be in Natania's life.

I quickly settled into my new routine. I had my work and a macrobiotic household with new friends. I didn't even think about the fact that my life as a disciple was over, that my focus and motivation had changed so dramatically. It was too easy to move on. It was too easy to forget the peace and content-ment I felt as a disciple, my divine love for Kirpal, my love for God, and my clear vision for my future. Kirpal often said the greatest attribute of the mind was forgetfulness, and my life had become a testament to that.

BOOK 3
THE ENTREPRENEUR

"Try not to resist the changes that come your way. Instead, let life live through you. And do not worry that your life is turning upside down. How do you know that the side you are used to is better than the one to come?"

-Rumi

∂1∾

It was 1979, five years since Kirpal died. I don't remember exactly when I stopped thinking of myself as a devotee. The change was gradual and subtle. I now saw the period of discipleship as a phase I outgrew, much like my hippie phase. As a 33-year-old professional, I was ready for a new chapter in my life, new opportunities to embrace, and new challenges to conquer.

Our house sold quickly and for significantly more than we had paid. We repaid the balance of the mortgage to my parents and realized a nice profit, which I split equally with Christy. I quit my job at Great West Steel, and Christy took her share of the money and started a clothing boutique near the university, which, unfortunately, was a poor investment.

I had an idea for a new business venture. Most accounting firms were downtown in fancy office buildings. What about a storefront/walk-in accounting service? I wondered. There were many stores in the Kitsilano section of Vancouver. I scouted my old neighborhood and saw no accounting practices in the area. I found a reasonably priced storefront on 4th Avenue, a few blocks from where the Golden Lotus used to be. It was perfect for a small accounting practice, and Ross Data Services was born.

I moved out of the macrobiotic house and found a great apartment in a high-rise building near Stanley Park. I also bought a black Fiat Spider convertible with red upholstery. I was all set to enjoy my newfound bachelorhood.

Once I got into the dating game, my ethical principles completely unraveled. I stopped meditating and being a vegetarian.

Once again, getting laid was paramount in my mind. I was ready for action with my hot car and cool poetry, but action wasn't ready for me. It had been ten years since I had played the field. People's values had changed. Hippiedom was dead, and disco was the flavor of the moment. Hardly anyone was taking LSD. Cocaine was the drug of choice, but I didn't care for that high. My stories dated me and weren't of much interest to younger people. Saying I was an ex-hippie draft dodger from New York wouldn't get me to first base with the ladies. Neither was saying I was an ex-disciple of a spiritual master.

My apartment was far from my friends, and I didn't get to see them much. Most of the time, I was alone, focused on building my new business. I wandered the streets of my new neighborhood. There were lots of bars filled with young people having fun. It felt weird walking into a bar alone. Most of the single women came with a friend. If I had gone with a friend, I might have had a chance to pick someone up, but none of my friends liked the bar scene, and most of them were still in relationships. Mostly, I looked forward to weekends with my dear daughter.

Vancouver has many beaches, and I liked going to them. English Bay was within walking distance from my apartment and was a great place to swim. On the Kitsilano side, my office was near Kits Beach and Jericho Beach. During the summer, Kits swarmed with people, with many bathing beauties to admire—but none to talk to.

My favorite beach was Wreck Beach, out near the University of British Columbia. The University is on a peninsula about a hundred feet above the desolate beach. Only a few steep trails lead to this wild, isolated beach. The beach runs for more than ten miles and is festooned with driftwood, including whole trees that washed up during storms, twisted, gnarled, and bleached from years in the sun. Some were works of art with colorful swirls and amazing shapes.

During the summer, a section of Wreck Beach became a

nude beach that I frequented. It reminded me of my days in Galley Bay so many years earlier. There was freedom in being naked among strangers—there I was with nothing to hide. All kinds of people were at the nude beach, including beautiful women working on perfecting their tans. It was a place where you respected other people's bodies under a blanket of cool. There was far more lust at the regular beaches.

But mostly, I enjoyed wandering the deserted parts of the beach in all kinds of weather. I liked when the ocean raged and the surf pounded the shore. I liked feeling the cold spray drenching me and how nature created this desolate spot without interference from man. I liked finding beauty in the little things: an unusual stone, a pretty shell, an enormous boulder, and the enchanting swirls in weathered wood. I enjoyed sitting on my driftwood throne, sometimes enraptured in the present moment and other times lost in the wreck of my life.

During this period, I wrote the following poem:

Mind's Fine Thorns

A long time on this beach
Dry this summer, digging eyes
Hungry mouths in search
Sighing under waves.
Whitecap marching bands
Where are the majorettes? Where are the stars?
Under the sea without reflection.

> Cold beer. Cold beer
> Carried on his head
> A momentary reprieve
> A dollar's worth of sweat.

A long time on this beach
The tide is blushing

The sun is close to the edge
Bleating sheep don't make waves
God's turning over
Nobody touches mind's fine thorns

    Relax. Relax.
    What effort does the sea expel?
    Naked thighs attract
    Bronzed and oiled so well.

A long time on this beach
A stage: A barnacle throne
A crown of wet seaweed,
Where do my footprints go?
Why do they hide the sun?
Faces for the fire, be prepared
Friendly driftwood staring.

    The stage is damned
    A beach of crab thighs
    All ground to sand
    Don't close your eyes.

A long time on this beach
The stage is gone
The beach is dying, faces prepared
Like Kosher pickles to meet the night.
Desire: hopeless as silver smelts
Crying in gill nets.
Mother Earth, kiss me
I need your nipple of love.

    Tweedle dee dee, tweedle dee dum
    Life is but a sweet ripe plum
    If meaning is not what you seek
    Then its juice runs down your cheek.

❧2❧

My dear daughter, Natania, spent every other weekend with me. We had fun. I took her bike riding in Stanley Park. We visited the monkey lady next door, who let her play with her rambunctious spider monkey. Natania was a beautiful child, and I adored her. She was smart, had started to read at an early age, and had already developed a fine vocabulary. During each visit, I would prepare a new word for her to learn. She loved language and books.

We rode on my bicycle, played in the Japanese Gardens, and visited the zoo. I tried to be fully present with her. She was growing so fast, and there was a certain sadness in this young child. I know she missed having her family under one roof, and sometimes I did as well.

Christy moved into a new apartment, and one night, I had a strong desire to see her. The memory of our love still lingered somewhere in the deep recesses of my heart. All I wanted was to see her, to reminisce, and to be friends. I needed a friend that night. But unfortunately, Christy wasn't ready for that. I was surprised she even agreed to my visit. I was gravely disappointed and wrote the following poem shortly after, another addition to *Wedlocks and Half Nelsons*.

Late Night Embers

My pain grew eyes
saw emptiness everywhere
and went blind to your door
squeezed in that small opening

Tea & one dry biscuit offered
empty kindness in an empty kitchen
managed a few drops of conversation
slim consolation for all our years

No heat
who turned off the heat?
heat's impoverished
I can't accept this cold

My pain grew legs
squeezed out your hardened door
as silently as the frost
as suddenly as a chill

The frigid night receives me
unseen
uncherished
unembraced

I wander empty crystalline streets
branches entombed in ice
twigs and gossamer hoarfrost
illumined by lamp light

Beguiling moonlight
on this clear night of desolate beauty
alluring remoteness
unattainable ebullience

I shudder but cannot scream
I whisper but cannot laugh or cry
I glisten like an icicle
afraid I'll crack or melt

I'm so alone
in this frozen wonderland
on a distant galaxy
a fading star

That night was the last time I reached out to Christy as a friend. It was clear that Christy wasn't interested in friendship. She was civil and polite when I came to pick up Natania, but I'm sure she was also civil to the delivery guy. At first, I felt disappointment, which soon turned to resentment. She had been my first love. We had some incredible times together. Did those amazing memories now mean nothing to her? How could she throw these away? How could she write me off like I was some insignificant acquaintance? Weren't we once deeply in love? I must have hurt her greatly. I wished she would just let it out, whatever it was. I wanted her to scream at me and pound me with her fists if that helped. But no such luck. All I got was that quiet indifference, that English stiff upper lip treatment.

But I could see Christy was having a hard time. The resentment didn't last long. I needed to forgive her and myself. I remembered that Kirpal advised us to forgive and forget. To her credit, she never bad-mouthed me to Natania. She wanted our daughter to know her father, for which I am genuinely grateful. I had to accept my role as the ex and make the best of my relationship with my dear daughter.

*　*　*

One day, a friend told me that Timothy Leary was in Vancouver and performing at a club downtown. He was billed as the "Stand-Up Philosopher." Somehow, merging hippie philosophy and stand-up comedy seemed weird. Still, I couldn't resist going to see his show. Perhaps I would even have the chance to see him backstage and catch up on the good old days.

I got to the theater, which was much smaller than I expected for someone so famous. I was fortunate to get a good seat. The stage had a bar stool and a mic, like what you would expect for a stand-up comic. Leary had aged a lot since I last saw him about a dozen years earlier. I knew he had lived through some hard times, including a couple of stints in prison.

Leary tried to be funny, but somehow it seemed contrived and inauthentic, like someone else had written his material. The new insights and revelations he promised at the start of his routine were old, and many no longer seemed pertinent. I couldn't help but feel bad for him. He was a caricature of his former self. A once brilliant mind was now spouting cliches and worn-out phrases. The world had changed; the hippie era was over. But Leary was lost in the past. And when his act was over, I chose not to go backstage. I didn't want to have to lie about his performance. I preferred to remember him as the LSD guru, the man who gave me a home at Millbrook and inspired a generation.

❧ 3 ❧

Ross Data Services was growing nicely. My clients were mostly mom-and-pop businesses—the bagel shop on the corner, restaurants, various stores, and individuals needing their taxes done. That all changed when Ian arrived at my office.

Ian was a TV producer looking for an accountant. I have no idea how he found me, but it was most likely from a client recommendation. Canada had recently passed an attractive tax credit program to promote the film industry. In essence, if someone invested in a Canadian movie or TV show, they could deduct the entire value of the investment from their tax bill. So, an investor had nothing to lose. To qualify for this tax credit required an accredited accountant to verify that each show met government standards ... and that's where I came in.

Ian produced a series of TV shows called *The Stan Kann Show*. Stan was famous for appearing on *The Tonight Show with Johnny Carson* 77 times, more than any other guest. He also appeared 89 times on *The Mike Douglas Show* and was somewhat of a celebrity in his own right. Stan was hysterically funny and known for his crazy hobbies, which included collecting antique vacuum cleaners, barber poles, and other unusual items.

Ian produced 24 episodes of *The Stan Kann Show* and needed them certified. Once that was complete, he could raise money from investors.

Ian asked if I would certify his series; the going rate was five hundred dollars per episode. I researched the requirements for certification and certified all 24 episodes in a couple of days. I

271

earned twelve thousand dollars from this project, a lot of money in 1979. I even found investors for his shows and got a ten percent finder's fee for my efforts. I became fascinated by this industry and wanted to work in it. I never imagined how lucrative the entertainment industry was. It sure beats doing tax returns and keeping the books of small businesses.

I heard that Lifestream had outgrown its Wang mini-computer and wanted to sell it at a reasonable price. I figured having a computer would help my business and image. My newly hired assistant could input each client's transactions on the computer and provide timely financial statements. Using the computer saved time and increased our profitability.

One of my clients, Werner, owned a large Swiss restaurant, but his passion was film. He had a script and was looking to produce it. He introduced me to Jim, a production controller who eventually became my mentor.

With Jim's help, I computerized the complex chart of accounts structure for feature films with its unique above-the-line and below-the-line costs. This provided an excellent tool for recording and quickly reporting costs, which helped productions stay on budget. As far as I know, this was Canada's first computerized film accounting system.

My first job as a production accountant proved a disaster. I was sent on location to Lethbridge, Alberta, for a film starring James Garner. I was paid handsomely for my services, plus an additional five hundred dollars per week for my computer, which remained at my Vancouver office. Each day, I would fax the account transactions to my assistant, and she would enter them into the computer and fax back reports. This worked well for a time. But once production was in full swing, the production manager called me into her office and unceremoniously fired me. She said I wasn't getting the reports to them fast enough. I was paid for my work and asked to leave.

I was devastated. This was the first time I was ever fired from a job. I didn't understand why until three weeks later. I learned that the production couldn't raise the money needed to continue. Firing me and my computer was about cost savings. The entire production folded, and most people left without getting paid for the last few weeks. It was most unfortunate. Jim consoled me and told me that this is part of being in the film industry. Many projects never see the light of day. Also, film people are paid well because there are sometimes long periods without work.

Fortunately, I still had all my accounting clients. But now that I had experienced the excitement of entertainment accounting, my work life was no longer satisfying. Soon, a new entertainment accounting opportunity came my way. Werner finally raised enough money to produce a feature film, *By Design*, starring Patty Duke and Saul Robinac. I became the production accountant on this film, and Jim was the associate producer. The film was a comedy about a lesbian couple, both successful fashion designers, who wanted to have a baby. This was long before adoption agencies would consider a gay couple suitable parents.

I learned so much from Jim about production accounting, and the entire shoot ran smoothly. Everyone greatly appreciated the computerized reports and financial statements. Regular account-

Ross Data Services in 1978, with Eva, my first friend from Bolivia.

ing was pretty dull, but this was fast-moving, complex, and satisfying. The film industry has many unions and guilds, each negotiating different job rates. There were the Screen Actors

Guild, Directors Guild, Teamsters, and the IATSE (International Alliance of Theatrical Stage Employees). There were specific rules for regular time, time-and-a-half, and golden time. There were also penalties for rest violations, violations associated with meal periods, and other complexities. Getting the payroll right each week required a great deal of work and was my number one priority.

Also, the production managers, set designers, and others needed cash for the right props and to get to the correct locations. It was common to have fifty thousand dollars in cash floating around and requiring receipts. Long days were a norm for this business, and I was hooked. Maybe one day, I could follow in Jim's footsteps and become an associate producer.

❧ 4 ❧

That Sunday was a glorious sunny day that would soon change my life. Michael and Helen were close friends and neighbors, also initiated by Kirpal, who no longer followed the path. That day, Michael invited me to join them on a walk around Stanley Park.

Michael and Helen were joined by Michael's sister, Elizabeth. I had known Michael for many years, but never knew he had a sister. We walked the seawall, a magnificent ten-kilometer path on the outside perimeter of Stanley Park. The walk offered endless ocean views and marvelous vistas of the mountains to the north.

Michael's sister, Elizabeth, was a very attractive woman in her late twenties with shoulder-length auburn hair, bright blue eyes, and a lovely figure. She was beautiful, confident, intelligent, cultured, and easy to talk to.

We walked together, and soon, our steps were in sync. I was fascinated by her and very attracted to her. Being with her was so natural; I felt like we were old friends in no time. I learned that she had danced with the Bolshoi in Edmonton when she was thirteen and now wanted to act. In fact, she was part of an actor's workshop in Vancouver. I told her about my work in feature films. Halfway through the walk, we were holding hands.

She invited me to her apartment for tea, which I gladly accepted. Once we got to her place, we immediately started kissing. Our clothes were off in no time, and we were soon in the throes of passionate lovemaking. And what a lover she was. She was daring, receptive, and could take control and leave me breathless. We made love multiple times, and I woke up in her arms the next morning.

From then on, we were inseparable. When I was not at work, I was with Elizabeth. She told me that I was soft and wanted to toughen me up. She was in excellent shape. Trying to keep up with her during our daily jogs in Stanley Park certainly helped my conditioning. Soon, I was able to run the entire seawall at a good clip. She also got me on a good, healthy diet. No more fast food, just lots of salad with sensible proteins.

She was very cultured, and we would attend programs by the Vancouver Symphony and the ballet. She encouraged me to continue writing poetry, and soon, I was writing love poems for her. She introduced me to foreign movies by Fellini and Bergman. We would have long discussions about their meaning.

But Elizabeth had a dark side. Sometimes, she became belittling and condescending. This could last for days; then she would suddenly be her sweet, caring self. She told me she had bipolar disorder and to not listen to her when she was depressed.

One major problem was that she was extremely jealous of my daughter, Natania. She was pleasant enough when we were together, but Elizabeth chose not to be around on weekends when Natania was with me. I couldn't understand why she would have such a strong aversion to my sweet, wonderful six-year-old child. She explained it wasn't rational, but she wanted our love to be new and wonderful, and she hated that I had a child with another woman. She wanted all of me, all to herself.

Early in our relationship, she told me, "What I love about you is your potential."

"What about who I am now?" I asked.

"You're wonderful, but you have the potential to be great, and I think I can help you achieve that," she answered.

I believe that in her mind, she thought she could mold me to fit her image. She was already molding me in so many ways: my diet, exercise, and cultural activities. I liked learning from her and gladly gave her my heart. I didn't mind that she was the alpha in the relationship. I wanted the relationship to work. I was finally over Christy, and I needed love in my life, true love. I thought I had found it with Elizabeth.

I met her parents, lovely, wealthy people. I could see why Michael and Elizabeth had nice apartments and didn't have to work. Her father was a Polish aristocrat who had emigrated to England just before the Nazi invasion. Once in England, he joined the army as an officer and saw action. After the war, he became a doctor. Elizabeth's mom was a sweet, doting Scottish woman with a thick accent and a fondness for whiskey—scotch, of course. They had moved to Edmonton after the war, where her dad had established a successful medical practice that included a fully functioning clinic.

In Vancouver, they ran a large health food store, and, as a doctor, he recommended lots of vitamins and natural remedies that his customers were happy to buy repeatedly. Naturally, the store was very successful. Both parents ran the store, and the children rarely needed to work there, although they were on the books as employees.

Elizabeth confided in me about an incident that occurred when she was sixteen and still living in Edmonton with her parents. She discovered she was pregnant and told her father. Her father said there was nothing to worry about and he would take care of it. She thought he would arrange an abortion at a clinic since she didn't want a baby at that tender age. But her father immediately escorted her to his clinic and performed the abortion. This really messed her up, and she felt it significantly contributed to her neuroses.

But that incident didn't affect her sexual appetite. Elizabeth was a very passionate woman. She loved sex and would often initiate it, much to my delight. She was always ready for sex, regardless of when and where. She was playful, daring, uninhibited, and always surprised and delighted me with her lustfulness.

I was starting to fall in love with Elizabeth. There were several months of incredible talks, profound honesty, and fun times. We were inseparable and got along perfectly. We seemed aligned about our goals for the future. I felt she would bring out the best in me and that I had finally found my soulmate. After a few months of soul-searching, I was ready to take this relationship to the next level. I decided to ask Elizabeth to marry me.

I proposed during a lovely walk through the Japanese Gardens in Stanley Park. She was delighted and told me she loved me, too, and wanted to be my wife more than anything else in the world. I was very moved by her response and believed I had made the right decision.

We went to her parents' house and told them the good news. Soon, Michael and Helen joined us. We went out to our favorite Chinese restaurant to celebrate.

Then we discussed the wedding plans. She was Catholic but not religious and thought getting married by a justice of the peace would be fine. We discussed dates, whom to invite, where to have the reception and our honeymoon, and other happy things. Then she dropped the bombshell. She was adamant about not having my daughter attend our wedding.

I couldn't believe it and asked, "How the hell can you exclude my daughter from our wedding? She's my beloved child and has done nothing to justify her exclusion."

She replied, "I know it's not rational. But I feel so jealous that you have a child with another woman. I don't want to be reminded of this on our wedding day. Please understand and do it my way."

I don't know why I gave in. What else in my past could make her jealous or angry? Was I making a mistake? Doubts were creeping in, but her kindness, caring, and focused attention to making me perfectly happy put my mind at rest. Once I proposed, I became the center of her universe. It was like all her energy was there to please me, and I must admit it was gratifying.

This time, I let my family know I was getting married again, and my sister Nancy came to our wedding from LA. It was a small wedding at City Hall with a reception at her parents' apartment. Maybe twenty or thirty people attended. We had a lovely wedding cake and lots of delicious catered food. We were married on December 8, 1979. I don't think anyone took photos.

The next day, I went to see Natania (who was six then) and brought her a large piece of wedding cake. She was sad to have been excluded. I could see how much this hurt her. I vowed to make time for her and show her how much I loved her. I later learned from Christy that Natania ate a tiny bit of the wedding cake every day for almost a year.

We planned a ski trip to Alta, Utah, for our honeymoon and asked our friends Jurek and Deirdre to join us. The day before leaving, we saw the movie *Kramer vs. Kramer*. This was an upsetting movie that drove Elizabeth crazy. The film was about a divorce in which the mother left, and the father had to take care of the child. In Elizabeth's mind, I suppose she saw a possibility that Christy could leave Natania with me. But if she knew Christy, that would never happen in a million years. But the chance of this happening drove her into a realm of rage, anger, and jealousy unlike anything I had ever experienced. This was a major flare-up; it was epic. I was ready to leave her with all the hysterical crying. And why? Because I had a daughter. No amount of explanation helped; no degree of reasoning succeeded. Something was seriously wrong, and I was scared the marriage would end before we even began our honeymoon.

The next day, she apologized and promised to let it go. We left for the mountains of Utah, where I would finally learn to ski. Elizabeth and Jurek were skilled skiers who were out each day on the most advanced slopes. So, I hung out with Deirdre on the bunny hill most of the week. By the end of the week, I felt confident enough to go down an intermediate run. Elizabeth and I finally got to ski together, and she was as graceful on the slopes as on the dance floor.

We had a wonderful honeymoon in the cold mountain air of Utah. Usually, Jurek and Deirdre joined us for dinner, and we had great conversations with lots of laughs. Jurek was a film and theater director of some prominence and shared some of his insights and adventures. We enjoyed being with these fun-loving, artistic people. Jurek would eventually move to Los Angeles and direct movies. His 1987 feature film *Anna* starred Sally Kirkland and Paulina Porizkova and received critical acclaim and a Best Actress Golden Globe for Sally Kirkland.

After a few months of marital bliss, Elizabeth got accepted into a Shakespeare and Company acting workshop in Lenox, Massachusetts. This was a great opportunity for her to develop deeper acting skills. She would be gone for about a month. I knew what this meant to her and, of course, agreed to this short separation.

I got long, detailed letters from her almost daily, telling me all about the program, the people, and how much she missed me. In her letters, she mentioned an Israeli actor and how well they worked together. I could tell from the letter that they seemed to be developing a close friendship. After a couple of weeks, her letters came less frequently and were shorter. The longing for me seemed less intense. I strongly felt she was having an affair with the Israeli actor. I even wrote her about my suspicion, but she never addressed it.

It was all hugs and kisses when she returned. She was happy to be back, and everything returned to normal. She was the same passionate lover as before. She seemed truly glad to be back with me. It was wonderful to have her back in my arms and back in my bed. But that doubt about her infidelity lingered. I couldn't shake it.

Finally, I couldn't stand the doubt anymore. One evening, I came right out and asked, "Did you have an affair with that Israeli actor?"

After some hesitation and discomfort, she said, "I did."

With a lump in my throat, I asked, "Why?"

"It just happened."

"Didn't you tell him you were married?"

"Yes, I told him right off that I was married. He respected that for a time. We acted together. We rehearsed together. We saw each other every day. He wanted me. He pursued me. I fought it until I couldn't."

My heart sank. She could see the hurt on my face. I walked away. I felt defeated.

She came after me with tears in her eyes and said, "I'm sorry. I'm so sorry. I came back to you because I love you, not him. Can you forgive me?"

All I could muster was, "I don't know."

"Let's try to put this behind us?" she asked.

After that painful encounter, things got better. She was super nice, so loving and attentive. And, in time, the pain subsided; it was almost like old times again. But in the back of my mind, I felt betrayed. Something broke, but I tried hard not to think about it or let it bother me. I hoped, in time, I could let it go completely.

I was busy with my work, and she was working on a play based on Sylvia Plath's poetry. Her brother Michael was writing the music.

Meanwhile, the Canadian government rescinded the tax credit for TV and feature films. This practically destroyed the film industry in Canada. It made it much harder to get film work in Vancouver. Elizabeth suggested we move to New York to pursue our careers, and I agreed. I was so entrenched in the relationship that I didn't even consider Natania when I decided to move to New York.

Elizabeth got an acting opportunity in New York, and we both went for a visit. I met her friend, Andre Gregory, a NY theater director. He invited us to his place in the Hamptons, and we spent the weekend with him, his wife, and two children. Andre wrote a script called My Dinner with Andre and was seeking backers. This was my opportunity to shine. I said, "I raised money for productions in Vancouver; maybe I could help." Andre was thrilled and gave me the script. My Dinner with Andre became a very successful movie, but I, unfortunately, couldn't find any backers in Canada.

Returning to Manhattan was exciting, especially now that I had money. I learned the film industry was flourishing, and there was Broadway, great restaurants, and clubs to enjoy. It didn't take long before I felt like I had returned home with a new wife to a new life in the city I loved.

I found out my family had a relative who owned a bunch of brownstones on the Upper West Side of Manhattan. I contacted him, and he found us a fantastic apartment on 85th Street, a stone's throw from Central Park. It was perfect. It was a large one-bedroom with a big living room that featured a beautiful brick wall. It also had a terrace overlooking the back of the building. Elizabeth was ecstatic. I saw my future right there. This fantastic apartment sealed the deal. Everything was working out perfectly, and I was more than happy to leave Vancouver behind. I was sure I could find a way to stay close to my daughter. Given Elizabeth's feelings, I didn't know how, but somehow, I believed I would solve this problem.

I went back to Vancouver with great excitement and anticipation. All I needed to do now was sell my business, get my immigration papers, and leave my daughter behind. Was I in some kind of trance? What power did Elizabeth have over me that I was so willing to disrupt my entire life for her?

❧5❧

It took a couple of months to settle everything in Vancouver. I quickly found a buyer for my accounting practice, which had a good clientele and a capable assistant who handled things well in my absence. I received a decent amount for the business.

Getting my papers proved more challenging. I thought that perhaps I could be a dual citizen. But I learned the United States only recognizes dual citizenship if it was the last citizenship taken. I told the consulate I didn't realize I would lose US citizenship when I became Canadian. The consulate officer said I could apply to reinstate it, but it would take a long time. If I wanted to immigrate to the US immediately, I must apply as a Canadian. But before I could do that, I needed to rescind my US citizenship, which I did. Getting a green card proved easy since my parents sponsored me and I was a professional with a good-sized bank balance.

I don't remember how I broke this news to Christy and Natania. But I remember promising Christy I'd continue paying alimony and would visit periodically and send for Natania for visits to New York.

I finally moved to New York in late 1980. I loved our new apartment and soon got back into the joys of the city. Elizabeth and I enrolled in a filmmaking course at the New School. I also enrolled in a feature film accounting course. I didn't need the accounting class, but hoped to make connections there.

The filmmaking course was a lot of fun. I wrote a script, found actors, chose music, and did the editing. Elizabeth worked on my project, and I worked on hers. She finished hers, but my film never made it past editing. Clearly, I wasn't a filmmaker; I was the money man. We were now getting along great, and I once again felt hopeful about our relationship.

Elizabeth got a part in an off-off-Broadway play called *Conference of the Birds,* based on a twelfth-century Sufi poem. I finally got to see Elizabeth act. She was terrific, and I enjoyed the play.

The marital bliss didn't last for long. Soon, the Israeli guy was back in the picture. I became extremely jealous, but she denied that anything was happening. I didn't believe her. She started visiting "friends" without me and sometimes came home late at night. Once, I checked her diaphragm case and found it empty. Now I was sure that she was screwing around. We were fighting, but I couldn't break it off for some inexplicable reason. She still had power over me. I figured if she was screwing around, I should too. It didn't take long before I was having an affair with Nora, clearly a passive-aggressive reaction. A short time after that, our marriage finally broke apart, and Elizabeth was the one who ended it.

I thought the Israeli guy would win her heart, but she surprised me. Our downstairs neighbor, Bill, was her new conquest. She came in with him, looking joyous, and announced they were in love. Then she asked me to leave.

"You're asking me to leave my apartment?" I asked incredulously.

She said, "Yes. I don't think you would be happy here if I were living downstairs with Bill. I think it best to have a clean break."

"You're right. It would be best if I never see your face again."

Leaving this great apartment was a small price to pay for my freedom. I was genuinely relieved—it felt like the end of a bad dream. I grabbed a few things from the closet and walked away, thinking of her and Bill. I pity the fool, I thought to myself.

It was good I was involved with Nora, or I wouldn't have

had a place to stay. I would have had to take a cab downtown and stay at a hotel like a lonely dog. At least I was staying with someone who liked me.

What amazed me about my relationship with Elizabeth was that I knew early on it could turn out badly. I remembered walking around Lost Lagoon in Stanley Park the night before our wedding, wondering if I was setting myself up for another failed marriage. I was distressed that I agreed to exclude my dear daughter from our wedding. I also remembered her mood swings and how controlling she was. The wedding ring I planned to give her the next day was in my hand, and I almost threw it into the water a dozen times, but I couldn't. I even swung my arm like I was throwing a baseball, but I couldn't open my fingers. Something stopped me. It was like I was on this karmic train and couldn't get off until it was my stop. Logic and sensibility dictated it was all wrong. But it seemed there was nothing I could do to stop it.

It was crazy. I gave up my beautiful, loving daughter, a successful business, and good friends for a disturbed woman who brought out the worst in me. All the ethical values I held dear went out the window. I looked in the mirror and wasn't happy with what I saw, what I had become.

How did I get so lost? It wasn't that long ago that I followed a great guru, living a life devoted to ethical values. How did they all fade away like footprints on the beach during the rising tide? When I followed the path, I examined my life every day and prayed to overcome my failures. During this last year with Elizabeth, I was lost in our drama, engulfed in a well of lust, jealousy, and deceit.

Perhaps I could start anew now that Elizabeth was out of my life. Hopefully, the guy who had integrity was still somewhere within me. Maybe there's a reason all this happened. Perhaps there was a reason I'm in New York City now. I never even considered going back to Vancouver. Maybe God had a plan for me.

❧ 6 ❧

Free at last. I felt like a man just released from prison. It was amazing how quickly I stopped thinking about Elizabeth. Miraculously, I felt no anger, no resentment. Would you care about an abscessed tooth that the dentist extracted from your mouth? Now that the pain was gone, I had no desire to analyze that relationship or figure out what went wrong. I was relieved it was over and fortunate I could close that book and start anew.

Soon, I rented a nice apartment on 88th Street off Riverside Drive. It was easy to settle into my new life. There were plenty of secondhand stores on Amsterdam Avenue, and I found most of the things I needed. I arranged to pick up my stuff with Elizabeth, and she said she didn't want to be there when I arrived. That was fine with me. Bill was there to ensure I didn't steal any of the stuff I had paid for. It didn't matter. I only wanted my personal belongings. I took a cab over and had him wait while I got my things.

It didn't take long to settle into my new digs and reconnect with old friends. I saw Steve, who was still playing gigs and promoting free jazz concerts. I learned from Steve that my friend Murray, from Middle Village, had recently died at the age of 35. This was a real shock. Murray was one of my best friends, and I wished I could have seen him one last time.

Next, I reconnected with Perry. He was the same wonderful man I remembered so fondly. He was living in SoHo and in a committed relationship with a sweet woman named Terry. He still made music and had a few new albums to his credit. I asked him about Florin/Ishvara, and he said he lost contact with her a few years ago. He thought she may have died. It had been ten years since I last saw her, and I would have loved to see her again. Perry didn't remember her address in Harlem, so unfortunately, I couldn't check if her center was still there. I asked about the rest of the 11th Street gang. Gene, the beat poet, was out of jail and living in California. He didn't know where Mac or Eric was. He also heard Andy was hooked on heroin and no longer living in the East Village, which made me sad. I wished that there was some way I could help.

The old neighborhood looked much worse. There was graffiti everywhere. Many stores were abandoned, and some buildings had been demolished. Some areas looked like a war zone. Most of the hippies were gone, and all that remained was dirt, grime, garbage, and some fond memories. My building on 11th and B was gone. I would have liked to have seen my "Hole in the Wall" mural again, but it was now dust in the wind.

My new neighborhood was wonderful, with many well-kept brownstones and restaurants. Riverside Park was a block away, with its fantastic view of the Hudson River and New Jersey. There were lots of people jogging the four miles of the park. Many young professionals lived here, and exploring my new neighborhood as a free man felt great.

One morning, I was having a late breakfast at the corner diner, where they made great omelets. I was enjoying one when Steve walked in. Steve was an old friend from Vancouver and an initiate of Kirpal. Steve came over and smiled. I stood up, and we hugged. It was great seeing an old friend. But I felt guilty about eating an omelet. It was a sign I was no longer following the teachings. I was caught red-handed, but Steve was cool. I wasn't the only one who had fallen off the path.

Kirpal often said the greatest attribute of the mind is forgetfulness. Once the bond of love and devotion is broken, it's easy to go astray. I had forgotten Kirpal. But he never forgot me. Sometimes, in the middle of the night, I would hear the holy sound reverberating in the darkness. I would see golden light sprout forth, and for a few moments, I longed for him. But in the morning, it was all forgotten. Now, here was Steve, three thousand miles away from Vancouver in a city with eight million people, and he walked into a diner at the precise moment I was there. What are the odds?

Steve asked, "Have you heard about Arran? He recently denounced Ajaib and proclaimed Darshan as the true successor."

"Wow, that's a shock," I said.

"Arran wrote about it in a letter. I have a copy if you want to read it."

"I sure do."

Indeed, this was big news. Arran, my old boss and *Satsang* group leader, was the one who found Ajaib and proclaimed him the true successor to Kirpal. Arran was one of the top officials in that organization, and to denounce Ajaib now must have required irrefutable proof.

"Two Fools" detailed how Arran and Richard came to realize that Ajaib was not a perfect Master. Arran, a scholar on the teachings of the Masters, found significant discrepancies in some of Ajaib's writings and discourses. This concerned him. He and Richard happened to go to Darshan's ashram in Delhi. There, they had a private meeting with Darshan. Ever the scholar, Arran had a long list of highly esoteric spiritual questions that Darshan answered perfectly. After a long conversation, Arran was convinced Darshan was the true successor. "Two Fools" was well-written and convincing. I read it twice. I connected with it. There was still a spark of love for Kirpal somewhere within me. But I remembered the pain of losing Kirpal. How could I give my heart to another Master? I felt hopelessly stuck in the quicksand of my current circumstance and thought my life as a disciple was over.

I imagined Arran was now ostracized from the *Satsang* community since most Vancouver initiates were deeply involved with Ajaib. I felt bad for him. It took guts to admit he was wrong and announce it publicly. Arran must have felt terrible since he misled so many people. But one thing about Arran—he has integrity and could never live a lie.

Steve and I spent a wonderful day together, and he brought me up to date on many of my dear friends and fellow initiates. It had been about four years since I stopped seeing these people, and it was great to hear how they were doing.

❧ 7 ❧

She walked into my life on Wednesday, November 18, 1981.

Stan and I were having a drink at Aesop's Fables, a restaurant bar in Brooklyn Heights. It was a slow night, and we were the only ones seated at one end of the horseshoe-shaped bar. Then, she walked in, cool and confident, wearing a gray fedora like gangsters wore in 1930s movies.

She walked right past us and sat down at the other end of the bar, right in my line of vision. She was a knockout: classy, sophisticated, and gorgeous, about 5'3" with a slender figure, wavy chestnut hair, and stunning large blue eyes. I couldn't stop looking at her.

Stan soon realized he was talking to the wall. He smiled, got up, and said, "Go for it." All I could think about was how to approach this gorgeous creature. I considered many introductions, but they all seemed lame. Time was running out; I would lose my chance if I didn't act now.

So, I got up and slowly walked over to her, cool, relaxed, and confident. I still wasn't sure what to say. All I could muster on the spur of the moment was, "Hi, can I try on your fedora?" Oh my God, what a stupid thing to say; you sound like a *shlemiel*, I thought. But she smiled and handed me the hat.

To our amazement, the hat fit. She said, "I didn't think it would fit you since I have a small head."

"What do you think it means?" I offered. And so began a most memorable conversation. I told her I was a feature film accountant, which sounded much better than saying I was an unemployed accountant trying to break into the industry. And she replied that she, too, was in the entertainment industry. She was a publicist for the Folksbiene Yiddish Theater.

"You speak Yiddish?" I asked.

"Yes, I speak it fluently," she responded.

"Me too. Are your parents Holocaust survivors?" I asked. And she answered that they were.

And so began an amazing conversation with this remarkable woman. The more we spoke, the more commonality we found. I felt we must be kindred spirits.

The bar was closing, and she invited me to her apartment on Joralemon Street. We spoke until the wee hours of the morning. She told me what her parents went through during the Holocaust. Her father was in Auschwitz, and her mother survived a brutal work camp. They met in a Displaced Persons camp in Germany and married. They immigrated to America, and she was born in New York.

I told her the story of my parents and how the Nazi Einsatzgruppen (mobile killing units) had destroyed both my mothers' and fathers' villages and how they had miraculously survived.

We talked about being the firstborn to immigrant parents and the responsibilities we had, even as young children. Rosie spoke about how her parents relied on her since they didn't read English. Not only did she feel responsible for them, but she also wanted to protect them because of all the pain and suffering they had experienced. Her poor father was an alcoholic and the superintendent at the tenement they lived in on the Lower East Side. Even at an early age, she had been the adult in the family, and many decisions fell upon her young shoulders.

She told me how her father had wound up in the Bellevue Psychiatric Ward. He had been very drunk, and when the police picked him up, he had been rambling in Yiddish, which they thought was gibberish. It was twelve-year-old Rosie who had to go to Bellevue to get him released, which had required convincing multiple people he wasn't a threat to himself or others.

I could see she was a remarkable woman, full of love and compassion. She was bright and articulate, and I became more fascinated by the moment.

I told her that my parents relied on me as well. I had been the responsible one even when I was in elementary school, and that experience gave me confidence later in life. But my parents learned English, and by the time I had started high school, they could manage quite well.

We discovered we were both spiritual seekers. She was involved with a group called Path Works, which was a mix of spirituality, body work, and psychotherapy. I considered myself a spiritual seeker even though I wasn't following my guru.

We freely shared our lives, and the hours flew by quickly.

At about 2:00 a.m., I asked if I could stay over since I lived in Manhattan.

She replied, "I think it would be better if you went home. A cab won't be too expensive at this hour."

We kissed, and the kiss became passionate. I was hoping she would change her mind; I would have liked nothing better than to make love to her that night. I was smitten and could tell she liked me. But she was resolute in her decision, and I respected her for it. And so began my delightful courtship with Rosie.

❧ 8 ❧

Rosie and I dated regularly, but not exclusively. I was terrified of jumping into another serious relationship on the rebound. I wouldn't allow myself to fall in love again so soon.

After about six months of dating, Rosie asked me if I would like to split a share in a summer rental on Fire Island. Our good friends Nancy and Peter were taking a share along with two other couples that Rosie knew. Being in a beach community every weekend sounded great, so I agreed.

Fire Island is off the south shore of Long Island and has no roads; getting there requires a ferry or water taxi. It contained about a dozen communities and was famous for its pristine beaches. The house we rented was in the Water Island community, which was small and private, with about fifty homes. It's secluded and quiet, unlike other parts of the island. Water Island was situated between two hotbeds of rowdiness. To the south was The Pines, primarily gay and known for its high tea celebration each afternoon. To the north was Davis Park with its swinging singles scene.

We usually drove to Sayville on Friday afternoon, took a water taxi to Water Island, and got to our bungalow by early evening. Once there, we could fully relax. It was quiet and beautiful. We would meet the water taxi and buy *The New York Times* on Sunday mornings. We shared the bungalow with interesting people, and everyone got along famously.

Each weekend, one of the four couples was responsible for feeding everyone. Each couple planned the meals carefully and tried to ensure we had everything we needed for the weekend. There were no stores on Water Island; the nearest store was about a mile away up the beach at Davis Park. Nobody wanted to make the trek for supplies, so stocking up well for the weekend was important.

Each couple tried to outdo the others with gourmet meals and fine wine. It was a friendly competition, and no one took offense. What we got were great, creative meals. Each couple was nice and laid back, and we enjoyed each other's company. One of our housemates was Mark, a writer for a comedy show, and he had a fantastic sense of humor.

Our bungalow faced the bay and was a short walk to the private beach. About a half mile south was a nude beach we all liked to frequent. Hanging out there was wonderful; it reminded me of happy times at Galley Bay.

Each couple also had a week on the Island to themselves. We planned our week when Natania was with us. Rosie was so loving and caring toward Natania, who was nine then. That summer, my admiration for Rosie grew tremendously. I could see how she was with other people, especially with Natania. Rosie was loving, caring, and funny—a winning combination in my book.

*　*　*

When Natania graduated from public school, I flew to Vancouver to be part of that happy event. She had been a brilliant student and a fantastic, loving child. I spent a wonderful week seeing Natania every day after school and all day over the weekend. I also got to see some of my old friends. It was great being back in Vancouver, but New York was now my home.

One night, I took Christy out to dinner. Christy looked great and was very open and friendly, perhaps even a bit flirty. We had a good time, the conversation was light and easy, and at one point, those old loving feelings cropped up, and I had a slight desire to see if we could get back together. I wondered if she felt the same. But red flags were frantically waving somewhere in the back of my mind. Thankfully, I heeded the warning. It was a lovely evening. It was cordial, and we enjoyed a pleasant evening as old friends.

Leaving Natania was hard. I felt she hoped to see Christy and me back together, to see her family as whole. I told her I loved her and we would see each other soon. My heart was breaking, leaving my dear daughter.

Every summer, Natania came to New York for a month or more. We always planned fun trips during her visit.

*　*　*

Rosie and I had been dating for well over a year. One day as we walked in Central Park, she turned to me and said, "You know we both spend a lot of money on rent. If we move in together, we could save a lot. We see each other every weekend. Why not move in together to save on rent?"

She knew my practical side and hoped this would appeal to me.

I laughed. "Are you proposing?"

"No, I'm just trying to be practical."

"Really? It sounds like you want to take the relationship to the next level."

She admitted that she hoped we could live together but was not proposing.

"I like the practical touch," I told her.

At this point, I had a good job at Pan American Properties, and she was working at the Transit Authority. I thought about our respective apartments and which one we should live in. The more I thought about it, the more I believed a clean break from our past would be best. I still had a nice nest egg and figured I should buy a co-op rather than rent a new apartment. We found a lovely little co-op at One Grace Court in Brooklyn Heights.

When I told my father about the co-op, he asked how

much interest the bank charged for the mortgage, just like he did when he lent us the money for my first house. The amount was considerably higher than the interest on his CDs, so he offered us a loan at the bank's interest rate.

Shortly after buying the co-op, I went to visit my parents. I told my father about Rosie and how I was scared to commit, seeing how wrong I was with my second marriage.

My dad said, "Bernie, Rosie sounds like a nice Jewish girl who has never married. You say you love her. You should ask her to marry you before she changes her mind. You're no bargain with two ex-wives and a child."

I laughed and said, "You're right, Dad."

After several months of living together, I felt confident that Rosie was the one. It was around Christmas. I wanted to do it right and propose with an engagement ring. But I was afraid of buying one she didn't like. So, I found a nice zirconia engagement ring that was in a fancy box and proposed. Rosie was delighted and accepted my proposal immediately. A few days later, we went shopping for a real diamond ring.

When we announced the engagement, both sets of parents were delighted. Rosie's parents had been praying for this day for years, and even though they weren't wealthy, they wanted us to have a beautiful traditional Jewish wedding. Of course, Natania would be a junior bridesmaid, have a beautiful dress, and be loved and celebrated by the entire family.

Rosie resurrected my Jewish roots. After my Bar Mitzvah, I lost interest in Judaism and stopped attending services. Rosie wasn't religious, but she clearly loved our religion. She wanted a traditional Jewish wedding, and we looked for the right synagogue, met with rabbis, and discussed what we wanted during the wedding service. Her enthusiasm rekindled my faith.

The rehearsal dinner was at Rosie's parents' house in Brighton Beach. Both of our immediate families were there to start the festivities. Both sets of parents and many others at our special dinner were Holocaust survivors. Their joy knew no bounds, and we were both beaming with happiness. The conversations were mostly in Yiddish, and it felt wonderful to be speaking my first language.

❧ 9 ❧

I'd never seen my parents happier; my mother in her lilac gown with her blonde hair so beautifully coiffured, my father in his tux smiling so broadly. I had given them grief most of my life, and now, at long last, they enjoyed an event they never thought they would see. They finally had some *naches* (joy and pride) from their son. They weren't even invited to my first two weddings in Canada, presided over by justices of the peace.

My beautiful bride, Rosie, looked so spectacular in her snow-white, off-the-shoulder wedding gown. Her parents were over the moon. Their brilliant, rebellious daughter finally married the perfect guy. Okay, not perfect, but still very good. They never discounted me as a serious suitor, even though I had been married twice before and had a nine-year-old daughter. They loved me. I spoke Yiddish, had a good job, and came from a good Jewish family.

I was so happy on our wedding day, May 22, 1983. I'd finally found my soulmate, my magnificent Rosie. I had never met a woman who was so caring, so loving, so understanding. At 33 years old, it was Rosie's first marriage. I knew she wanted children, and so did I. I wanted to be a better father than I was for Natania. My beautiful, sensitive Natania was there to celebrate with us, and Rosie loved and always thought of her as her own daughter from day one. Her loving, nurturing, and welcoming nature was one of the many attributes that made me realize she was the one. They say the third time's the charm. It certainly was for me.

My father walked me down the aisle, and I stood, topped with my *tallit* (prayer shawl), before the rabbi under the *chuppah* (marriage canopy), beautifully decorated with flowers. *Pachelbel's Canon* started to play as I watched my bride walk toward me. Everyone stood as my beautiful Rosie, more radiant than any Tiffany jewel, walked slowly down the aisle, flanked by her beaming parents. The rabbi proceeded with the wedding ceremony. I lifted her veil and saw her smiling face; my happiness knew no bounds. We had written our vows, and Rosie's were eloquent and poignant. Rosie

May 22, 1983, our wedding day

circled me seven times, a tradition among Ashkenazi Jews who believe this ritual creates a magical wall that offers protection from evil and temptation. Then, a wine glass wrapped in a cloth was laid on the floor, and I stomped on it. The breaking of the glass is to remember the destruction of the Holy Temple in Jerusalem. Then, everyone shouted *Mazel Tov* (congratulations), and we were officially married.

We continued to the festive banquet hall. The receiving line seemed endless, but the joy was infectious. Our wedding was like a return to our roots, with Yiddish spoken freely and many loud relatives gushing with happiness. The photographer took hundreds of shots in the magnificent synagogue with its beautiful stained-glass windows. The band played our song, "Time in a Bottle," by Jim Croce, and we had our first dance as husband and wife, a waltz. Then everyone joined in the traditional *hora*, an exuberant circle dance that culminated with us being lifted on chairs to wild cheers from our guests. Our band was great, the food was delicious, and the joy and laughter were infectious. Everyone enjoyed the reception, and we couldn't have been happier.

We spent so much time going to every table and talking to every friend and relative that we didn't have a chance to sample the delicious food. Our meals were served, but by the time we returned to our table, the staff had already cleared them. By the end of the evening, we were starving. I don't think we even tasted our beautiful, multi-tiered wedding cake. But after the wedding, after the last guest had left, we went to our favorite Chinese restaurant for our wedding meal. It wasn't kosher, but it sure was satisfying.

❧10❧

Israel was the ideal place for our honeymoon in the summer of 1983. We were excited to see this miracle, this garden grown from the ashes of the Holocaust, this thriving democratic country in the Holy Land. This was the spiritual home of our ancestors that had survived eight wars with its Arab neighbors since declaring independence in 1948.

We didn't want to be part of a tour, so we planned three wonderful weeks of activities. We took El Al Airlines, and when we were about to land, they started playing "Jerusalem of Gold" over the intercom system. This brought tears to our eyes and to those of most of the people on the plane.

Jerusalem was a delight both visually and spiritually. The city truly turned golden when the sun was low in the western sky. I felt something special as I walked the streets, something ancient and holy.

One of the first things we did was visit the Western Wall, also known as the Wailing Wall, the holiest site in Judaism. It was part of the great Second Temple built by Herod. Many people prayed at the wall, and seeing these various segments of Jewish society praying together was inspiring. There were Hasidim, Orthodox, and secular Jews, and soldiers with Uzis strapped to their backs, all praying to our one God. It was a common belief that your wish would come true if you wrote it on paper and pushed it into a crevice on the Western Wall. Rosie wrote that we wanted babies.

Even though there was fighting on the northern border

with Lebanon, we felt safe throughout our Israeli trip. Both men and women soldiers were there protecting the country. Military duty was compulsory for all Israelis except the Hasidim, the ultra-orthodox sects.

We were invited to share a meal with a Hasidic family on the seventh night after our wedding. This was arranged because we spoke Yiddish, the Hasidim's primary language. Our hosts were a young couple with half a dozen children, and it was delightful to speak Yiddish with them. They found out it had been seven days since our marriage. Traditionally, the *Sheva Bruchot*, the seven blessings, is recited after the wedding to celebrate the sanctity of the marriage. We weren't sure if the *Sheva Bruchot* had been recited at our wedding, so the host said now would be a perfect opportunity to bless our union. I couldn't read the prayers since I'd forgotten my Hebrew training. But our gracious host happily recited the blessings, and I repeated them. He was very understanding and didn't make me feel ashamed or inadequate.

After our meal, we went to their synagogue, where the congregation welcomed me. Someone helped me recite the prayer for putting on my *tallit*, my prayer shawl. I was so moved by the passion and fervor of their prayer that it didn't matter that I didn't understand the words. I understood the love of God reverberating in the prayer.

The women were sequestered in the balcony with a barrier in front of them, so we couldn't even see a finger sticking out, which Rosie tried to do.

I spoke to a Hasidic man after the service. To my surprise, he was an ex-hippie and ex-acidhead from Australia who found his spiritual master, a Hasidic rabbi. He had come to this path about twelve years earlier, about the same time I came to Kirpal. What impressed me was his devotion, his love of God. He said he made his living as a scribe and was in the middle of writing a Torah scroll. He told me this would take about eighteen months to complete, and the scroll would be unusable if there were even one mistake. He bubbled over with love and enthusiasm as he told me his story. Once, I had deep feelings for God and my guru. I envied his devoutness, his simple, focused life. I started to miss the feeling of spiritual love bubbling up in my heart, the joy that devotion brings, the peace from meditation, and the clarity of purpose one feels while on a spiritual path.

We said our goodbyes to our host and returned to the King David Hotel. From our window, we could see the Western Wall and the great Muslim mosque called Dome of the Rock, the fourth most holy site in Islam. Looking out at this incredible city, the ancestral and spiritual home of our people, Christians, and Muslims, I couldn't help feeling the holiness of this city of gold.

The next day, we walked the Stations of the Cross—the Via Dolorosa—the path Jesus took on his way to crucifixion, which started in the Muslim quarter and ended at the Church of the Holy Sepulchre. We learned there are fourteen stations, each an actual location where a significant event in Jesus's martyrdom occurred. The first station was where Pontius Pilate condemned Jesus to death. The last station was where Jesus was laid to rest in a tomb. Each station was clearly marked. Walking in the footsteps of Jesus was profound. People were praying and sobbing along the route. I couldn't help but feel the holiness and sanctity in every step where Jesus suffered, dragging a heavy cross as he staggered toward martyrdom.

* * *

One of the most intense experiences was Yad Vashem, the World Holocaust Remembrance Center in Jerusalem. In Hebrew, *Yad Vashem* means "a memorial and a name." The center is dedicated to preserving the memory of the Jews who were murdered, telling the stories of the survivors, honoring Jews who fought against their Nazi oppressors, and memorializing the Gentiles who selflessly aided Jews in need.

The center displays the systematic persecution of the Jews

by the Nazis. The oppression had started in 1933 with the stripping of their citizenship and vandalizing of their businesses and escalated into pogroms in which Nazi-instigated attacks had killed Jews. By 1938, many Jews had been sent to one of the numerous concentration camps or evicted from their homes in occupied Nazi territories and forced into slum-like overcrowded ghettos. The ghettos had been a stepping-stone to the extermination camps, where millions of Jews were slaughtered, or to forced-labor camps where Jews were often worked to death. In 1941, the Nazis had unleashed the Einsatzgruppen (mobile killing units), who had been responsible for killing another million Jews, including most of my family. In total, an estimated seventeen million people had been killed by the Nazi regime, including more than six million Jews.

The exhibit showed heartbreaking photos of this barbaric progression from persecution, destruction, and slave labor to wanton murder. While looking at photos of Jews just liberated from Auschwitz, Rosie noticed a picture of her uncle Rachmil, who survived. There he was, among the emaciated, among the walking skeletons. This made it even more personal. As you go through the exhibit, your heart breaks and keeps breaking the deeper you wander into that hell that the Jews and others went through. This was the hell that Rosie's and my parents experienced firsthand. Rosie's father survived Auschwitz, and her mother survived being in a forced labor camp.

Another exhibit that tore at our hearts was the Hall of Names. Displayed here were thousands of photographs of those killed in the Holocaust. We saw faces that looked so familiar. It was like looking at our family photo album. These were our relatives: our grandparents, aunts, uncles, cousins, all murdered during that genocide, family that we would never get to know and love.

Yad Vashem also honored the non-Jews who risked their lives to aid Jews during the Holocaust by creating "The Righteous Among Nations." We saw pictures of Oskar Schindler, Raoul Wallenberg, and many other brave souls. I asked my mother if she had submitted Jakub's name, the farmer that hid her for three years. Unfortunately, she couldn't because she didn't remember his last name. But in my heart, he was there, recognized and thanked.

Despite all the suffering, death, and destruction that my people underwent, we persevered and succeeded, and now we had our homeland, the glorious miracle of Israel. I was so proud of this magnificent, tiny country, democratic and prosperous, despite being surrounded by enemies.

*   *   *

Jerusalem is a cosmopolitan city with great restaurants, clubs, and an active nightlife. One night, we were at a restaurant enjoying a delicious meal when we heard our wedding song played, "Time in a Bottle," by Jim Croce. We were so moved that we got up and danced.

We spent a glorious week in Jerusalem, and now it was time to see the rest of this amazing country. We rented a car for two weeks and traveled the length and breadth of Israel. First, we went south. We bathed in the Dead Sea, where we floated like corks, unsinkable. On a scorching hot day, we found Ein Gedi and cooled off under the waterfall. In Jericho, we saw the remains of a ten-thousand-year-old civilization. At that time, it was still under Israeli rule, but it returned to the Palestinians in 1994.

In Eilat, we enjoyed this resort city on the Red Sea. The highlight for me was scuba diving in the Red Sea, one of the best locations in the world. We stayed at The Sonesta, the only five-star hotel in Israel at the time. The hotel was in Taba, which was part of Israel, but was later returned to Egypt.

We also dined with a Bedouin family. We were invited into their tent and sat on carpets. We enjoyed how our host made traditional bread on an open fire. Our meal was delicious, and our hosts were most gracious. We were even introduced to their camels. One took a fancy to Rosie. I have a picture of this large camel smiling down at Rosie.

We then traveled north, along the Mediterranean Sea, to Tel Aviv, a thriving metropolis with great beaches, where we enjoyed swimming in the Mediterranean Sea. Then, we traveled to Natanya, Caesarea, and Haifa and wandered the beautiful Bahá'í gardens.

We stayed in a kibbutz near the Lebanese border, where Rosie's relatives lived. During our tour of the kibbutz, we marveled at the rich agricultural land forged out of a desert. Everyone lived communally and ate together in a large common hall. No one had apartments, just motel-like rooms with small bathrooms. Things were well organized, and everyone had assigned tasks. Childcare was communal, and children lived in separate barracks from an early age. The family unit was the entire kibbutz. The kibbutz hosted many volunteers from America and Europe, and the vast majority were from Germany. Maybe some were even the children of Nazis.

Next, we headed west to the ancient city of Safed, located in Upper Galilee and perched atop one of the highest mountains in the area. Safed is one of Judaism's four Holy Cities.

After the expulsion of the Jews from Spain in 1492, many prominent rabbis, including the great Rabbi Isaac Luria, found their way to Safed, which became the center for learning Kabbalah, a set of mystical teachings meant to explain the relationship between the unchanging, eternal God and the mortal, finite universe.

This beautiful city was a joy to explore, with its cobbled streets, ancient sites, vibrant art galleries, and panoramic views.

From Safed, we went to the delightful port city of Tiberias on the Sea of Galilee, another one of the four Holy Cities (Jerusalem and Hebron round out the four). There, we enjoyed eating St. Peter's fish, a kind of tilapia.

Our three weeks flew by, and it was time to return home. What a glorious honeymoon this had been! We felt great pride in what the Israeli people had accomplished in 35 short years among hostile neighbors who had waged multiple wars. We felt a deep connection to our roots and vowed to return.

❧11❧

We were back in New York for a couple of months when we heard that Sant Darshan Singh, Kirpal's true successor, was on his 1983 world tour and in New York. In fact, he was speaking at Hunter College the next day, and Rosie was interested in attending.

We got to the main auditorium, which was filling up quickly, and took our seats. I didn't remember anyone from the *Satsangs* I attended in New York thirteen years ago. I could see people greeting each other with the traditional folding of their hands. I could see the excitement on their faces, the anticipation of seeing their guru, which was so familiar. Could it be? Could the love and light of Kirpal once again fill my soul?

When Darshan entered the stage, he slowly walked its length with folded hands, showering everyone with his loving glance. He began to speak, but I couldn't understand half of what he was saying. Kirpal had had a deep, resonating voice, but even with his thick Indian accent, I could understand every word. Darshan's pitch was much higher, and most of what he said was lost to me.

While sitting there, all I did was compare him to Kirpal. He looked smaller; he didn't have a long, flowing white beard; his gaze wasn't intoxicating me. I started doubting he was a true Master, regardless of what Arran wrote in the "Two Fools" letter. As the evening progressed, I even started questioning Kirpal despite my incredible spiritual experiences. Maybe I had outgrown the path. I convinced myself that following a guru was just a phase of my youth.

At the end of the talk, the people who wanted to get the Master's blessing formed two rows facing each other with room for Darshan to walk between. I don't know why I joined a row, considering how I felt about the path at that moment. I thought of leaving, but my feet wouldn't move.

As Darshan walked toward me, I couldn't help myself. I said to him, "I remember you when I was at Sawan Ashram with Master Kirpal back in 1970."

Master Darshan looked me in the eyes so lovingly and sweetly and said, "Dear brother, I remember you. You should come to Kirpal Ashram (Darshan's new ashram in Delhi)." He then gave me a wonderful hug.

I felt waves of love flow through me. I felt bliss I hadn't felt since being at the ashram in India all those years ago. I was so blissed out that I almost walked into a telephone pole.

I walked with Rosie for a while without saying a word. She saw what had happened, and after some time, she asked, "Are you now back on the path?"

After a moment's reflection, I replied, "No. That was my past."

What amazed me was how the path kept cropping up every few months. It seemed like Kirpal wasn't ready to let me forget entirely.

❧12❧

I'd been working at Pan American Properties since 1981. This company was a large real estate investment trust owned by the British Coal Board Pension Fund. They held a portfolio of high-end properties valued at more than one billion dollars. One of its holdings was the Watergate complex, made famous by the Nixon administration.

My job title was data processing manager/internal audit manager, and I was an expert at using the TenMan system on IBM System 36/38. TenMan was a Chicago-based software company that sold an excellent tenant management software system. I had many dealings with TenMan and was instrumental in getting them SOX compliance to meet the requirements of the Sarbanes-Oxley Act that Congress had recently enacted. This act detailed the accounting standards for public companies. Being SOX-compliant was a boon for TenMan, and the management was grateful I helped make it possible.

One sunny Sunday in early 1984, I was walking across the Brooklyn Bridge with my trusty Canon A1 camera. I had developed a love of photography and often sought inspiration through the camera's viewfinder. What I found that day was inspiration of another kind. I had an epiphany as I got closer to Manhattan, scanning the thousands of buildings. The idea for my next business venture was born right there on the bridge. I thought to myself, why not sell the TenMan Property Management Software? I saw thousands of opportunities. And the strategy for forming my new venture became clear. I even conceived a name for my new company, Skyline Computer Systems.

After my epiphany, I called Frank, the president of TenMan, and made an appointment to see him the following week. I explained I wanted to create a dealership in New York to sell his software. He was intrigued, and we selected a day to meet.

I arrived at the office, conveniently located near O'Hare Airport. Frank showed me around and introduced me to his staff, some of whom I knew from telephone conversations.

When we were in Frank's office, he asked, "Why do you want a dealership? I would love to hire you as a salesman. You'd have a good base salary and make lots more on commission."

I said, "I think your software is great, and I know there are a lot of opportunities in New York and New Jersey. I know your software inside and out, and I also know what management wants. I can get people excited about TenMan, and I'm confident I will succeed."

Frank replied, "What do you know about the sales process? What do you know about marketing software? Do you know how much this venture will cost? Do you know how long it will take you before you make the first sale? There's a long sales cycle selling high-priced computer software. When you have your own business, the expenses pile up quickly. You better be well funded."

I took this in and realized he was right. What the hell was I getting myself into?

He added, "I like you and think you will succeed. How about starting off as a salesman? I'll set you up, and we can make a deal so when you're ready, you can have your own dealership."

It was tempting, but in my gut, I knew if I went down that road, I would be his salesman for a very long time. I thought about his proposition, carefully composing an answer.

I said, "Frank, your offer is very tempting. I started two successful businesses in Canada, and I like being my own boss.

I have money to invest, and I'm willing to take the chance. What I need is help with the sales process and marketing. What I need is assurance that all leads for my territory are exclusively mine and a list of your customers in my territory, so I can build a good reference list."

Frank looked at me for a long moment, smiled, and said, "Kid, you got balls. I like your passion. By starting a business, you will work your ass off to make it successful. I think you just may succeed. I will help you."

Frank then introduced me to his top salesman, Nate. We spent many hours going through the pricing and marketing literature. He also did a detailed demonstration of the software as he would for prospective clients. His presentation was excellent. He showed the system's strengths, with compelling reasons to buy it. I learned a lot from him.

I stayed for one more day. We ironed out an exclusive marketing and sales agreement for New York and New Jersey the next day. Frank was generous with the margin; I got 40% on software, 15% on hardware, and 100% on implementation.

He then asked me if I had a budget. I didn't have a detailed budget, but I did a rough calculation of what I needed to start the business. We sat down and reviewed the numbers: an IBM System, office rent in New York, a security deposit, furniture, and a secretary. Frank suggested it could take three or four months before my first sale. That was more expensive than I anticipated. I knew I could swing it if the hardware was out of the equation.

I asked, "Is it possible to lease the hardware?"

He asked, "What collateral do you have?

I said, "I own a co-op in Brooklyn Heights."

"Never put up your home," he advised. He said, "I'll arrange a lease and cosign. Also, I have a new customer in New York. I'll pay you to do the training. This way, you can earn some money while getting set up."

I was floored by his generosity. The set-up and training of a new customer could provide weeks of work and earn me thousands of dollars. I thanked him profusely.

His final advice was, "Get a nice office in a good location; it doesn't have to be big. I have a good feeling about you. I think you will succeed and make us both lots of money, providing you survive the first six months."

I figured that Frank felt he had a winning solution. If I were successful, he would win. If I failed, he would win by hiring me as a salesman with an established office. Frank was a smart businessman, and I had great respect for him. Perhaps he could be my mentor. He built a very successful business with top-notch talent.

❧13❧

A few weeks later, in early 1984, I signed a lease for a small office in the Helmsley Building on 44th and Park Avenue. I called Frank and told him the good news. He said I picked a good location, right by Grand Central Station. Setting up my IBM system and having my furniture delivered took a few more weeks.

My office consisted of three rooms: an entry where my secretary Rosemary sat, an empty office for future expansion, and a large office that also served as a demo center. I leased an IBM System 36 computer, a twelve-inch monitor, and a dot matrix printer. One of the first things I did was compile a good reference list. TenMan had some clients in New York, including my old firm.

I visited each and asked how they liked the system. Most of them needed some help or clarification, which I provided. They were happy to have a resource in New York, and many agreed to serve as references. TenMan gave me a list of leads, and I called them and invited them to my office for a demo. We advertised in property management journals. We bought mailing lists and sent out informative mailers. We did telemarketing to get prospects to come to the office for a demonstration. Both my secretary and I did marketing.

It was a challenge to get people excited while viewing our software on a tiny monitor. So, I peppered my sales pitch with questions about their business and showed them the comprehensive management reports the system produced. My knowledge of property management combined with my expertise in TenMan resulted in sales. In a short time, we were doing well, and

I hired more people. Selling TenMan, along with IBM mini-computers and implementation, produced sales between $75,000 and $125,000, netting 30% to 40% profit. But, during my marketing efforts, I found many smaller property management firms that wanted to computerize but couldn't afford the TenMan system.

In 1985, I attended the Computer Expo and was impressed with the growth of the personal computer market. I learned that IBM had released the AT personal computer, which was business-worthy, and Novell had issued NetWare, enabling multiple PCs to work together as a multi-user network, like mini-computers. I thought I could make a fortune if only a PC-based property management program existed.

A few days later, I called Frank and asked if TenMan was working on a PC-based solution.

Frank said, "PCs are toys, and I don't see a major market for them. However, there is a small software company in Chicago that just came out with a PC-based property management system. It's the Softa Group, and its software is Skyline Property Management System."

I thought this could be what I was hoping for, and the name was perfect. I took a few seconds to calm down, not to sound too excited.

I said, "From my marketing efforts, I came across small property managers looking for an inexpensive solution. Do you mind if I evaluate the PC-based solution?"

Frank said, "Give it a try if you like. But I bet you'll find it's not worth the effort. You'll be spending as much time on these little deals as you do on one of ours. You'll make pennies rather than dollars."

Frank gave me a contact at the Softa Group. After I hung up, I called and made an appointment to meet the owners and see the software.

I flew to Chicago that week and met the three guys who started Softa, and I had an in-depth demonstration of the Skyline System. It was easy to use and powerful enough to do the job, even for property managers with a large portfolio. They were delighted to sign me up as their second independent distributor. I also got certified on NetWare, the Novell networking system that enabled me to offer a turnkey multi-user system using PCs.

In 1985, I had two proven software solutions. By 1986, ninety percent of my sales came from PCs. I showed both systems to my larger prospects, and most wanted the PC. Frank was wrong about making pennies with PC sales. These sales were profitable, and it took significantly less time to close a deal.

By the end of 1986, it became clear I needed to drop TenMan, but I didn't want to get stuck with an expensive IBM System 36. I had one promising prospect. To seal the deal, I sold my IBM hardware at a good discount.

I had sold TenMan for about two years and had been able to close about sixteen deals. Frank was delighted since this was much better than he had expected. I had more than doubled his client count in New York.

With PCs now in the mainstream for businesses, I hardly had any prospects left for mini-computers. With a heavy heart, I knew I had to call Frank.

I said, "I want to be perfectly open with you. Most of my sales come from PCs. Selling TenMan is getting harder. I always lead with TenMan, but many clients also want to see the PC solution. Are you planning to come out with a PC solution?"

Frank said, "No. My strategy is to add more functionality to our software. We are adding features that will blow up the market. The PC solution will only do a fraction of what we will soon be able to do."

"When will your new version be ready?" I asked.

"In about a year," Frank answered.

I knew that software manufacturers always exaggerate new releases. I couldn't understand why Frank could not see where the industry was going. I had to cut my ties and knew it would be painful.

I said, "Frank, selling two competing systems is killing me. It confuses prospects, makes my job much harder, and lengthens the sales cycle. I asked both you and Softa for features unique to the NY residential market. They delivered, and you passed on it. They are hungry for sales and turn around enhancements quickly. I'm sorry, but I must go with them. I really appreciate all you did for me and will be eternally grateful, but I have a business to run, and I must do what's best for it."

Frank was clearly upset. He could only say, "What about the lease on the System 36?"

I said, "It's already paid off. I sold it to one of my new clients."

This finalized it. Now, I didn't even have the hardware to show TenMan. He wished me good luck and quickly hung up.

It didn't take long for PCs to become the preferred computer solution. Property managers raved about the Skyline System, and we installed our system in some of the largest firms in the greater New York area. TenMan quickly disappeared as a competitor. We even converted TenMan clients to Skyline. I loved my business and devoted much time to making it successful.

Incorporating the ethical principles that I learned from Kirpal became the key to my success. I did my best to be honest and genuinely care for my clients and employees. I understood you can't fake respect and succeed. To be authentic, you need to not only have respectful words, but also respectful thoughts. When you genuinely like people and treat them well, they will trust you and become your customers, provided your product satisfies their needs.

❧14❧

Rosie and I decided to start a family when I was 38 and she was 33. Many months had passed without luck. We finally went to a fertility clinic and even tried in-vitro without success. Rosie wouldn't give up hope; she even agreed to a surgical procedure as a last-ditch effort.

A few days before her surgery, Rosie came to my office and nonchalantly asked, "Have you seen today's newspaper?"

I said, "No, why?"

And then she showed me the headline.

Bernard Ross is going to be a father!

Rosie had stopped at one of the souvenir shops in Times Square and created the headline. I couldn't believe my eyes. I was so happy. I grabbed Rosie, and we started laughing and jumping for joy all over the office. My staff was also delighted. I left work to be with her and celebrate our good fortune. Rosie's prayer at the Western Wall in Israel was answered.

After nearly seven months of pregnancy, Rosie started to have contractions. We were very concerned, and the doctor put her on some medication to stop them. This was a crucial time since the baby needed at least another month to grow.

But our Jonathan couldn't wait to enter the world, and Rosie went into labor at the start of her seventh month. Jonathan was born at Mount Sinai Hospital in New York City on November 29, 1985, and weighed about four and a half pounds. Fortunately, the hospital had an excellent neonatal unit. Even so, they gave him a fifty percent chance of survival right after his birth. He had a brain hemorrhage and needed blood. I donated my blood for the transfusion. After surviving those first few days, Jonathan's chances became considerably better.

Jonathan was a fighter and made good progress. Our tiny son was in an incubator, and we decorated it with our pictures. Rosie practically lived at the hospital, and I went every day after work and stayed late into the night to be with him as much as possible.

After a month, we came home with our precious son. He was growing nicely, and there weren't any serious problems with his health. Once he was home, we realized our tiny one-bedroom co-op wasn't adequate for a family. So, Rosie began to research where to relocate.

We chose Westchester County since Long Island was very congested, and traffic was notoriously bad. Rosie decided on Chappaqua, since it had the best schools. Our son wasn't even a year old, and Rosie was already planning his education.

We found a beautiful Tudor in Chappaqua in our price range. We sold our co-op in Brooklyn Heights for more than double what we had paid and, thus, had a solid down payment for our new home.

Rosie wanted more children, and this five-bedroom house would be ideal for our family. There were lots of new babies in the community, and Rosie made many new friends. She loved being home with our baby and was dreaming about more children in the future.

My commute from Chappaqua to Manhattan was easy. It took about fifty minutes to get to Grand Central Station. The commute provided a perfect time to write proposals and plan my day using my laptop. Many prospects came to our office to see a demonstration of our software, but some prospects wanted us to come to them. This became the norm as portable demonstration equipment got better. During our third year, I hired a salesman to handle demonstrations outside Manhattan. Our territory was all of New York, New Jersey, and Connecticut.

The Softa Group, which had developed Skyline, were adding dealers all over the country. We met in Chicago each year, and my dealership always won the trophy for the most sales. One year, the Softa Group was generous and rewarded me with an all-expense paid trip to Club Med in The Bahamas. We took young Jonathan and had a blast.

With dedication and focus, I had built a very successful company. As we grew, I expanded our offices twice and even opened an office in Boston.

❧15❧

"Sunlight fell upon the wall; the wall received a borrowed splendor.
Why set your heart on a piece of earth, O simple one?
Seek out the source which shines forever."

-Rumi

One day, Rosie got a card in the mail stating that Darshan was returning to New York. It was interesting that the card came to her rather than me. Darshan was scheduled to be in New York for about a week, and the meetings were all at the Roosevelt Hotel, only a few blocks from my office.

The card advertised the New York portion of Darshan's 1988 World Tour and was due to begin in a few days. I attended the first event of the tour, a meditation session. This was the first time I sat in meditation in many years. Soon after closing my eyes and repeating the sacred mantra, I had an incredible inner experience, resulting in tremendous joy and bliss. I felt a section of my heart, one that had been closed for years, open and fill with love, the sweet, wonderful love of God. I had forgotten how beautifully intoxicating meditation was.

That evening, I attended the *Satsang*, the Master's talk. As I watched Darshan speak, I saw his form transform into Kirpal's many times. I witnessed a golden aura around him and now understood what he was saying. Darshan spoke of Kirpal, and I could see his tremendous love for him. Even though sixteen years had passed since I last saw Kirpal, I felt the same love welling up in my heart. This was a magical evening. I hadn't been expecting such a strong reaction, but I could not deny it. The program ran late into the night, and many people spoke of their experiences with Master Kirpal. Hearing those experiences fueled my longing for my Master. It was already very late, and the moderator asked if anyone else would like to share remembrances of their time with Kirpal. I found my hand raised and was called on before I realized what I had done.

I was ushered to the podium and wasn't sure what to say. I looked out and saw more than a thousand people looking at me. I was nervous and began by introducing myself, saying when I was initiated and when I was in India with Kirpal. Then, suddenly, I was telling the story of the hair from my Master's beard. Tears were in my eyes as I described Kirpal's beauty and what this precious gift meant. My heart overflowed with love and gratitude for Kirpal as I relived this magical event. I looked toward Darshan, and he looked directly at me. His look of love and understanding filled me with bliss. I knew right then and there that Darshan was the true successor, and I was now back on the path. That night in the Master's assembly changed me forever.

How will Rosie deal with it? I wondered? Well, it didn't take too long to find out.

Rosie had never seen this side of me before. She saw me with other initiates and didn't understand the *bhakti*, the love and devotion spilling out of everyone. She thought she knew me. Now, I was acting so differently, so strangely. She was worried this could end our marriage. She thought perhaps she had married a Martian. She wondered if I was part of some crazy cult.

I couldn't explain the phenomenon that overtook me. The more I tried to explain it, the weirder I sounded and the more concerned she became. Fortunately, Tom, a dear friend I knew from my days with Kirpal in India, came to the rescue. He explained everything clearly and logically. Tom stayed with us in Chappaqua, and he and Rosie spoke late into the night. She finally realized I wasn't a different person. I was still her loving husband, but now there was another dimension to my being.

The last day of Darshan's visit was hard on us all. This was especially true for me since the Master had only been back in my life for a few blessed days. Darshan's son, Raji was often on the stage with him, and on the last day, he could not hold back his tears. I felt a strong sense that Darshan was going to die soon. Behind all the love and joy, I felt a sense of foreboding. I remembered the unbearable pain when Kirpal died. I wondered, Lord, will I have to go through it again?

I remembered that during the 1983 tour, Master Darshan had invited me to the ashram. I knew I needed to go to India again before it was too late. I wanted to be there for Kirpal's birthday on February 6. I wrote and was permitted to come at the beginning of February. I went for two weeks since I couldn't leave the business for longer.

During the months leading up to my trip, I followed all the precepts of the path again. I meditated regularly, ate a strict vegetarian diet, and wrote my diaries and devotional poetry again. I also attended *Satsang* each week, reconnecting with old friends and making many new ones. And Rosie was mostly fine with it. She could see I was happier, less stressed, and, hopefully, a better husband.

~16~

I arrived in India on January 31, 1988, and stayed at Darshan's new Kirpal Ashram. There were only a few Westerners there. The Master's wonderful greeting made me feel like a prodigal son returning home.

Darshan called me his dear brother and called his own initiates his dear sons or daughters. I was amazed by how much access I had to the Master and saw him often. He was so charming, so open, and so loving. One of my worries was I would take him as my guru in place of Kirpal. But I knew that Kirpal was my guru. What amazed me was that everything Darshan did reminded me of Kirpal. He was reconnecting me to Kirpal, not to himself. I had lost that connection, and Darshan was reestablishing and strengthening it. It was uncanny how his words and actions brought Kirpal to the forefront of my mind. We were having dinner with Darshan one evening, and he started to chew his drink. Immediately, I remembered a talk where Kirpal recommended that we should "chew our drinks and drink our food for good digestion." Drinking your food meant chewing it until it was liquid, and chewing your drink helped the digestion of liquids. It was the little things, the endearing remembrances of my time with Kirpal, that Darshan somehow rekindled.

One day, I was in the meditation room when somebody announced the Master was coming out of his house. People started lining up to get his *darshan*. People were hurrying to get a good spot as if a few feet closer would make a big difference. As I walked, I saw a frail older woman escorted by two younger women. The woman was shaking uncontrollably, and the two women were practically carrying her. Once we were lined up, someone brought a chair for her. Her shaking continued as we waited for the Master.

After a short wait, I saw the Master walking toward us, lovingly greeting each person. Just as he got to the older woman, she forced herself to stand, even though her body was severely shaking. When the Master met her eyes, her shaking stopped. The Master showered her with divine love. I could see her smile, forgetting all her pain. And then the Master did something I had never seen before. The Master blew a kiss to her like one would to a dear child. It was such a soft and tender expression of his boundless love. I felt privileged and grateful to have witnessed it. I was so moved I could have melted on the spot.

Then, it was my turn to receive the Master's *darshan*. I looked into his beautiful eyes as he showered me with love that filled me with bliss and happiness. It filled me to the brim. And then, to my surprise and delight, he also blew a kiss to me. No words can express the love and gratitude I felt at that moment.

I was invited to speak during Kirpal's birthday celebration. Thousands of people attended, and I recalled some of my time with Master Kirpal and read a poem. This was a great honor, especially for someone who had left the path for twelve years. At times, I didn't feel worthy of all this attention, of all these honors. But most of the time, I was in bliss, and the past didn't matter.

I was sitting six to eight hours daily in meditation, having tremendous experiences. Usually, speaking about our inner experiences is not allowed, but Master Darshan permitted me to share a particularly memorable experience. During one meditation, I saw an enormous bright golden light. Out of that light, the radiant form of Baba Sawan Singh (Kirpal's guru) appeared, and as I looked in awe and wonder, he changed into Master Kirpal, and after a time, he changed into a young Sikh with a black beard. The radiant forms I saw were crystal clear, especially the eyes of each Master. I was in absolute bliss as I viewed them. Each one lasted for several moments before turning into the next.

Seeing the radiant form of the Master is our hope and prayer before every meditation. It is a blessed milestone signifying entry into the astral plane, a starting point of one's spiritual journey into the higher regions. The radiant form cannot be obtained simply by one's efforts, regardless of how hard we try or how many hours we sit in meditation. It comes by grace and brings sweet bliss and deep gratitude for the guru. It affirms this path is real, for the mind cannot conjure up the radiant form. After this experience, I felt profound joy and tremendous gratitude, but also a deep sadness.

As I sat in the stillness of the meditation room after my sitting, I began to wonder what the meaning of this vision was. How come Master Darshan was not there? Why was there a new radiant form? I had the dreaded feeling that this was a sign that Darshan was going to die soon, and this young Sikh—Darshan's son Raji—would be his successor. I was distraught. I had been back on the path for less than a year and was destined to have my heart broken again. At the first opportunity, I requested a private session with the Master.

I saw him late that night. I was alone with him in his office and told him of my vision.

He looked at me with loving eyes and said, "You know when the Master calls, I have to go."

My heart sank when he said this. He further clarified, "But it's not imminent." This gave me a bit of hope. He also permitted me to share this experience with others. Perhaps this experience would help with the transition to the new Master when the time comes.

While there, I thought this was a golden opportunity to ask questions.

I started by saying, "Master, I don't understand. I had so much love for Master Kirpal, and after his death, I left the path. I didn't follow the teachings for twelve years. Then, when I saw you in New

York on the last tour, the love and devotion was suddenly back, as strong as ever. It was like a switch in my heart was flipped open."

The Master looked at me sweetly and said, "This was your karma."

These simple few words triggered a clear understanding. I knew being off the path for all those years was absolutely necessary. If not, I wouldn't have moved to New York, married Rosie, or had my son, Jonathan. All the guilt for being a fallen disciple vanished. I could see clearly that this was all part of the divine plan. It was all meant to be.

While I was at it, I thought of another question. "When I was in India in 1970, I met you and asked if you would send me some of your poems. But they never arrived, and I foolishly believed that you weren't the true successor because I didn't get them."

Master smiled and said, "I remember that several people asked for my poems, which I sent. You know the Indian postal service is notoriously bad. Can I be held responsible for them losing the letter?"

I apologized for asking such a stupid question. And he said, "Not at all. It's good to get that off your chest."

My short visit was ending. The final day arrived, and with a heavy heart, I was leaving the Master. One of the attendees led me to Darshan's office. There, he gave me a beautiful woolen meditation shawl, and his wife—Mata Ji—offered lots of *prashad* (blessed food) to take for our *Satsang*. Master and Auntie walked me out since the taxi was already waiting. Master looked lovingly at me and gave me a big hug.

With tears in my eyes, I said, "Master, I'm leaving heaven."

He responded, "Then take heaven with you."

I left his residence and got into the taxi, trying to hold back my tears. Then I realized I didn't have my shoes. I stopped the cab and walked up the steps to retrieve them. Master and Auntie were still there, smiling and waving goodbye.

Shortly after leaving the ashram, I wrote the following poem about meditation on my third eye:

HEAVEN'S DOOR

In this world of turmoil and uncertainty
Your door is my safe harbor.
It is a calm and tranquil lagoon
Where I can focus on Your gifts
And enjoy the celestial rhapsody.

Your door is the launching pad of my aspirations
And the breakwater against an ocean of desires.
Tucked away behind my eyebrows,
It's the core of my heart.
The beginning of the end
Of mind's endless dialogue.
Your door is the womb of my soul
Where the embryo of my attainment
Is nurtured by the nectar of Your love.
It's the inlet to the sea of immortality
Where I can swim in eternal bliss.

Your door is my prayer mat and my Mecca
Your door is my temple and my confessional.
It's the secret
Behind my almost imperceptible smile
That melts away adversity.

Amidst my prayers and supplication
Amidst my pining and yearning
for higher experiences and greater bliss,
I pray that I may ever be grateful
For this gift, this seat at Your golden door.

When I returned to New York, there was talk that the
Master was planning another world tour next year. This bright-
ened our hopes. I remembered him saying his death was not

Sant Darshan Singh Ji Maharaj
(1921 – 1989)

imminent. But three and a half months after I left India, the gracious Master, Sant Darshan Singh Ji Maharaj, died on May 30, 1989.

ᔧ17ᔨ

After Master Darshan's death, Sant Rajinder Singh became the Master. He was there to wipe away our tears and soothe our broken hearts. More than two hundred thousand initiates of Kirpal and Darshan needed consolation. He visited all the centers and filled our hearts with hope and love. We needed to see him often, for great was our loss and deep was our despair.

This period was especially hard for me. It had only been nine months since I reconnected with Kirpal through the loving grace of Master Darshan. I was back on the path after so many years of being away, and I was afraid I would slip back into the fog of forgetfulness. In India with Master Darshan, I had prayed for a short rope to tether me to this sacred path. I hoped that Master Rajinder would keep me close.

One of the first meetings with Rajinder was in Bowling Green, Virginia. I drove down with Rosie and three-year-old Jonathan. Once the Master arrived, he walked through the crowd and greeted each person. When he got to us, I introduced Rosie and Jonathan.

Jonathan looked up at the Master with defiance and said, "I'm not Jonathan; I'm Mickey Mouse."

The Master smiled, patted me on the back, and said, "Don't worry, he will turn out all right."

Right then, I knew Rajinder would help us grow on this path of love and light.

A few months after my meeting with Rajinder, one of the Science of Spirituality representatives asked if I wanted to be

330

a group leader for Westchester and Rockland counties in New York. This entailed preparing weekly meetings for existing members and outreach to attract new people. It also involved being the local face of the mission. I didn't want to take the responsibility alone, so James offered to do it with me. We rented space in a yoga center in Nyack, NY.

Preparing for the weekly *Satsang* was fun. We found a topic, researched the literature for quotes from the Masters, and took turns running the meeting. One day, a Hasidic man came to our meeting. Afterward, he asked many questions about our meditation practices and mantra, with a particular interest in the regions or planes of creation. He told us he was a rabbi and a Kabbalah teacher. We answered his questions as best we could and invited him to return. We also told him our teacher, Rajinder, was planning a tour stop in New York in the next few months. He gave us his address so we could notify him when the Master visited New York.

It was most unusual that a Hasid would venture out of their small circle. We weren't surprised when he didn't return to our weekly meetings. After many months, Rajinder came to New York and held a program in one of the hotels by the airport. On Sunday, the Master gave a talk and offered initiation later that afternoon. About fifty or sixty people stayed for initiation, and to my surprise, the Hasidic rabbi was among them.

I sat in on the initiation, which took about two hours. Afterward, the rabbi approached me, somewhat excited. He said there are also five planes of creation in Jewish mysticism, and there are names of God for each one. He wondered if he could use the Hebrew names rather than the Sanskrit ones. I said he needed to ask the Master and led him to someone who could take him. Later, he returned and told me the Master asked him to write the names. The Master blessed them and told the rabbi he could use the Hebrew names for meditation. I found out later that the Master had also allowed Sufis (Muslim mystics) to use the Islamic names of God once the initiate had asked.

This information was intriguing. Clearly, the teachings of Judaism, Islam, and Hinduism have significant commonalities. These ideas about the planes of creation and the secret names of God are shrouded in ancient texts. But the names themselves have no power until a living Master infuses them with his attention.

❧18☙

Our company was very profitable, and we decided it was time to upgrade our family home from a lovely old Tudor to a brand-new six-thousand-square-foot post-modern colonial in a beautiful new neighborhood, an executive enclave, as one of our neighbors called it. The designer home had six bedrooms, five baths, a large full basement, two fireplaces, and an amazing modern kitchen. The Rosses had arrived.

All we needed now was more children to fill this huge house. When Jonathan was two years old and finally walking, we decided we wanted more children. It took a couple of years for Rosie to conceive again, and soon Evan was born. Evan was born six weeks early but was big enough to be in no danger.

When Evan was over a year old, my father's illness worsened, and I flew to Florida to be with the family. Dad was in hospice, and my mom, sisters, and I visited with him each day. He was very frail, and you could see that his time was nearly up. One day after our morning visit, my family was going to have lunch and planned to return in the afternoon. I didn't feel like eating for some reason and chose to stay behind with my dad. I was alone with him, looking at this frail older man who had suffered so much. I was thinking about how much he loved us, sacrificed for his family, and everything he had done for me. Now, his breathing was getting shallower and shallower. I felt that he was going to leave the body soon. I held his hand and started to repeat my mantra, trying to keep my tears at bay. After a short time, he gave my hand one last squeeze and was gone. I felt he knew he was leaving, and that was his way of saying goodbye. I was grateful to share that last moment with him.

My family returned after lunch to the sad news. We had the funeral three days later, which he had paid for years earlier. He had arranged everything perfectly. He had left written instructions with all the details for the funeral home. We had nothing to worry about; he had taken care of everything. Such was his style.

Right after the funeral, I meditated in the living room after everyone was fast asleep. At one point during the meditation, I could smell a wonderful fragrance of jasmine and remembered that a true Master has the aroma of jasmine and roses. The next day, Master Rajinder called to tell me my father was in a good place. I was so grateful for the call.

Eighteen months after Evan's birth, we were blessed again with a beautiful daughter, Alexandra. Now, our family was complete. Alexandra was named after her grandfather, who had died three months earlier.

Natania, my eldest daughter, was soon engaged, and we attended that festive wedding celebration with the entire family in Vancouver. Christy had also remarried and had another daughter the same age as Jonathan. The wedding was a joyous affair, and we welcomed Michael into our family.

* * *

Satsang remained an important part of our lives. Rajinder lived near Chicago. About a year after he became the Master, the mission bought a church in Naperville, a Chicago suburb. A hotel was next to the property, making it convenient for a weekend visit. He also held special programs during the summer and on Thanksgiving and Christmas. I had many opportunities to see the Master each year, and the entire family would often attend these programs. The *Satsang* consisted of many wonderful, caring people. We formed many friendships and had *Satsang* parties in our homes. Many followers became lifelong friends.

In 1993, Master Rajinder was in New York City for a tour stop. Before the scheduled talk, he went to bless a store owned by a member of our group. I happened to be there with many others. He showed great interest in the establishment and asked several questions about it.

At one point, he turned to me and said, "Bernard, don't you have a business nearby?"

I said, "Yes, my office is a few blocks away."

"Would you like me to come to your office?" he asked.

"I would greatly appreciate it."

This was something that I wouldn't have asked for or even hoped for. I was so touched by his kindness. I rushed off to get Rosie and the kids and tried straightening up my office before the Master came. After a time, he came with his lovely wife, Rita, and about a dozen initiates. I showed the Master around my office and explained what we did. He took his time and asked about each employee.

Our entire family was there. My son Evan, who was two,

With Sant Rajinder when he blessed my office in 1993.

had already memorized the location of every state in the country and every country on a world map. We told the Master about his gift and produced a map. Rajinder pointed to a location on the map, and Evan identified Illinois, the state where the Master lived. The visit was a special grace that I greatly appreciated. We were even blessed with photos of this wonderful event.

In 1994, Rosie decided to become initiated. She wasn't a full vegetarian, but was committed to being one.

As the children grew older, they no longer wanted to see Rajinder, and rarely did Rosie. To her credit, Rosie was always supportive when I wanted to see him, even for multiple weeks at the ashram, and she was always impeccable about preparing vegetarian food.

I continued to see the Master multiple times each year. It was easy to fly out on a Saturday morning, get to see Rajinder twice, and return Sunday night. There was always a Saturday evening program and a Sunday afternoon *Satsang*. During the Saturday program, the Master would bless each person individually. In the beginning of his mission, when attendance was in the hundreds, we would line up and get his *darshan* along with *parshad*. This was an opportunity to ask questions, which he happily answered. As the mission grew and attendance became greater than a thousand, the *Satsang* was held in the hotel ballroom. Even with this mass of people, the Master still blessed each person individually and answered their questions. He walked slowly across each row, and when a row was completed, the chairs would be moved so that he could bless the next row of people. He did this so that we didn't have to stand in line to see him. He walked for hours while we sat waiting for those magnificent eyes to brighten our souls. That one glance, often accompanied by a pat on my head or shoulder, filled me with divine love.

Every five or six years, I went to the ashram in India for a couple of weeks of focused meditation and daily *darshan*.

At the ashram, everything was provided, and our objective was to put the maximum time into our meditation practices. The volunteers at the ashram were incredibly gracious and attended to our every need. They were a perfect example of living the principle of selfless service.

Near the ashram was a large meeting area called Kirpal Bagh, where *Satsang* was held each Sunday. Usually, thirty or forty thousand people attended. Even in this multitude, Master Rajinder's love filled every heart. It was a joy seeing all those smiling faces with gratitude and hope radiating from their eyes. Those experiences helped me appreciate the magnitude of the Master's mission. Only a totally enlightened being could care for so many souls.

✑19✑

Greed killed a good thing. The Softa Group had visions of going public. In 1989, it achieved growth of 581% during a three-year cycle. It was also listed as number 497 in the Inc. 5000 rankings. A strong dealer channel and a good product got them to this point. In 1994, they went all out to go public and hired experts to help make it happen. They had a new president and new executives experienced in preparing an IPO, an initial public offering. The focus of the company had shifted to impressing Wall Street.

Part of Softa's strategy was to cannibalize its dealer channel and sell directly, competing with its wholesalers. My reward for being the number one dealership for the last nine years was to have Softa steal my top salesman. Then, a few months later, Softa recruited my Boston salesman, effectively closing our Boston operation. Their policies were systematically destroying my company. I was left with seventeen employees and drastically reduced sales. It was no use complaining. The new management considered us competitors. They wanted to sell at retail rather than wholesale. The sales margin for most of the dealers was fifty percent; by selling directly, they could double their sales. The new management understood little about our market and what the dealers provided.

Softa's drastic change of policy and attitude threw me into a depression. My once profitable company was losing money each month. My cash reserve was shriveling up, and if it continued, I would face bankruptcy. To make matters worse, I pulled my back out and was bedridden with pain for days. My world was falling apart; my dream was dying. I didn't know what to do. There, bedridden, I prayed. I prayed to God, and I prayed to the Master. I tried to empty myself and focus all my attention on prayer and meditation. Then I had an epiphany.

YOU DON'T SELL SOFTWARE; YOU SELL SOLUTIONS.

There it was, clear as a bell. The value of our company wasn't that we sold the Skyline Property Management program. Our value was our ability to provide solutions to the unique requirements of our customers. Property management is a complex industry, and each type of management has unique needs. We were experts at selling software, implementing it, and supporting our clients. All we needed was to market different software.

I was energized by my realization. After a few days of searching, I found a property management software that could potentially replace Skyline. I was impressed with Yardi, a California company whose software was written for Windows, which was becoming the new industry standard. The company's owner, Anant Yardi, was a programmer who had a real estate portfolio, so he understood the needs of property managers. The reviews I found were all positive. So, in 1995, I persuaded them to meet with me. I flew to Santa Barbara and met with the CEO and executive team for a few days. They were growing fast but were not yet doing well in the Northeast. I told them it was because I was their competition. By acquiring my company, they could become established quickly in this region. We had a great staff, more than seven hundred active clients, and plenty of prospects in our pipeline.

Within a few weeks, we hammered out an agreement. My prayers were answered, and I couldn't have imagined a better outcome. Yardi paid me for my company, hired all my staff, and we agreed on my salary plus a commission structure. I was hired as Vice President of Sales, Northeast. I was excited to have a great new product and couldn't wait to start selling it.

It didn't take long before we destroyed Skyline in the marketplace. Yardi's software was modern and powerful, and we knew all of Skyline's weaknesses. They were never able to go public, and within a few years, the Softa Group was purchased by another company at a bargain-basement price. I didn't feel bad for them since their greed had brought about their demise. Their actions had hurt many of their loyal resellers. We were fortunate to have secured our future with Yardi.

Working for Yardi was great until it wasn't. As VP of Sales, I had three or four salespeople working under me. We were doing very well. In fact, I brought in the largest sale in Yardi history, a two-million-dollar deal with the NY Metropolitan Transit Authority.

At the end of my three-year contract, Mr. Yardi called me into his office and wanted to renegotiate my compensation. He thought I was earning too much and offered me a slight increase in my base salary, but now my commission would be based solely on my sales rather than what my staff—the team I had hired and mentored—brought in. This would mean a significant reduction in my earnings.

I told Mr. Yardi, "I'm involved in most of the sales, and my staff often want my help finalizing orders. Not getting compensated for my work is unfair and would mean a large cut in my compensation."

Mr. Yardi said, "I have faith in your ability. You can sell more to make up the difference."

At this point, I was tired of working for someone else, tired of the games, and tired of the limitations. It was time to start another new business. Timberline was one of Yardi's main competitors, and they had been trying to recruit me for the last year. I met with them and told them I wasn't interested in a job—I wanted an independent dealership. They wanted me very badly. During the negotiations, I mentioned I was owed sixty thousand dollars in commission from Yardi, and if I walked away, I would lose it. They said they would give me a sixty-thousand-dollar signing bonus. That sealed the deal. In 1998, I started Core Systems Inc. and opened an office in Mount Kisco, New

York. This was the third company I had started.

Timberline even gave me a salesperson and consultant. They were closing out an underperforming dealership and introduced me to Gary, a knowledgeable salesperson. On day one, I had Gary do demos and close business while I learned the software. I also had John for implementation and training. Gary was my first employee at Core Systems, and he would also be my first employee at my next venture.

❧ 20 ❧

Happiness is working for yourself. This is especially true if you're making a good living. In my case, the critical factor for success wasn't location—it was timing. I started Core Systems in 1998, just before the Y2K issue. Timberline was Y2K-compliant, and many property management software programs couldn't handle processing dates in the year 2000. Many opportunities came our way, and we made plenty of sales. Also, it became clear Microsoft Windows was becoming the predominant operating system. Companies that were abandoning mini-computers and DOS systems wanted the latest proven technology. And we were there with a great new property management solution.

One of my early sales was to Heron Properties. Frank, one of its VPs, was a brilliant guy and self-taught programmer. He could figure out how to simplify complex manual processes by writing a custom program. He showed me some programs he created for Heron that eliminated tedious manual processing and offered improved accuracy. I respected his talent and often ran automation ideas by him.

One of my clients wanted a paperless accounts payable approval solution, and Frank jumped at the opportunity to create it. The company was a real estate investment trust with 125 approvers across seven regional offices. They had been spending a lot of money on overnighting invoices to the various regions for approval. Having a programmatic method of approving invoices would save them a fortune.

After a year and a half of programming, Frank developed a

finished product. He had quit his job at Heron and was living in Florida. His full-time job was programming a product he named TimberScan, designed to work exclusively for the Timberline Accounting System. Neither Timberline nor any third-party add-on programs offered this capability, and with twenty thousand customers, this program offered enormous opportunities.

Once TimberScan was ready in 2004, I began selling it. The first version of the program was designed for property managers, and most of Timberline's clients were construction companies. We successfully got a few sales, but more importantly, it piqued people's interest in automating the accounts payable approval process.

Frank had to return to the drawing board and reprogram the software for contractors, which took another year. Once completed, sales took off. I became the exclusive distributor of TimberScan—and the company's sales, marketing, and distribution arm. I built a dealer channel of a dozen or so resellers of Timberline and established pricing, provided marketing materials, created demos, and closed sales. Frank focused on adding features to the software, fixing bugs, and managing programmers.

By 2007, it was clear this would be a major success. The great recession hit around this time, and companies had to become more efficient to survive. TimberScan not only saved our clients a lot of money but also improved the efficiency of paying vendor invoices.

Still, I realized I was building a company I had no stake in. Frank could fire me once the dealer network was established, and I would get nothing. I approached Frank with a plan to form a new company with each of us as equal partners. The new company would buy the rights to the TimberScan program from Frank, and we would run it together. I told Frank I would give up Core Systems and focus all my energy on the new company. I sold Core Systems to another Timberline dealer. By that point, I had about 350 clients, and the sale gave me a nice annuity stream.

Having my own software program had always been my dream. As a reseller, you're always at the mercy of the manufacturer.

We came to an agreement, and Core Associates was born on January 1, 2008. I lived in New York, and Frank was in Florida, so out of necessity, we worked virtually. During our first year, we added about a dozen employees, some from different states, all working from home. Telecommuting became our reality. Our challenge was to keep everyone focused, informed, and motivated.

Frank's neighbor, Jeff, was a corporate coach who advised large companies on building an improved corporate culture. Hiring him helped us immensely. We invested in annual retreats at beautiful tropical resorts held every January. Jeff didn't like the term "retreats" because it denotes going backward, so we called our meetings "corporate surges." These were intensive team-building and planning sessions where every voice was heard. These motivated and inspired us to build a great company run by dedicated people. These meetings helped develop a clear vision for our company and define our strategy for achieving it. We also made sure there was plenty of time for fun and socializing.

Right from the beginning, we were dedicated to building a great corporate culture. Our employees were the soul of our company, and we ensured they were heard and appreciated.

In twelve years, Frank and I built Core Associates into a sixty-person company with multiple products, over twenty-two hundred clients, and more than forty thousand users. We focused on creating great software, providing exceptional service to our clients, building a powerful dealer channel, and taking great care of our employees. We accomplished all of this by establishing a great culture and attracting wonderful, caring people who stayed with us for many years.

In December 2020, we successfully sold Core Associates for an excellent price. The new owner, AvidXchange, had a strong culture and a great future vision. They retained our entire staff.

I never had a partner in any venture before Frank. And Frank was a great partner and a wonderful friend. We were both retained by AvidXchange as VPs; they wanted us to stay for at least three years and offered us great bonuses for each year. We committed to staying, not so much for the money but for our desire to make TimberScan the predominant purchase-to-pay solution for the construction industry. A year and a half after the purchase, I chose to retire. At that time, TimberScan was well integrated with AvidXchange, and it was an opportune time to walk away and focus more on my spiritual journey.

Our Surge – January 2020, Playa del Carmen, Mexico

∾21∾

I'd like to share one of the most shocking and disturbing events from my time at Core Associates. This event affected my entire company and me deeply.

When my company had been in business for two or three years, it became clear we needed a project manager to direct our programming efforts. We tried one guy part-time, but it didn't work out.

I was in India celebrating the wedding of Arran's son Arjan to Master Rajinder's daughter Rimjhim in 2010. Late one night, after one of the pre-wedding celebrations, I was on a bus back to the ashram when I started a conversation with Karen and learned she was a highly experienced project manager with an MBA. I told her about my company, and she expressed an interest in working for us. She applied for the position when she got back to Chicago. Karen lived there with her husband and two sons and were active members of the spiritual community.

We hired Karen, who turned out to be an effective project manager. In time, she was promoted to VP of Programming, became a member of our strategic leadership team, and contributed to the smooth running of the company.

After about seven years on the job, she went through an epic life change, a complete reversal of everything she previously held dear. She divorced her husband, left the spiritual path, and moved in with a much younger guy. She became more critical of how we ran the business and more demanding. Since she had an MBA, she made it clear she could do a better job running the company and wanted to be Chief Operations Officer, my title at the time. Not only was the executive committee finding her difficult, but her co-workers were also complaining. This difficult period lasted about a year, and we tried to work with her and find common ground. As time went on, she became more difficult. The final straw came when she sent Frank and me a long, disturbing email with demands, threats, and ultimatums. She thought the company would fall apart if she left and wanted the COO title, recognition, and compensation she considered worthy of her talent.

After much discussion and soul-searching, we decided to let her go. Because of the many years of good service to the company, we offered her a generous severance package. Our attorney drafted the agreement, which stipulated she could not contact any of our employees for one year. This is a standard requirement in severance agreements. We knew she would be angry, and we didn't want her spewing vitriol about us to our employees. When we told her of the termination, she became upset but reluctantly accepted our agreement.

About six months after the termination, I got a call from one of Rajinder's secretaries asking if I could come to Chicago for a meeting in three weeks on a particular Saturday. He also suggested I take an early flight to arrive in Chicago before noon. It sounded a bit mysterious, but, of course, I accepted.

Three days before I was scheduled to fly to Chicago, I learned that Karen died by suicide. I was in shock. She had hung herself from a rafter in the new house she had recently purchased. I shared this news with my fellow workers, and everyone was distraught. We were sure the termination contributed to her suicide. These were dark days at our company; we felt the burden; we felt the guilt, and we all felt the pain. Her son worked at Core, and speaking with him made it even more traumatic.

I was especially devastated since I had always considered her a dear friend. I had brought her into the company. I knew her husband and children well. We all were on the same spiritual path and saw each other multiple times each year when I visited the Chicago Center.

Once I landed in Chicago, I got an email informing me that Karen's funeral was being held that very day at noon near Rajinder's center. With a heavy heart, I went to pay my last respects. About a hundred people were at the funeral home, most of whom were members of our spiritual community. I knew many of them; most knew Karen had worked for my company. I wondered how many of them thought my company contributed to her suicide. My guilt was building by the minute. I felt like running away, but I forced myself to stay. Her ex-husband, Phil, was there with their two sons. Phil came over, gave me a big hug, which was much needed, and said he was glad I came.

I found a seat in the crowded funeral home. Karen's open casket was in the front of the chapel. Many people spoke, including Karen's mother and boyfriend, but I was in a fog. I was lost in misery and found it hard to comprehend what was said. Finally, people lined up against the back wall, preparing to view the open casket. I found myself in the line. I don't know why. I felt like I was in a trance, with tears in my eyes and a big lump in my throat. I got to the casket and looked down at Karen's body. I couldn't believe it was her. She seemed so many years older. It was like the anguish and suffering she went through in the final months of her life were written on her face. My heart went out to her. I prayed, hoping she was in a better place and asking for forgiveness. I asked God and Karen's soul for forgiveness for anything my company or I did to contribute to her suicide.

I passed her mom and offered my condolences. I passed her boyfriend, and before I could say anything, he said, "Karen was devastated that you fired her, and to not allow her to talk to her friends at Core was cruel."

I didn't think I could feel more pain and guilt, but I did. I felt that if we hadn't listened to the lawyers, maybe Karen would be alive today.

I walked out and got into my car as quickly as I could. I didn't want to see or speak to anyone. I felt like pure unadulterated crap.

Master Rajinder's talk that afternoon was at the Benedictine University, about ten miles from the funeral parlor. I was a mess emotionally and somehow made my way into the large auditorium. Many people were already seated. An usher led me down to the first row, right in front of where the Master would speak, as if this were my assigned seat.

Master gave a compelling and powerful talk. It was clear that what he said related to Karen's suicide. Many of the people in the audience knew and loved her. How could this happen to someone following our spiritual path?

Rajinder explained that no matter what difficulties we face on our journey through life, we should remember we are deeply loved. Not only are our friends and family, teachers, and community available to help us through life's hardships, but God, too, will never forsake us. God's love and light always exist to brighten our day.

He stated that our society has taught us to excel and solve problems as individuals. We sometimes don't ask for help when difficulties arise, since we consider it a sign of weakness. Sometimes, we can spiral into hopelessness and depression. Help is there. We need to know it's okay to ask for it. We must remember what we have experienced so many times—this too shall pass.

Rajinder reminded us we are a community and need to help and look out for each other. Times of trouble come, but they also leave. We are here to love and serve one another. But unfortunately, sometimes people don't want help.

He said this much more eloquently and poignantly than I ever could. He lifted our spirits and helped us cope with the loss and suffering we all felt. He looked at me many times, and my heart felt the healing rays of his love.

When the talk was over and I was ready to leave, an usher

came over and said that the Master wanted to see me. I followed the usher to a small room where Master Rajinder and his wife were seated.

He looked at me lovingly and said, "It's not your fault." Nothing else needed to be said. Those few words lifted the burden from my heart, but I was still sad for Karen and, especially, her two wonderful sons.

I thought about the events that led me to be in Chicago on this sad day. There was no way I would have been there if the Master hadn't asked me to come three weeks earlier. The Master healed many hearts that day. This is a small example of what it's like to have a spiritual Master. He looks after each disciple and is the catalyst for our spiritual growth. The teachings tell us that the Master is not the body but has the power of God working through him.

Sant Rajinder Singh Ji Maharaj

❧22❧

The COVID-19 epidemic hit our family hard. In May 2020, Rosie's uncle Rachmil died. He was a 94-year-old Holocaust survivor who was fit and still possessed all his faculties. He had survived Auschwitz, but not this dreaded disease. He had been the patriarch of Rosie's family and a kind and generous man. His loss hurt us deeply. He had lived in California, and because of Covid, we couldn't attend his funeral. Rosie spoke to her cousins and FaceTimed with them, but that was not the same as being there. Part of the tragedy of this disease was that people could not say goodbye to their loved ones face-to-face.

On July 10, my mom caught Covid. My sister Nancy was with her in Florida when her breathing became very labored. Nancy immediately called an ambulance despite my mother's objections. The hospital couldn't save her. She passed away at 8:40 p.m. on Sunday, July 12, 2020. She was 97 years old, blessed with a sound mind and a heart full of love and caring. Her body, however, had deteriorated, and she had suffered physically. I had seen her a few months earlier when she had gotten to hold her youngest great-granddaughter. She took such joy and delight in family.

Now she was gone, and we were stuck in New York, unable to travel due to Covid restrictions. I called my children and relatives the next morning to relay the sad news. Those were some of the most difficult days of my life. The loss of my mother hit me hard. I've never felt so distraught, so devastated. And what made it especially hard was that we couldn't attend the funeral. In the Jewish tradition, the immediate family wears a torn black garment representing the tear in your heart when losing a loved one. Usually, the funeral home provides torn black ribbons to the family members. But we made our own from a black garment cut in the shape of ribbons and wore it near our hearts.

My children were wonderful. Jon, Evan, and Ali all came over on Monday and were a great comfort. Natania and her family, who live in Toronto, were on the phone and FaceTime, offering comfort. The funeral took place on Wednesday, July 15. My sister Nancy and the rabbi were the only ones physically at the gravesite. The rest of us had to attend via Zoom. We could see the casket but couldn't place a rose or soil from Israel on it. We couldn't see her casket placed next to her beloved husband's. I felt awful for Nancy, all alone without the comfort of family.

About forty people attended the Zoom funeral. Many people shared memories of my mother. Part of my remembrance was to tell her Holocaust story, which many people didn't know. The Zoom call lasted well over an hour. It was bittersweet. In the Jewish tradition, after the death of a close family member, we typically sit *shiva*, which consists of seven days of mourning. Friends and family bring food and provide solace to the bereaved. We couldn't sit *shiva* because of Covid.

A couple of days after the funeral, Master Rajinder called to offer his condolences. He said my mom was in a good place and that she loved me and didn't want me to be unhappy. What a joy it was to receive that call. It was a soothing balm on my lacerated heart.

Once again, I benefited from having a guru. I'm just an ordinary member of our group, yet Rajinder took the time to comfort me in my time of need. Rajinder has more than two hundred thousand followers. I've heard many stories of how the Master is always there when a disciple needs help. He is love personified. He works tirelessly for his disciples and all

humanity, teaching the benefits of meditation and ethical living. I am so grateful to God and the three great Masters for all
they have given me.

❧23❧

I decided not to include more details about my wonderful children and grandchildren. If I conveyed even half of the marvelous times we've had together with the joy and *naches* I got, this memoir would be much longer.

I'm blessed with a wonderful family. All four of my children turned out to be good human beings. They are all bright, successful, and caring. My four grandchildren are amazing. Our family is close-knit, and we see each other often. Everyone loves one another. What more can a parent ask for?

Rosie is the love of my life. I am grateful every day that she is my wife, partner, and better half. We have our health and are enjoying growing older together. Family is the center of our lives.

I am now 77 and recently retired. My health is excellent except for arthritis in my knees. I don't need to take any medicine. My weight is under control because of my vegan diet and a good exercise program (tennis, pickleball, and the gym). But the most important contributor to my overall well-being is regular meditation.

Many studies extol the benefits of meditation for physical, mental, emotional, and spiritual well-being. *Inner and Outer Peace through Meditation* by Rajinder Singh (Lisle, Illinois: Radiance Publishers, 2007) is an excellent book for anyone seeking to learn the benefits of meditation at all levels.

There are numerous benefits to practicing meditation, but the following are the most significant to me:

SIPPING SUNLIGHT: A MEMOIR

- Meditation allows me to enter a place of peace. Regardless of how tumultuous my day is, my meditation practice calms me and lets me return to my center. This is not to say I never get rattled or frustrated, but regular meditation reduces these incidents. The peace I get from meditation significantly reduces worry, which is the main cause of stress and anxiety. The peace I get radiates throughout my day and positively affects those around me.

- Meditation opens my heart and helps me be more loving and compassionate to others. After all, we are all souls; we are all brothers and sisters in the eyes of God. We all struggle to find our purpose in life and deserve love and understanding.

- Meditation helps me realize I am not the body, but the soul. Experiencing the inner light and sound during meditation helps me rise above body consciousness and see with the eyes of my soul. The bliss I get makes me want to go deeper and spend more time in meditation. The body is a temporary vehicle and will die one day. Most of us identify with our mind and body and have numerous attachments that keep us chained to this earth. Meditation helps me overcome many of my attachments and desires, but I still get roped in. It will take a lot of focused awareness and prayer before I'm totally free of them.

Now that I have written my story, I see my life more clearly. God's unseen hand has always guided me through trials and tribulations as well as joys and disappointments. I've had adventures, incredible experiences, and maybe even some miracles. I've had enough drama in my life; now, I long for peace. I want to live a life of love, gratitude, and service to others (with a few fun vacations thrown in). I want to heed

Kirpal's advice and spend my final years perfecting my meditation. Only God knows how much time I have left. I've started this work in earnest. I hope to progress on this glorious path to enlightenment with God's grace. I still have a long way to go, but hopefully, I'll be able to make significant progress toward the goal before I leave.

Rosie and me in 2020.

Note 1 – Meditation Instructions by Sant Rajinder Singh:

"Meditation does not require any difficult postures. The technique involves sitting in a pose most comfortable, one in which you can sit the longest without moving, and that is not conducive to falling asleep. Any movement keeps the attention on the body. No part of the body should be touching anyone since if one moves, it will disturb the other."

Meditation Instructions:

- "Close your eyes very gently, in a relaxed way, as you do when we go to sleep.

- Your attention should be fully alert. Try not to put any strain on your eyes or try to look up.

- Focus your eyes about eight to ten inches into the field of darkness in front of you on the horizontal plane.

- Mentally repeat a calming word

- Sit lovingly and calmly to see what comes up, as if you were watching a movie screen and waiting to see what appears on it."

For more information about Sant Rajinder Singh, Science of Spirituality, and SOS Meditation, go to SOS.org.

Note 2 – The Book Title:

"Sipping Sunlight" refers to a key to successful meditation. In the esoteric teachings of most religions and wisdom paths, there are many references to inner light. During meditation on the third eye, we experience degrees of light, from mere flashes to intense bright sunlight, culminating with seeing the inner sun. To rise above the physical region, we need to pass through the inner sun, and once that's accomplished, we see a being of light – the radiant or astral form of our guide or guru.

We cannot advance our meditation practices by force of will, visualization, or imagination. My guru, Kirpal Singh, said that it takes focused concentration along with effortless effort to break through. To achieve a state of effortless effort, we need to sip the inner sunlight, savor every ray, and drink deeply of that magnificent brightness. We need to be grateful, for progress only comes through grace. As we go deeper into meditation, we experience divine intoxication, sublime joy, and heavenly bliss. No earthly high can compare.

ACKNOWLEDGMENTS

Many people helped and influenced me in publishing my memoir. I'm grateful to my wonderful family for its encouragement. Rosie, my dear wife, has been there from the beginning of this endeavor, encouraging, proofing, and making constructive comments. My son Evan was especially helpful in proofing my early work and making recommendations. He helped greatly with the book's structure and the sequencing of events. He encouraged me to be bold and expose my weaknesses.

My challenge in writing is my dyslexia, and even after careful reading, there were many incorrect or missing words. Also, my grammar isn't great. My first editor and dear friend, Rhonda Shore, spent many hours cleaning up my manuscript, tightening my sentences, and advising me on content. She is an extraordinary editor who honed my manuscript, making it fit for publication. She also encouraged me to get my memoir published and, in fact, recommended Atmosphere Press.

Nathaniel Lee Hansen, the editor Atmosphere assigned, proved excellent. He spent two hours taking a deep dive into the weaknesses of my manuscript. After our most enlightening session, I cut the manuscript by about ten percent, eliminating paragraphs and chapters superfluous to the story. He also helped identify problems with tense and structure. It took a few months to rework the memoir, which was significantly improved by his editing skills.

Others also helped sharpen my memory. I'm grateful to Steve Tintweiss and How Wachspress for helping me remember my hippie days in the '60s in the East Village, New York.

Christy Wayne and Brian Nation were most helpful with recalling the Galley Bay hippie commune. I'm also grateful Helena Sutton for her superb proofreading and excellent suggestion regarding the title of my memoir, to Bea Pohl for her insight and recommendations, and to Arran Stephens for his kind words of encouragement.

ABOUT ATMOSPHERE PRESS

Founded in 2015, Atmosphere Press was built on the principles of Honesty, Transparency, Professionalism, Kindness, and Making Your Book Awesome. As an ethical and author-friendly hybrid press, we stay true to that founding mission today.

If you're a reader, enter our giveaway for a free book here:

SCAN TO ENTER
BOOK GIVEAWAY

If you're a writer, submit your manuscript for consideration here:

SCAN TO SUBMIT
MANUSCRIPT

And always feel free to visit Atmosphere Press and our authors online at atmospherepress.com. See you there soon!

ABOUT THE
AUTHOR

BERNARD ROSS is an author and has worked in feature film accounting and computer technology. Retired at 76, he splits his time between his homes in Delray Beach, Florida, and Brewster, New York. Ross attended City College of New York and the University of British Columbia in Vancouver, became a CPA, founded three companies, and co-founded another. Ross, a child of Holocaust survivors, was born in Poland and immigrated to America with his family when he was five years old. Hard work and frugality were the survival tools of his family. He began working when he was twelve, and those tools served him well throughout his life.

Ross has practiced meditation since 1969 and attributes his success in life and business to the benefits he gained through meditation and following the ethical principles of his spiritual path. His hobbies include tennis, pickleball, travel, photography, gardening, nature walks, and writing. Ross is happily married and is blessed to have a wonderful, close-knit family of four children and four grandchildren.

Milton Keynes UK
Ingram Content Group UK Ltd.
UKHW011135220424
441551UK00006B/561